TEA WITH SISTER ANNA

Anna McNulty Lester

1862–1900

TEA WITH SISTER ANNA
a Paris journal

SUSAN GILBERT HARVEY

For Will Enloe
309 E. 3rd St

with best
wishes
Susan Harvey

GOLDEN
APPLE
PRESS

The author has made every effort to ensure the accuracy of information contained in this book, but she assumes no responsibility for errors, omissions, or inconsistencies regarding people or places.

First printing 2005

ISBN 0-9768956-0-9

Cover art by Frances M. B. Blaikie 1898

CONTENTS

ILLUSTRATIONS

All cartoon sketches were gifts to Anna Lester from Frances M. B. Blaikie

Charcoal drawings by Anna Lester in 1897 and 1898

> *If I should come home now I would have absolutely nothing to show for my winter except these charcoals and I suppose Rome people would be too modest to look at them—but All studios here have them framed and hung around the walls to show that the pupils can draw from Life.*
>
> Anna Lester, April 1898

CHRONOLOGY

1862	Anna McNulty Lester born in Conway, SC, on December 9
1868	Bannester and Eliza Mary Lester move from Georgetown, SC, to Rome, GA, with Mary Margaret (Minnie), Fleetwood, and Anna
1876	Edith Lester born in Rome, GA, on September 24
1878	Mary Margaret Lester dies in childbirth at age 21
1878	AML studies at Rome Female College
1884	AML graduates from Augusta Female Seminary in Staunton, VA, with degree in business and gold medal in art
1884-85	AML studies at the Art Students' League, NYC
1885-86	AML assists Miss Helen Fairchild at Augusta Female Seminary
1886-87	AML teaches at AFS, studies china painting in NYC in summer
1887-90	AML head of art department at Shorter College, Rome, GA
1893-96	AML head of art department at Augusta Female Seminary
1893	AML and EL visit Women's Building, Chicago World's Fair
1894	EL graduates from Shorter College, Rome, GA, studies at Southern Conservatory of Music, Rome, GA
1896	EL goes to Berlin to study music
1897	AML goes to Paris to study art
1898	AML and EL spend summer in Germany and Switzerland
1898	AML leaves Paris on December 8 for Rome, GA
1899	AML paints miniature portraits and gives private lessons
1899	EL leaves Berlin, teaches music at Agnes Scott Institute, Decatur, GA
1900	AML dies in Rome, GA, on October 17
1905	Edith Lester marries William P. Harbin, M.D.
1937	Susan Cuttino Gilbert born in Rome, GA, daughter of Mary Cuttino Harbin and Warren Gilbert, M.D.
1957	Susan Gilbert on Hollins Abroad-Paris program
1959	Susan Gilbert degree in Art History, Hollins College, VA, marries David D. Harvey in October, moves to Okinawa
1960	Edith Lester Harbin dies on September 9
1998	Susan Gilbert Harvey explores Anna Lester's Paris

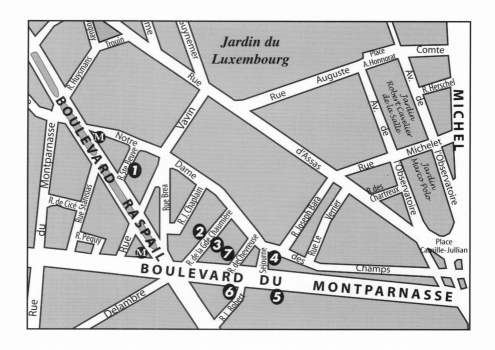

ANNA LESTER'S PARIS

1. Madame Grégoire's pension:
   9, rue Sainte-Beuve

2. Académie Colarossi:
   10, rue de la Grande Chaumière

3. Chapel of Saint Luke:
   5, rue de la Grande Chaumière

4. Académie Delécluse:
   84, rue Notre-Dame-des-Champs

5. Mademoiselle Berthier's pension:
   144 bis, boulevard du Montparnasse

6. Madame Bazin's pension:
   2, rue Léopold-Robert

7. The Girl's Club:
   4, rue de Chevreuse

PREFACE

Every family collects anecdotes and legends from previous generations. Some characters from the past snag the imagination; others remain names on tombstones and genealogical charts. As a child, I heard stories about Anna McNulty Lester, my grandmother's artist sister. Anna taught at women's colleges in the South and studied in New York and Paris. When I inherited Anna's journal and letters, I saw fin-de-siècle Paris through her eyes: she sketched in the parks, attended the Salon exhibition, and drew from live models in academic studios. In spite of ill health and stingy landladies, she preserved her joie de vivre. By going to Paris in 1998, I connected with Anna's spirit, but I also relived my year on the Hollins Abroad-Paris Program.

This book is creative nonfiction and should be read as a story, not as a historical record. The characters, locations, and letters are real, but some contemporary time sequences are composites, and conversations are not verbatim. I edited Anna's letters for clarity, but I left her grammar, erratic capitalization, and loose punctuation intact. I followed her use of "The Girl's Club," possibly short for The American Girl's Club. She used "don't" for "doesn't," "Buss" for "bus," and misspelled some French words. Anna copied poems and quotations into her 1898 journal. I include some of these, with sources when known. The cartoon drawings were gifts to Anna Lester from Frances M. B. Blaikie in 1898.

I admire Anna's talent and tenacity, and I have enjoyed walking her streets in Paris. The surprise was finding passion in my great-aunt's solitary life. She burned some letters, but a typed quotation in her papers encouraged me to investigate her relationship and to examine my own life as an artist. Perhaps this directive came from Anna's "Dear Friend":

Let us hang our life on the line, as painters say, and look at it honestly.

Drawing from Life

The spirits of coming things stride on before their arrival.

October 1998
Rome, Georgia

Music has deserted my mother's house. From the attic window, I look down on her patio where the rain plasters gold leaf fans to the bricks. When the piano restorers carried the Steinway grand across the garden, they broke stems of dead Tropicana roses and brittle maidenhair ferns. Several years ago, somber men from the funeral home rolled my father out the front door; my mother left down a back door ramp on a nursing home gurney. Downstairs, only memories remain in the empty rooms. Chopin is gone; *La Bohème* is silenced; Strauss has waltzed back to the Vienna Woods.

For months, my siblings and I have sifted layers of a Southern lady's household: the silver tea service, Haviland cream soup bowls, embroidered linens from Portugal. We divided the beds and chests from Biggs in Atlanta and the walnut tables and chairs made by Georgia craftsmen. Clearing this attic was an archaeological dig through generations of memorabilia. We discovered our clay handprints from kindergarten, our father's Army Air Force insignia from World War II, and our mother's photo as May Queen at Shorter College. We hauled off chipped Russell Wright china, operetta costumes, and white enamel canisters from our father's medical office. As our mother's mind began to calcify, she hid things. We found two hundred dollars in the piano bench and an IRS refund check stashed in Walt Whitman's *Leaves of Grass*.

My brother, Peter Gilbert, has returned to his medical practice; my sister, Edith Ethridge, has resumed teaching. I am here to unpack the last unopened container in the attic: Sister Anna's trunk. Anna McNulty Lester was the sister of our grandmother, Edith Lester Harbin. Anna taught art in women's colleges, and her oils, watercolors, and painted china are family heirlooms. I construct art from junkyard objects, but despite our different media, Anna and I have things in common. We left Rome, Georgia, to attend colleges in Virginia, and sixty years after Anna packed this trunk to study life drawing in Paris, I enrolled in the Hollins Abroad-Paris Program.

———

In February 1957, thirty young women from Hollins College overcame tugboat and longshoreman strikes to board the RMS *Carinthia*, our shuttle ship from New York to Halifax, Nova Scotia, where the RMS *Queen Elizabeth* awaited. We were the third group of students to abandon our idyllic Virginia campus for the exhilaration of Paris. Like Anna, I packed a trunk. The Hollins Abroad pioneers gave us a mimeographed list of essentials:

> Two dark heavy coats. Heels, flats, and a pair of walking shoes. Nylon and
> Dacron blouses. Nylon dickies or collars. Gloves: fur-lined, smart dark,
> and white. One garter belt and two girdles. One stiff crinoline. Stockings,
> washed and balled as if used (to fool customs). Cigarette lighter and fluid.
> A full skirt to wear over Bermudas on summer tour. Millions of bobby
> pins, but no white bobby sox.

My mother, Mary Harbin Gilbert, kept my Paris souvenirs: passport and identity photos of a nineteen-year-old girl with a brown ponytail and a wide grin; blue airmail letters addressed to my family and to David Harvey, a student at Georgia Tech. In a photograph made beside a ship life preserver, I'm wearing a pillbox black velvet hat and a charcoal gray suit under my wool coat. On my shoulder is an orchid corsage from "Aunt" Joy Harper, my grandmother's best friend. Her bon voyage advice translated a French proverb: "One cannot have too much of a good thing." Another friend of my grandmother's had lived in Romania with her diplomat husband. Her farewell note warned me to be wary of "naughty French men."

From the deck of the *Carinthia*, I waved to my mother on the pier. I was living her thwarted dream. In 1934, she cancelled her trip abroad when her father had a heart attack; she went home to teach her mother's music pupils. As the gap of water between us widened, I'm sure she worried about sending me to Europe during cold war tensions. Only four months earlier, Russia had crushed the Hungarian uprising. Because the Suez Canal crisis occurred during our Hollins Abroad orientation, the college scratched Egypt from our summer itinerary, denying us the pyramids and the Sphinx.

At the first dinner aboard the *Elizabeth*, I sat with classmate Nina Terry. Our waiter looked like Ray Bolger and was much more fun than the Argentine businessmen at table number 26. Nina and I were to room alone in Paris, but we discovered common interests in art, architecture, and music. On the night of the shipboard gala, while our classmates danced the Hokey Pokey, we stood on the stern of the ship, pondered our future, and watched the wake churning back toward America.

I can't thank my mother for saving my Paris memorabilia because she is mired in Alzheimer's quicksand; no one predicted she would outlive our mountain-climbing dad. From "Doc" we inherited defunct gold mine claims in Colorado. Our beautiful "Mamie" kept diamonds and pearls in the bank, but the true family jewels were stored here, in the walk-in attic on the second floor of her home. Edith inherited Anna Lester's steel-pointed alpine walking stick from Zermatt; Pete claimed our great-grandfather's Civil War surgeon's kit. Because of my middle name, I have ancestor Peter Cuttino's portrait. Dried hydrangeas and yarrow no longer hang from strings on the attic rafters. The Mexican sombrero—Grandfather Harbin's souvenir from the Spanish-American War—is gone from its hook. With the packing boxes removed, Sister Anna's trunk sits like a family altar in the empty space.

When I was an art history major at Hollins, my mother gave me Sister Anna's art books and her letters from the Augusta Female Seminary—later Mary Baldwin College—in Staunton, Virginia. When I opened Anna's books, her spirit popped out. What energy will escape when I open this trunk? I touch the wooden ridges that support the canvas backing. The leather handle straps are cracked and stretched from the hands of porters on trains and transatlantic ships. Before Anna sailed to Europe in 1897, she marked the end panel: Anna M. Lester, Rome, Georgia, U.S.A.

Grandmother Harbin had a rustic farmhouse near Rome, a refuge from the city for her physician husband and heaven-on-red-earth for her grandchildren. While we picked daffodils in March and Hickory King corn in July, Granny filled our heads with family stories. After the Civil War, her parents, Bannester and Eliza Mary Lester, left Georgetown, South Carolina. "Not for financial reasons," Granny insisted. "Papa's dry goods store was flourishing." In 1868 they came to Rome with their children: Mary Margaret (Minnie), Fleetwood, and Anna. My grandmother escaped the war's trauma; she was not born until 1876. In Rome the Lesters found schools for their children. Fleetwood studied at "Mr. Proctor's school." Anna and Minnie enrolled at the Rome Female College where, according to the College brochure, "the methods of instruction are to make earnest, thinking women, not automata." Minnie was a musician. Anna also loved music but didn't want to look at "all those little black notes." Anna studied art at the RFC with Miss Helen Fairchild, a graduate of the National Academy of Design. Miss Fairchild entered her students' drawings in the 1878 Paris Exposition; Ellen Lou Axson, a future First Lady of the United States, won a bronze medal. When Miss Fairchild went to teach at the Augusta Female Seminary, Anna enrolled there and received a gold medal in drawing and painting. My grandmother said that Sister Anna "had a head for figures." Her degree from the AFS School of Business was in bookkeeping.

In October 1884, Anna and Ellen Lou Axson enrolled in the Art Students' League in New York City. Talent, not gender, was the sole basis for admission to the prestigious League. The Rome women studied with George de Forest Brush and Frederick Freer and enjoyed the bohemian atmosphere of New York. They visited museums, galleries, and studios, and one Sunday, they walked across the new Brooklyn Bridge to hear Henry Ward Beecher speak.

Ellen Lou Axson abandoned her art career to marry Woodrow Wilson; Anna returned to the Augusta Female Seminary to teach china painting and drawing with Miss Fairchild. In 1887, Anna became head of the Shorter College art department in Rome. When Miss Fairchild retired in 1893, Miss Mary Baldwin hired Anna to direct the AFS art department. The Staunton letters my mother gave me show Anna's life as a spinster schoolteacher. She wrote her father:

> I am not much for society, and here we know no one. When we are
> invited out in town it is always to a ladies party, not a gentleman to be
> seen. I have never been in the society of gentlemen, either at home or
> here, and naturally shrink from making a beginning, especially so late in
> life. I feel out of place and cannot enjoy myself or be at my ease. I wish
> that it were otherwise, but I cannot undo what is past.
>
> I don't want to be old maidish and I am going to try my best not to
> be, but as for being "sweet as a violet and fresh as a rose," that don't
> belong to me. I am not much given to having the blues, and I always try
> to be cheerful and look on the bright side.

The year 1896 was pivotal for my grandmother and her sister. Edith had graduated from Shorter College and had completed two years of post-graduate teaching at the Southern Conservatory of Music in Rome. She described the shock in the Lester family when her professors recommended further study in Berlin, Germany. Her "Papa" could not pay for European study, but Sister Anna had savings from her teaching salary and real estate investments; she offered to pay Edith's Berlin expenses. After insuring her life for repayment to Anna, Edith Lester sailed for Germany in July 1896 to study with master piano and organ teachers.

In Staunton, Miss Baldwin hired a "French lady of high culture and great literary attainments" to teach foreign languages for the 1896-97 session. Mademoiselle Henriette Ballu tutored Anna in German and advised her about European life. As Miss Baldwin's health declined, the assistant principal, Miss Ella Weimar, assumed more control and antagonized the teachers. Anna confided to Edith that the "two-sided" Miss Weimar might fire her new friend, Mlle Ballu. Exhausted from loading the ceramic kiln and disciplining mischievous girls in the dormitory, Anna thought about leaving Mary Baldwin Seminary. She thanked her father for sending food packages to cheer her up:

> The grapes are delightful and I will *look* at the olives a while before I open them. Nobody in these parts has as nice olives as I do. Every one remarks on their "beauty and fatness" and you ought to have heard them talking about the "Poetry in the Coffee" and such nonsense. I have heard before today of "Poetry in washing dishes" but I failed to see it. I would rather have it in the Coffee and Tea.

In the spring of 1897, Anna was 34. Weary of school politics, she submitted her resignation to Miss Baldwin. I imagine that Mlle Ballu encouraged her to study art in Paris instead of returning to teach at Shorter College. From Berlin, twenty-year-old Edith agreed.

March 7, 1897
Berlin, Germany
Dear Sister,

> You must not do it [stay in Staunton], you need *rest*. Your health is of more importance than anything else. I think it would be almost a sin for you to teach next year. I wish I had some way of *making* you, but no one can *make* you, so all I can do is to beg. Come over here for a year even

if your friend don't. For my part, I hope you will never be in a school again, and I don't wish to start that way. I am not undecided as to what you *ought* to do, if you are.

Please remember me to all of your friends. Mr. Jett [the minister], Mlle Ballu, and Miss Duncan especially. No "true love runs smooth" you say. I never asked you before, but why have you never married? If you think that is impertinent, why, don't answer.

Lovingly,

Edith Lester

March 12, 1897
Mary Baldwin Seminary
Staunton, Virginia.
My dear Father,

I had just gotten under way studying, when there was a knock and the girl said Miss Baldwin wanted to see me in her room. I went down and there found Miss Strickler. Miss B. had sent for all the teachers it seems. She said she was very sorry to give me up, etc. but did not say anything of being willing to pay the same and keep me. So I consider the resignation accepted. I told her I had always been fond of her and how much we all missed her. Miss Baldwin can never get well, she gets worse and she will never be able to do more than she does now.

I am glad I am out of it and that the matter is decided. My head does not feel as if it was in a condition to be worried with uncertainties. I hope you all keep well.

With much love,

Anna M. Lester

April 1, 1897
Mary Baldwin Seminary
Staunton, Virginia
My dear Father,

I am glad you are all well. I feel a good deal better, and something in that medicine makes me awfully hungry. I have been sleeping much better this week. I have heard from Miss Douglas last night, she has been real sick. She has not decided yet if she can go to Europe but I guess if she went we would never come to terms on the Steamer for she wants to go on an expensive one and I *will not*, as $60 is as much as I wish to pay for crossing. I have written to the Red Star Line for terms. When I hear I will let her know what I intend doing. If she wants to do the same all good and well, if no—she will just have to meet me somewhere over there.

The jasmine must have bloomed very well this year. I am glad all the pets keep well. I hope your collections will be good and I trust Mr. F. will pay up in *full*. Don't let him get such a headway again. Good night and pleasant dreams.

Lovingly,

Anna M. Lester

April 11, 1897

Berlin, Germany

Dear Sister,

It makes me laugh some times when I wonder how some of these people [in Europe] will strike you. Do come with the intention of seeing the funny side of things, or you will lose a lot of enjoyment. If you wish to sleep well, drink a glass of beer before going to bed. Beer would be good for you anyway and when you come I am going to build you up on it. At present the only time I really care for the beer is at night when I come home late from a concert or opera. A glass then is certainly delightful.

Last night we went again to hear de Pachmann. His Chopin is perfectly charming, fully as beautiful as Paderewski's. He was a few years ago said to be the best Chopin player in the world and then he is so funny. Mama knows I wish to stay three years, and has said several times that she hopes when the two years are up that I can stay longer, but I know Papa is going to say he wants me home. Don't write anything to him or Mama and I will tell you what [Professor] Barth says, when I manage to ask him, and if he advises me to stay, I want you to make Papa see it in the right light. I am sure Barth will give me his candid opinion, and I am really afraid he will tell me not to stay. He will not tell me so unless he believes it, and if he believes it I suppose I will have to do so and acknowledge my self beaten, but *no*, I'll never do that. *Why* have I too much ambition for my capacity? I don't want to be a one-legged teacher, but to be able to command a good price and to stick up to it.

With love,

Edith Lester

July 4, 1897

Berlin, Germany

My dear Sister,

Bring as many little light pretty things for your room as possible. I want some Spencerian Pens, No. 1, a whole *lot*. That little black fascinator you knit for me with pink ribbons, if Mama hasn't given it away. And two small American flags for Frances and me. We have done our best to get some here and they are not the right color. Look as if they had been in the rain a month. If you have any extra room in your trunk you can just slip in Papa's store, hominy, Boston baked beans, canned tomatoes and corn and anything else nice, *olives*. I have seen none here. I don't care for candies. Bring enough handkerchiefs to last till you get home, and shoes too. It pays to have a good steamer rug. Take your big shawl on the steamer and winter jacket, underskirt, and dress. I did not find my flannels necessary. Take nice pillows for your back and head, too. And have as nice a time as possible *snoozing* when you are not walking. Be sure to get the seasick medicine and don't wait until you *are* sick to take it.

I expect you will be so gay and giddy when you come that I will have to play chaperone. And then you will find some nice widower without any children and take him. Don't you dare to unless he is rich and awfully nice.

Goodbye with lots of love,

Edith Lester

Anna got recommendation letters from her past employers and researched art studios in Paris. She packed this steamer trunk, took a train to New York, and sailed at noon on July 28, 1897, aboard the SS *Noordland* of the Red Star Line. Edith was waiting on the other side of the Atlantic in Antwerp, Belgium.

My fingernails break as I shake the trunk clasp. Pete, Edith, and I never found a key to fit. We know our mother took things out of the trunk. Did she lock it or is it rusted shut? I wiggle a large nail from one of the low rafters and using the brick doorstop—a souvenir from the demolished Harbin Hospital—I hammer the nail under the clasp until it snaps open. The hinges resist as I lift the lid, then a plume of dust rises like incense in a French cathedral. I step back, cover my nose, and let the dancing motes settle. The nineteenth-century air will not help my pesky cold and cough.

On the right side of the trunk tray, a box holds art paraphernalia: a wooden palette, some horsehair brushes, pointed sticks of charcoal in adjustable brass holders. The ceramic mixing tray for china painting has dried pigments, crusty with age but vibrant gold, orange, and green. When Anna put these things aside in 1900, did she know it was the last day she would paint or draw? On the left side are museum guidebooks, sketchbooks, an address book, and a black leather Book of Common Prayer. Cardboard boxes hold receipts from studios in Paris and stationery with quotations typed in purple ink.

Here's a maroon journal with gold letters on the cover—*Agenda Buvard du Bon Marché 1898.* I turn to the signature on the first page. Anna M. Lester. Paris 1898. The ink, once black, has faded to sepia. Political cartoons and maps of Paris separate Anna's daily entries; at the end of each month, she filled a page with poetry and quotations. With difficulty, I read the faint handwriting to learn what Sister Anna did in October, a hundred years ago.

October 3, 1898
Entered at Julian's. Rooms very good, much better than I expected. Good model. Then stopped at Colarossi for my apron.

October 8, 1898
Worked all I could today, then had to rest my eyes. Washed my hair! We got seats for the Opera.

October 9, 1898
Have been to service. The chapel was almost full. I thought of my Dear D. all the time and wished she [or *he?*] was with me. Have written this afternoon by an open window, now I am going to have tea!

Anna's comment about hair-washing amuses me. Even in 1957, a rare shampoo rated an exclamation point. I think that Julian and Colarossi were famous studios in Paris. Where was the chapel? Who is Dear D.? Anna's cursive script has an ambiguous scroll before the *h*; I can't tell if the person she missed was male or female. I don't think she ever had a suitor, but I can't be sure.

I pick up Anna's calf leather address book and imagine her hand rubbing the raised AML monogram just as my fingers are doing. Inside are alphabetized hotel and pension addresses in Amalfi, Baden Baden, Berlin, Chamonix, New York, and Paris. I see addresses for Académie Colarossi and Académie Julian but no address for a chapel or church.

Under the letter *D*, there are two entries: Dresden, Germany, and Decatur, Georgia. Anna knew Miss Douglas and Miss Duncan in Staunton, but I see no addresses for them and no first names starting with *D*. The letter *M* designates a whole page of medicines: Ox gall Capsules, kidney tonic, Emo's Fruit Salt, Angier's Petroleum Emulsion, Glycones for constipation from Ely Lilly in Indianapolis, and Oil of Eucalyptus for a cold. Under *P* for Paris, Anna notes sources for gloves, tea, canvas, drawing paper, ivory, and frames. At the end of the book, she wrote ingredients for fruitcake: a pound of butter, a pound of sugar, a pound of flour, a dozen eggs, spices, fruit, nuts, and a wineglass of brandy. The grocer's daughter thought this family recipe rated space alongside the European addresses.

Another small volume, *Baedeker's Handbook for Paris*, is hand-covered in protective black silk. In the margins, Anna wrote the dates she first visited Notre-Dame, the Cluny Museum, and the Louvre. I shiver as I think about my great-aunt stepping into my favorite places; this *Baedeker* could serve as my guide for a centennial trip to Anna Lester's Paris. Using her address book and diary, I could retrace Anna's steps as well as some of my own. It would not be my first spontaneous trip to Paris.

Since my Hollins Abroad group sailed home to America in January 1958, a bungee cord tethered in Paris has stretched across the Atlantic, tugging me back to France. The freedom of my year abroad did not keep me from tying the knot with Ensign David Harvey. In the spring of 1959, he telephoned the Hollins library and persuaded a disapproving librarian to find me in the stacks. His "emergency call" was a marriage proposal. He had orders to the Pacific. Would I go with him? In a fateful second, my plans for graduate school at NYU and a return to France dissolved, and I said yes. The Navy sent us to Okinawa, where I used my Hollins education to birth one baby, conceive another, and mop muddy water from fifteen typhoons. In 1964 we returned to Rome to start a business and raise our children near their grandparents.

In July 1977, I was rushing through the library to find beach books for a family vacation when I felt an inner nudge: Go look at *Art in America* magazine. My three children were in the car, and I had no time for magazines, but the urge was strong. At various points in my life, I've felt a vibration between my shoulder blades when my intuition tells me that something cosmic is happening. Perhaps the sensation comes from God, or a universal feminine spirit, or ancestral ghosts directing my path, but when I've paid attention, vistas have opened. The situations often involve a leap from the status quo: making a risky phone call, writing to a stranger, or exiting the interstate on an illogical whim. Some people raise eyebrows when I describe these events; others nod in understanding.

That afternoon in the Carnegie Library, I opened the magazine to a full-page advertisement. I read it as an invitation and a command: Fly to Paris in October with *Art in America*. After our return to Rome, I had studied design at Shorter College, had exhibited fiber work at the High Museum with the Georgia Designer Craftsmen, and had seen art shows in New York, but this Paris trip sounded like a two-week feast of visual manna. I decided to give myself Paris as a fortieth birthday present. Going to France every twenty years did not seem indulgent. The deposit was due immediately; my savings from a part-time job would cover the cost. If I had seen the ad after vacation, I would have missed the trip. I got questions from some acquaintances: You're spending money on yourself? I knew the answer: My Self needed Paris.

In October 1977, I left multiple lists for a platoon of babysitters and went on the *Art in America* excursion. We toured an international art fair in the Grand Palais, gawked at the new Centre Pompidou, slurped garlicky snails, and sipped Kirs at the Georges V.

One evening in Paris, Paul Shanley of *Art in America* asked, "Susan, what exactly do you *do?*"

My mind hopscotched through carpools, PTA cupcakes, and dirty socks. My biggest excitement, other than buying new dish towels at the mill outlet, was sitting on the washer during the spin cycle. In a burst of self-affirmation, I claimed my identity.

"Paul," I said, "I'm an artist in search of a medium."

Some of the work I saw in Paris inspired my future constructions and assemblages. On my return, I saw exhibits by Joseph Cornell, Man Ray, Marcel Duchamp, and Robert Rauschenberg. I met New York visiting artists who lectured at Berry College near Rome. In 1978, I decided that, instead of taking art classes and hearing lectures, I would *be* an artist. Saying the words "I am an artist" was frightening but liberating.

While my courage was high, I called Dr. Tommy Mew, head of the art department of Berry College. He encourages new artists and had included some of my wooden shadow boxes in a show of women artists in 1976.

"Tommy, I'm ready for a one-woman show."

"Oh? You got lots of work?" he asked.

"None," I said. "Just give me a date."

"OK, February 1979."

Under deadline pressure, I scoured the gutters and junkyards of Rome and gathered wooden crates, ammunition cartridges, oxygen tanks, and fragments of a pipe organ. Just as Cézanne painted his landscape in Provence, and Louise Nevelson's art came from the gutters of Soho, I created sculpture from my own backyard.

For *Juxtapositions*, I filled the darkened Moon Gallery with statements on war, peace, social injustice, gender politics, and religion. One piece, composed of a shipping crate and a gear-ring from a dump truck, had five empty oxygen tanks behind a ring of symbolic fire. I named it *Resurrection*. I meant resurrection in the biblical sense, but in hindsight, I see the piece represented my birth as a professional artist. I had found my medium.

After two strong men and some students helped me unload and install the show, David arrived to help with the lighting. When we directed a spotlight onto *Resurrection*, it vibrated with life. We sat on the floor and ate a picnic supper in the shadows between circles of light.

"Now I get it," David said.

"Get what?"

"What you've been doing all these months. All that varnish, the scrub brushes, the rusty metal joints soaking in the kitchen sink. The junk turns into art when the light is focused."

I blessed him for his insight. After the show, the spotlights went out, and the materials reverted to junk under our house. The oxygen tanks became actors in repertory theatre, anticipating their next performance.

In March 1979, with photos from *Juxtapositions*, I went to Washington, D.C., to help my sister with her first baby. Waiting for their release from the hospital, I telephoned Ruth Gancie, an artist I had met on the *Art in America* trip.

"You don't remember me, but…"

"Of course, I remember you," she said. "We're having a board meeting at Gallery 10 tomorrow. Come by and show us what you've been doing."

When I arrived at the gallery on Dupont Circle, the board members were seated on the floor discussing who would bring the chicken salad for an opening the next night. I thought: Chicken salad? I could have stayed in the Green Thumb Garden Club and discussed chicken salad!

"Leave your photographs. Go downstairs to Afterwords Café and have lunch. We'll be finished with our meeting in an hour."

While I ate shrimp and avocado salad, the acoustic system switched from loud rock to a meditative Lord's Prayer. Was I the only one who saw the light intensify on my table? I went upstairs to reclaim my portfolio.

"Here she is," Ruth said.

I turned around to see who was behind me, but she was talking to me.

"You won't believe this, but while you were eating lunch, an artist called to cancel a show. The gallery is booked for two years, but we'd like to exhibit your work in this open spot. This fall."

I thought about trucking my crates and oxygen tanks from Georgia and hauling them up the steep steps to Gallery 10. I took a deep breath. "Wow, I accept."

Larry Ethridge, my brother-in-law, retrieved Edith and my niece from the hospital. That night, during our celebration dinner, I began to shake. What had I done? In a month, I jumped from the Moon Gallery at Berry College to a gallery on Dupont Circle.

In October, a friend and I drove a truck to Washington, Larry's friends unloaded my boxes and crates, and relatives came from afar to the opening of *Syncrisis*. David signed the guest book as "Mr. Susan Harvey." The art critic from the *Washington Post* wrote that I had "great evocative powers."

On the flight home, I saw the city of Washington below. Somewhere down there on Dupont Circle was a gallery filled with gears, tools, and crates from Rome junkyards and Army salvage stores. Junk from my hometown, transformed by arrangement and light, was now Art in the capital of our country. My seatmate on the plane did not understand why I burst into hysterical laughter, from ironic amusement and total exhaustion.

That show in 1979 grew out of listening to the voice in the library in 1977. I would have missed great adventures if I had clenched my jaw and walked past *Art in America* like a martyred good mother.

Now, in 1998, I'm at another intersection, a *carrefour*. Debris in gutter trash piles no longer lures me out of my car; I don't want to spray-paint any more piano crates or scrub rusty metal. I'll probably close my studio since I haven't had a solo show since 1996. Going to Paris in 1977 jump-started my art career; maybe Anna Lester's Paris holds inspiration for my future creative work as well as insight into my family history. Perhaps I crave Paris for professional resuscitation as well as for *crème brûlée*.

I lift the tray from Anna's trunk and set it on the plywood floor. Exposed are silk shirtwaists, eyelet-embroidered petticoats, and pleated nightgowns. Rolled between the layers of starched cotton are two bundles of envelopes. The stationery rustles like dried Vidalia onion skins as I loosen the confining knots of once-white ribbon and spread the letters on our worktable. The postage stamps are French; the envelope postmarks say Paris. I have struck pay dirt: Sister Anna's Paris letters. I should have known they were hidden somewhere.

One pile of letters has postmarks from September 1897 through June 1898; the second group starts in late August 1898 and ends in December 1898. The two stacks are bookends of the summer of 1898. July and August are missing, and I know why.

A year ago, my sister and I opened a hatbox in my mother's bedroom closet. We found the summer letters that Anna and Edith Lester wrote home from Switzerland and Germany in 1898. At the time, I thought we twentieth-century sisters might retrace Anna and Edith's itinerary in 1998, but when summer came, we could not arrange a romp in the Alps. As a vicarious alternative, I copied the one-hundred-year-old letters into a file on my computer. When Anna wrote home that she was determined to "live this summer to the fullest," did she have a premonition that she had only two summers left?

Day by day, I followed the Lester sisters on trains, lake steamers, and hiking trails. I intermingled their letters with diary accounts of my mundane summer: I saw bears at Grandfather Mountain while Anna and Edith saw the famous bears in Berne; I went to Kingston, Georgia, the day the sisters went to Königstull in Heidelberg; when the Lester women read Mark Twain's *A Tramp Abroad*, I read the same book. For two months, I charted their itinerary on a map and planned a small book for my family called *The Summers of '98*.

Anna's 1880s Staunton letters had introduced me to her personality, like *amuse-gueules* from an epistle chef. The 1898 summer letters were the sorbet course, an *entr'acte* between the sisters' work in Paris and Berlin. These Paris letters from the trunk are the main course, the *plat principal* of Anna's life. At the least, they are windfall apples, dropped at my feet. Who knows what will be the *fromage* and dessert.

The letters give Anna's Paris addresses: the Lafayette Home on rue de la Pompe and the pensions of the Berthier sisters and Madame Bazin in Montparnasse. Through a chance discovery two years ago, I already know that Anna's final address, *chez* Madame Grégoire, is now a hotel. The last letter is dated December 6, 1898. If I hurried, I could get to Paris before Sister Anna sails home.

Snippets from the letters are tantalizing. I could sit here and read them all if I had time and better light. In one paragraph to Edith in November 1897, Anna shows enthusiasm for her work in Paris:

> We have a fine fellow for a model this week. I am so glad I am learning to draw from Life full length. I always have wanted to and I like the work immensely! When you get here [for Christmas] you will wish you had *come to stay*. One cannot help being in love with Paris!

In another letter, she gives advice:

> Mother, if you need a new dress, why not get it *now*. Expenses are surely not much now, and you may as well use your money while you live. Take out *all* your things and *use* them. Don't save for some one else to slight. That is what I am going to do. I have come to the conclusion it is best—I wear my good cloak every day and so on—fur cape too—One might as well enjoy what he has as to *save* it.

I'm hooked. I raise my hands to the ceiling in capitulation: All *right!* I'll *do* something with these letters. I must have reached the age of memorabilia. At sixty-five, my mother wrote a book of family history, including some of Granny Harbin's letters from Berlin; at age eighty, my grandmother wrote her memories of family personalities and a postscript to her Berlin diary. I may be like the blindered mule at Granny's farm, following hereditary commands to gee, haw, and preserve family history. Or, exploring Anna Lester's Paris life may be the next step on my own artistic path.

I scoop the letters into plastic bags because I must finish today's task. The next thing in the trunk is an orange and black paisley shawl, wrapped in an old linen sheet. A note pinned to the challis wool says the shawl belonged to Eliza Mary Cuttino McNulty Lester, my great-grandmother. Anna and I were named for *her* mother, Anna Susan Cuttino McNulty. The Cuttino Huguenot blood dates to seventeenth-century France, to île de Ré, a small island near La Rochelle. With the shawl around my shoulders, I sink into a Windsor rocking chair and recite the Cuttino beads in a DNA rosary from maritime France to me: Jérémie, Pierre, Jeremiah….

In counterpoint to the creaking rocker, the rain telegraphs a message on the roof: Go to Paris. Go to Paris. Find Sister Anna. Find Sister Anna. Sounds like military orders, but since childhood, I've loved a mission. Pete played Dick Tracy, while I was Nancy Drew. During World War II, the neighborhood boys were soldiers and doctors; we girls were nurses and occasionally drove the pretend Jeep. My questing nature may date to those games of going behind enemy lines to rescue comrades.

More recently, in 1995, I spent weeks in Virginia tracking my Native-American ancestor, the "Princess" Nicketti. The resulting show, *The Dew Sweeper*, was my last solo exhibit. As I dismantled the work, I knew I had turned a corner in my visual art career: the *search* for Nicketti had been more exciting than making the sculpture.

Since then, between one-way conversations at my mother's bedside, I've played with my grandchildren and hunted for turf mazes and ancestral graves in England with my sister. A trip to Paris is tempting, and I'm ready for a new project, but my pragmatic voice says this is not a good time to travel. I have a raw sore throat and cough, I'm on my second antibiotic, and my hormones are in chaos. The stock market crash slashed our retirement funds and my mother's portfolio. The rain on the roof doesn't care: Go to Paris. Go to Paris.

Stacks of yellowed newspapers and art journals rest on the bottom of the trunk; I sneeze at the thought of picking them up. As I lower the trunk lid, I change my mind, put on a dust mask, and remove the papers. Ye Gods. The journals covered a large black folder on the trunk floor: an artist's portfolio, filled with crinkled-edged drawing paper. Why did Mamie bury it on the bottom of the trunk? With care, I lift the cardboard folder onto the table and untie the closure knots. This is a holy act, like opening a huge family Bible or a book of Smithsonian engravings.

A nude woman stares up at me. She stands erect, her head tilted, a finger at her lips in indecision or impatience. She seems to say, "What took you so long?" Her one exposed breast is a pointed muffin between scrawny shoulders. Her pompadour threatens to tumble around her ears, while her pubic hair is a curly triangle.

I page through drawings of sagging breasts, bulging bellies, shimmering flesh, and bare feet. Some women perch on stools. The men have handlebar moustaches and bushy eyebrows. One bearded man with outstretched arms resembles Jesus. A haughty man holds a long stick as if he were too good to be posing in a studio. He wears white briefs. Perhaps it was indecent for female artists to draw male genitalia— even in Paris. Only one drawing is signed Anna M. Lester, but this is her work; the dates range from October 1897 to November 1898. Anna was sketching full-length figures, but the heads and facial features are the most detailed. Her portraits capture the emotions of these Paris models: boredom, resignation, arrogance, and despair.

My mother never mentioned these drawings. Pete and Edith will not believe that I've struck the mother lode of Sister Anna's work. Drawing is not one of my natural talents, so I admire Anna's dexterity and her gift for portraiture. My gift is to take discarded objects and turn them into art. Perhaps this afternoon I've found the raw material for a written portrait drawn from Anna's life and my own. My favorite part of research is putting my feet on the earth where history happened; I think I'm predestined to walk Anna's Paris streets. Thanks to my pack-rat family, I have Anna's physical artifacts. Can I connect on a metaphysical level with a great-aunt I never knew? What, other than tea and olives, gave Anna joy? What obstacles frustrated her search for artistic salvation? What regrets did she have when her career stopped in midlife? If she left a piece of her soul in Paris, where would I find it?

After restacking the drawings, I close the portfolio and replace it in the trunk until a dry day. The lid descends with a whoosh and a sharp click. I look around the attic, remembering our months of work and the pleasure my mother had in preserving things. This afternoon I have received my inheritance. Am I too old for a solo adventure to the nineteenth century?

⎯⎯ ▭ ⊏▯⊐ ▭ ⎯⎯

On Hollins Abroad, I often went sightseeing or to the theatre or opera alone. The lack of a companion was not going to keep me from seeing Ingrid Bergman in *Thé et Sympathie*. The matriarch of my French family always asked with a dropped jaw, "You are going *alone? Toute seule, Suzanne?*"

"*Oui, Madame, toute seule.*"

I sounded confident, but her concern was legitimate. Hollins officials had warned us of white slave traders who might spike our drinks and abduct us for harems. We went out anyway. We exchanged money on the black market and met soldiers in nightclubs. On theater class nights, I joined Nina at a self-service restaurant for steak, pommes frites, and a carafe of wine. After the play, she walked to her apartment through Les Halles, the belly of Paris. In the open market, carcasses swung from hooks and vendors stopped for onion soup. I took the Métro to rue de la Pompe and hurried through deserted streets by moonlight. I jumped when cats screeched from doorways and rattled the *poubelles*. My high heels clicked on the sidewalk, and the shuttered storefronts echoed the sound. Nina and I confessed that we whispered *"Au secours! Au secours!"* in rhythm to our footsteps. Fortunately, we never needed to shout out loud for help.

I thrived in Paris at age twenty. I've been back several times, but this would be the first time alone. I'm sixty-one and the world is more dangerous, but I don't require any nightlife, and I will not be wearing high heels.

I turn off the attic lights and lock the silent house. With the rain pouring, it feels like night, but it's only four-thirty. I drive to the bank and open the safety-deposit box that guards the residue of generations: my father's Krugerrands, the silver bullet he cast in an antique mold, Bannester Lester's gold cufflinks, and the mourning jewelry of Eliza Mary Lester. Yes, my passport is valid. The funds in my savings account are modest, but as in 1977, they could send one person to Paris. I unwrap Anna Susan Cuttino McNulty's coin silver spoons, a wedding gift in 1959. What am I saving them for? They've rested long enough in their tarnish-resistant flannel. I drop the talisman spoons, the passport, and my savings book into my tote bag and drive home.

Water in the teakettle boils while I compose a still life in front of the fireplace. On Aunt Joy's Chinese lacquer tea table I place one of Anna's miniature portraits, her plaster cast of clasped hands, the edelweiss she and Granny picked in Zermatt, and the last coral geranium from my porch. Anna's blue-and-white Paris teapot comes off the shelf of my grandmother's secretary. I splash copper-colored tea into two porcelain cups—one for me, one for Sister Anna. I add lump sugar and lemon, and stir with my great-great-grandmother's spoon. The hot nectar soothes my throat and my spirit.

When David comes home, I give him a cup of tea and the news of my discoveries. He knows how a new project brings me energy; he agrees that I should invest my savings in a search for Sister Anna. When financial times are better, we will go together. Before going to bed, I ask Sister Anna to send the angels. I need a hotel room, a plane ticket, and a healthy body.

I dream I am in my grandmother's house at 309 East Third Street. The house is being restored. Upstairs, the bay window view is similar to that from my mother's house, but one of Rome's church steeples looks like the tower of Notre-Dame. From my grandmother's closet, I gather fifty pairs of black shoes and construct a seven-circuit labyrinth on her living room floor.

Like Granny Harbin, I wear sturdy black shoes, and I've been constructing labyrinths since a trip to Glastonbury, England, in 1994. The Cretan labyrinth design is unicursal with one path leading to the center. When Theseus killed the

Minotaur, he had a helpful clew, a ball of golden thread from Ariadne. In Paris, I will have clues from Anna's address book and letters. Whether my journey is a classic labyrinth or a multi-branching maze, I will put one black shoe in front of the other. I hope to find the sanctuary where Anna hides in Paris, the place where her life will intersect with mine.

At daybreak, I check the Internet. My favorite hotel has no rooms until the ninth of November. I reserve for nine days. I'm at my travel agency when it opens.

"Alice, I need a flight to Paris."

"Next summer?"

"November 8!"

"Gonna be cold and wet. David going with you?"

"Nope, I'm going solo."

"Here's a $435 seat on Air France."

"Book it."

Next stop is Waldenbooks, where I buy a large-print Paris map and two full-color guidebooks instead of checking out a battered *Frommer's* from the library. With ticket and books beside me, I drive over the hill past 309 East Third Street. I open the window and shout to whatever spirits may be hanging around the former Lester homeplace.

"I'm going to Paris. I'll bring Sister Anna home!"

"Caw," a crow answers from the top of a pin oak tree. I hear it as affirmation.

I assemble my gear: warm clothes, comfortable shoes, travelers' checks, and francs. I read as many of Anna's letters as my eyes can endure and take massive doses of vitamin C and echinacea. In contemplative moments, joy bubbles to the surface like the spring water at my grandmother's farm. My spirit is already in Paris. I walk on damp stone and sniff roasted chestnuts in the brittle air.

Toute seule, Sister Anna, I am coming to Paris.

Dreams grow holy put in action;
Work grows fair through starry dreaming,
But where each flows on unmingling,
Both are fruitless and in vain.

                                        Adelaide Anne Proctor

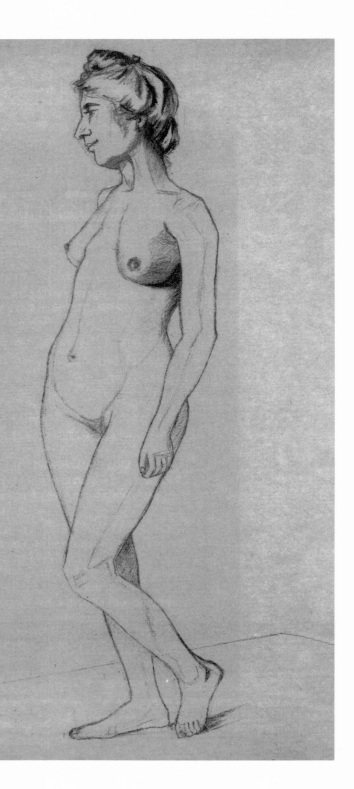

Oct 23 91'

En Route to the City of Light

November 8, 1998

Everyone has in himself a continent of undiscovered character. Happy is he who acts Columbus to his own Soul.

Sir J. Stevens

Air France flight 345 is also Delta flight 22, an auspicious number because my childhood nickname is TuTu. The flight is not full so I spread my coat across adjacent seats to stake out sleeping room in this flying cocoon. I have brought sustenance for my transformation from Georgia caterpillar to Paris butterfly: nuts, V-8 juice, a hard-boiled egg, earplugs, a mild sleeping potion, heavy wool socks, and a black beret to pull over my eyes. The flight personnel slam the overhead bins shut and distribute newspapers.

"*Atlanta Journal-Constitution? New York Times?*"

"*Non, merci. Le Monde et Paris-Match.*"

I plunge headfirst into French. In a news report, Newt Gingrich sends his *porte-parole*—his "word carrier"—to speak for him at a press conference. The expressive French language will give me more pleasure than the microwaved chicken in the galley. One newspaper describes the exchange of "friendship" rings by Charles and Camilla. Another story is about Bill Clinton's brother, Roger. I ignore advertisements for the Hard Rock Café and Chili's—low on my list of Paris landmarks. Headlines announce a possible United States bombing attack on Iraq. I must watch for retaliation against Americans as I conduct reconnaissance in the past. Anna was in Paris during the Spanish-American War; in 1957, France was at war in Algeria; on my 1977 trip, I exited the Métro into squads of riot police with plastic shields and tear gas. Travel can be dangerous, but Paris is worth the risk.

When Anna crossed the Atlantic Ocean, she adjusted to time zones over a period of twelve days. During the past week I used my own jet-lag prevention method. I pretended I was on an ocean liner, the SS *Suzanne*, and set my alarm clock to ring one hour earlier each morning. After I forced my eyelids open, I took a hot shower and read Anna's letters until the sun came up. I stirred my café au lait with a souvenir spoon from my 1977 Air France flight. The plane heads up the East Coast, and I turn my watch to the hour in France. If I can bypass the set meals of the airline, I will go to sleep on Paris time and avoid some fatigue on my first day. Stretched out on three seats, I wedge pillows in the places where my body hits seat belt metal. My wool socks stick out from the skimpy blanket. I wish I had the hot water bottle Granny Harbin gave me when I spent nights at her house.

My grandmother's white frame house on the East Third Street hill buzzed with activity. She taught music, organized a symphony orchestra, and held regional offices in the Music Lovers' Club. A revolving cast of family members and friends surrounded the Harbin dining room table. The piano tuner stayed for vegetable soup and cornbread after working on the Steinway grand; distant relatives arrived for short visits and then moved into the upstairs bedrooms for months. A room was reserved for our adopted aunt, Joy Harper, when she visited from New York or Europe.

When Granny returned from the city of Berlin in 1899, she did not want to live in a provincial town, but Joy introduced her to a young Rome doctor. The subsequent marriage of Edith Lester and Dr. William Harbin produced three physician sons, a piano-playing daughter, and seventeen grandchildren. While Granny made ambrosia at Christmas, she taught us to sing "O Tannenbaum" in German. She never went back to Europe; until "Dr. Will" died in 1942, every Harbin penny went to building his hospital.

Granny and I slept upstairs on the screened sleeping porch where six iron beds stood in a row. She insisted the outdoor air was healthy for our lungs, but by morning, the hot water bottle was cold and dew had congealed on the sheets.

"Hast du gut geschlafen?" Granny asked, when I came downstairs dressed for school. Frau Welle, her landlady in Berlin, used the same words in 1896.

"Ja. Danke," I learned to reply.

"Practice your scales; the grits and bacon will be ready in a minute."

In the music studio, I swiveled on the piano stool. "Tell me about Venus," I called, looking up at a charcoal drawing of Venus de Milo.

Granny came into the room, drying her hands on a towel. "Sister Anna drew her when she studied in Staunton. We saw the original statue in the Louvre in Paris. Now, play your Chopin waltz, then breakfast."

"But I haven't memorized the last part."

"Just do your best."

On winter nights after supper, I curled up before the fireplace and traced the Oriental rug design with my fingers.

"Do you remember Sister Minnie?" I asked.

"She died when Lafoy was born. I was only two, but I heard she was beautiful and had a fine voice. My sister Alberta died as an infant in Georgetown during the Civil War. Sister Anna was the only sister I knew."

"What about Great-Uncle Bubber?"

"His name is Fleetwood. He worked out west when he was young; now he lives in Florida."

Granny's attic was a treat for Saturday mornings. In the dusty storage area on the fourth floor, boxes held costumes and rhythm band instruments for the Junior Music Lovers' Club. Sister Minnie's trousseau trunk contained her wedding dress and petticoats; Sister Anna's Paris trunk sat in a corner under the eaves.

"Can I see Sister Anna's pigtails?"

Granny opened a box and unfolded tissue paper. Anna's hair was the color of the pine needles my cousins and I plaited and wove into baskets in the woods.

"They cut off her braids when she had the measles," Granny said.

I stroked the auburn bundles. "They feel like silk embroidery thread."

She creased the paper around the braids and, with a sigh, replaced the box on a shelf. "You know, Sister Anna lent me the money to study music in Berlin for three years. I never got to pay her back." She blew her nose, stuffed the handkerchief in her bosom, and closed the attic door. "Let's go feed the goldfish."

⊰ ❖ ⊱

Champagne corks explode in the forward cabin. Passengers behind the closed curtains will carve steak; we'll eat shriveled peas. Like the multiple classes on a steamship, we will arrive in Europe at the same moment, but those in first class have a more luxurious crossing.

The Saloon passenger manifest of the SS *Noordland* listed sixty-eight persons, including Miss Anna M. Lester, four doctors, one general, two "Honorable" gentlemen, and the Count G. de Lichtewelde, Envoy Extraordinary and Minister Plenipotentiary of Belgium to the United States. Their time at sea was longer than the nine days I will spend in Paris. Combining her artistic and accounting skills, Anna diagrammed the voyage on *Noordland* stationery. She marked the longitude and latitude with straight lines and made a daily mileage chart on a curved line across the ocean. The ship traveled 3,417 knots from New York to Antwerp. Tonight, the airplane icon on the cabin video screen makes similar calculations as we drone above the black Atlantic.

Facts for Travelers, the Red Star Line orientation manual, urged passengers not to crowd the ship with unnecessary articles. Steamer trunks in cabins had to fit under the stateroom sofa—the 1897 equivalent of rules against oversize luggage in overhead bins. The steamship line offered passengers deck chairs for the nominal sum of fifty cents—to avoid the "trouble and annoyance" of bringing their own. A line drawing shows a lady in a wide-brimmed hat, seated in a deck chair; she stares out to sea through binoculars. In the page margin, someone made a check mark in red ink and wrote instructions for Anna: Find deck steward as soon as possible and have him place chair where you want it—sunny side—midships. The ship's booklet says a steamer rug is "desirable," but the word "desirable" has been crossed out and the word "necessary" inserted in red ink.

Between the book's pages, slips of paper contain instructions in similar handwriting. Perhaps Mlle Ballu, Anna's colleague in Staunton, gave this advice: Be sure to take carriage *to* places in Italy—carry wrap to wear *inside* of cathedrals—then *walk* home. Drink black coffee with cognac if you feel chilly. *Never* travel at night.

The handwritten *Noordland* lunch menu for the first of August reflects the Victorian penchant for uppercase letters: Bouillon Tomato Soup, Marrow on Toast to Order, Curried Mutton and Rice, Fresh Pigs Feet Lyon with German Sausage, Oysters with fresh Lobster Caviar, Soused Mackerel Sardines, Rollmops, Dutch Herrings, Anchovies, Beetroots, Gingersnaps, Stewed Rhubarb, Huckleberries, and Camembert, Chester and Neufchâtel cheeses, Café and Thé.

That evening, passengers chose from: Little Neck Clams, Mock Turtle Soup, Boiled Dennebec Salmon, Vol au Vent, Ris de Veau, Agneau Rôti-Sauce Menthe. After Petit-Pois and Haricots Verts, there were Filet de Boeuf aux Macaroni, Quail on Toast, Plum Pudding Brandy and Hard Sauce, and Blanc Mange à la Vanille.

Sunday, August 1, 1897

Aboard the *Noordland*, Just off the "Banks"

My dear Mother and Father,

One week ago I was just leaving you and in one week more I hope to see Edith. I hope to send you the Cablegramme "Ablation" when I reach Antwerp. Aunt Susie and Susie stayed on the dock until I was way down the river. I saw them turn and go inside. I then came down to the stateroom and opened my things enough to get out the shawl, then went on deck and stayed until lunch. After lunch, I went again to the deck and stayed until dinner in a heavy rain and wind, to say nothing of the heavy sea! I went down but was afraid to stay long, it was so *warm* and I did not want to keel over so soon. They had the storm fixtures on the table at dinner. The next morning I got up and went to breakfast (goose that I was) and then after breakfast came down for my hat and before I could say Jack Robinson, I *lost* the breakfast. However I did not *feel* sick so I went on deck, got fixed in my chair and did not move until 7:30 P.M.

For once in my life I am taking things easy. I suppose because there is no other way. I have sewed a little, mended my gloves, hemmed my veil, read a little. This would all be fine if I had a congenial companion. Edith was fortunate to have Mr. Teddy [Tedcastle] to take her all round. If I muster the courage I will go out to the end of the boat by myself...someday.

In case I forget to tell you later, I will now. When you express the package to Mlle Ballu be sure and *pre*pay the Express and *mark* it so. And I want it to leave Rome the *afternoon* of August 30—so she will receive it the *first* day of school, which will be Sept 1st. *Don't* send it *one bit sooner* than the 30th on any account.

August 5

There has been a very heavy sea since yesterday morning. I could have stood on my head about as well as my feet on deck. Ropes were stretched along deck for us to hold on to, but to walk was "out of the question." It was *fun*. I did not mind the sideways motion but the one from end to end made my stomach feel as if it would drop out.

August 7

Well, you would laugh to see how we have been tied up—to keep us from sliding off the deck. Our chairs were first tied to the pole at our backs. Then a heavy rope fixed like a swing for each chair and after we would sit down, Max [the deck steward] would put the rope over our heads and under our arms to hold us in like babies, then the *fun* would come, we would all tip at once.

At dinner last night nearly everything upset in spite of the storm protectors—bottles of wine played tag with glasses and pickle jars. Down in the staterooms, things danced generally—the Highland fling, I think.

I want Father to tie up Mlle Ballu's box and address it. Put heavy paper on or it will tear. *Do not* put who it is from. The note inside will tell. You see I would not, for the *world* have Miss Weimar to suspect where the package comes from and she, you know, is in charge there now. And then too I want to surprise Mlle Ballu when she opens it in her own room. I believe now that is all I have to say about the box being sent and come to think of it, you may not get any other letter from me before the 30th if this takes as long to go home as *I* am taking to come. We went 305 miles yesterday. Love to Miss Beall [the Lesters' housekeeper] and the pets.

Your daughter,

Anna M. Lester

August 9 7:30 AM

I wanted to add this. The captain said this was the roughest trip for this season he has made in ten years! So, I have stood one test. It was not too bad. We have seen Bishop's Rock and Lizzard's end and are in the English Channel.

Antwerp

We got here at *11 P.M. last night!!!* I never dreamed they would land in the middle of the *night.* Finally I spied a porter from the Hotel de Flandres and the man said, "Yes, there is a Miss Lester registered at the hotel and yes, yes, she engaged a room for 2, and I have just *telephoned* to her the steamer was in sight." Well, I was glad. So he took my bags and I scurried round in and out among the men, women, and bags and after about 20 minutes I got the customhouse man and offered very politely to open the trunk but did not have to. He put on his little mark and then I squeezed in the Buss and we got up here, all our trunks on top. Edith was asleep supposing I could not come til morning. Well, we talked until 3:30 A.M.!! Edith says that we kept the man in the next room awake all night for we heard him give a *meaning* cough about 3 A.M. However we were so wide awake that sleep was out of the question. Edith is well and sends *Love*.

Most lovingly,
Anna M. Lester

According to my grandmother's diary, Anna coughed violently that night but dismissed it as "just a cold." From Antwerp Anna sent a cablegram to her father. Because charges were by the word, she had given him a code list:

Ablation means:

Arrived, all well, pleasant passage, found everything all right

Edith waiting for me and quite well

No trouble understanding language

Abominate means:

Arrived, all well, stormy passage

Was very sick, but am better now

Edith here, and is well

Ablution means:

Arrived all well, had a splendid passage. Edith not here, will wait for her

Anna's inventiveness impressed me until I saw that she adapted this method from the Cable Codex, a seven-thousand-word code used by voyagers of the nineteenth century. The Red Star Line *Facts for Travelers* lists a portion of the Codex. The word *Adjunct* translated to "Have had no letters from you for a fortnight or more. Are all well?" *Adulteress* signified "Have started for home, and shall sail by the Chester from Southampton on_____." *Aromatic* represented "Your husband has been taken ill." *Balderdash* equaled "Will you honor my draft for the sum of____?" Transatlantic cables hummed as single words like *Analeptic*, *Arboretum*, *Busybody*, *Octahedral*, and *Odiousness* conveyed complicated business and personal transactions.

Seen from this age of jet travel, my voyage to France in 1957 seems as archaic as Anna's trip on the *Noordland*.

16 February 1957 Halifax, Nova Scotia

Cunard Line R.M.S. *Carinthia*

Dear Family,

Famous last words: "Me? Get seasick?" Well, I can truly say that "mal de mer est *mal*." After lunch yesterday I went to bed feeling wretched, got up today and had tea and cheese and crackers. We get to Halifax tonight about 9. Hope the "Queen" is less rocky. Lunch yesterday was awful: me with 5 strangers and 10 pieces of silver and a menu I knew not what it said. I survived. Slept 16 hours. There are some darling children. Gave me quite a start to hear a *child* speaking French. You all are going to love your boat trip [in June]. Boats were made for children like E-E [Edith]. She'll have more fun.

One Hollins Abroad girl brought 50 pairs of stockings and everybody has at least three bags. I'm not worried, however. I just want to get to Paris and get settled. Am going to walk the deck before "tay."

Love to all,

TuTu

February 19, 1957

Aboard the *Queen Elizabeth*

America—Rome—Hollins feel like a dream. Can make no contact with them. Like *Brigadoon*. I like to think of this year as more than an "adventure" or a "good time." It is that, of course, but it is more an opportunity for widening my outlook, my scope. The more I see, hear, and do, the more tolerant I ought to become. I hope it works out this way. I want to be able to see people in strange surroundings, try to understand them (as much as possible) try to understand my *self* mainly, watch my reactions to various things, develop a poise and security to carry with me all my life. Some people's worries in life seem to be boys (scuse, *men*) and clothes. I don't suppose I was cut out to be a party girl. Who "cuts us out" anyway? Or do we cut ourselves out??

February 20, 1957

Aboard the *Queen Elizabeth*

Dear Family,

Well, this "tug" is *much* smoother than the last one. I haven't been sick on it. Have had more fun. No lists, no exams, nothing pressing! Sleep til noon, lunch at one, movie at two, tea at four, dinner at 7, dancing til 1 or 2. The man shortage is *awful*. Everybody is married, that's taken for granted, but they all want to have fun: a shoe salesman from Michigan, 2 short fat bald Englishmen, a psychologist from South Africa wanting to compare their and our race troubles, a suave Hungarian who asked me to "tanz" and kissed my hand. Dancing is a farce. All the men come up to my waist and both of us go sliding all over the floor with each sway of the boat.

You should see the red tape for customs and debarkation. Please give Granny my best, and everybody else. Can hardly believe I've only been gone a week. It's incredibly like 2 months.

Love to all
Tu

Vendredi, le 22 Fevrier 1957

15 bis, boulevard Jules Sandeau

Paris!!!

Ma chère famille,

No, I'm not going to write in French although the mind is buzzing with it. At several points I didn't think we'd make it but we did and I'm all settled avec les Jungs. They are charming and I feel right at home.

We reached Cherbourg at 7 A.M. yesterday. Well, much pushing and pulling of hair but all 33 of us got off the *Elizabeth* and on to the tug. Then to Cherbourg and the boat train. Eight in a compartment and 16 bags. I dreaded dinner but it was délicieux, all 6 courses. We reached Paris about 3:30. The customs inspectors on the train took one look at all our bags and gave up. About 5 we started delivering girls. I was last so it was about 7:30 before I got to 15 bis. Mlle de Ram took me in. You have to punch a button to make the street door open. Then up 6 flights on the elevator. I could walk up faster than the elevator but it's easier. Monsieur Jung met me at the door—a tall, erect man, gray hair and a little moustache. Madame Jung is very nice, a big smile and so very kind.

Love to all,
TuTu

My room at the Jungs had a marble mantelpiece and a large armoire. From the tall window, I looked out onto roofs and chimney pots. The bed had sheets the size of mainsails, a neck-cramping bolster pillow, and a blue velvet coverlet. Rooming alone was nice after the crowded boat cabin, but I was a stranger in a foreign household. Should I come out of my room for dinner or wait to be summoned? Do I sit with the family after dinner or go back to my room? How do I eat an orange with a knife and fork?

On the first day, I learned how far I would travel to the Guaranty Trust Bank at Place de la Concorde and to classes in the Latin Quarter. Hemingway and Steinbeck were my companions on the long Métro rides. Occasionally, I'd splurge and ride bus number 63, so I could see Paris above the ground. At breakfast, Monsieur Jung made toast in a wire contraption designed to char a split baguette. As he passed the orange marmalade, he might mention that the government had fallen overnight. French politics were peripheral to the logistics of my daily routine. I rushed to class in the morning, came home for lunch, went back to school in the afternoon, returned home for dinner before leaving for a play, movie, or opera. In addition, I had translations to prepare, irregular verbs to memorize, and stockings to wash. On Sunday nights we square danced and ate chili at the American Cathedral club. Although I met and dated "boys," my nineteen-year-old heart was linked to a Georgia Tech student.

March 1, 1957

15 bis, boulevard Jules Sandeau

Dearest One,

I'm in Paris! I have to keep telling myself and other people cause the light *definitely* hasn't dawned. Sometimes I know I'm in Paris but *definitely* not in Europe. We arrived on a bright blue beautiful day. (I'd expected dark gray cold) Had *no* trouble with customs (They took one look at our 70 bags and gave up!)

My family is wonderful and were so nice and friendly from the very first (I'd expected cold icy stares). The food is delicious (even cauliflower which I detest).

I haven't gotten lost yet. Have only been pinched once and had on too many clothes for that to be very effective. Have done a great deal of sightseeing—been to the Louvre twice—and have walked my feet down to the ankles. Five blocks to and from the Métro about 3 times a day—and *miles* when I get wherever I'm going.

School starts next Thursday. I'm taking an intensive French course and one in Art History (with visits to museums) and one in the Theatre (with trips to plays and discussion thereof). My family speaks English (which I didn't expect) so I am able to make myself understood when my French fails me (as it often does).

This afternoon Madame J. is gonna take me for a walk in the Bois de Boulogne. It's very dangerous to go alone—even in broad daylight—it has an awful reputation. I think that's where the expression "to the woods" originated. Of course *I* don't know.

Well, don't study too hard and have fun and never forget that I love you.

Always,
Tu

In August and September 1897, Anna and Edith visited museums and cathedrals in Antwerp, Brussels, Cologne, Dresden, and Leipzig. In Berlin, Anna saw Edith's pension; Edith came to Anna's pension for three weeks at Christmas. In June 1898 they met in Cologne for two months of travel. They spent twelve weeks together in Europe, before and during their music and art training. Anna's first address in Paris was in the *seizième arrondissement*. Mlle Ballu had recommended a boardinghouse for single professional women.

September 21, 1897
The Lafayette Home
187, rue de la Pompe
My dear Edith,

I am here and considering I could not speak French got on very well. I did not send a telegram because I had too much to say and did not know how to send the telegram. Got to Paris 6:15, could not find a Porter, so tried to carry *all*, staggered a few steps, stopped, and hailed every man who passed with "Factor la Baggage" until I got one. Then the baggage had to be put on a stand and examined again, 3rd time. He went inside and unwrapped books, etc, then left and my factor put me in a cab and I thought I was riding all over Paris. Passed Arch de Triumph, could see it in the dark.

I finally saw Madame Higgins and had supper. Dining room had an open fire and was very warm. I have only a candle to write by. I will have to get a lamp first thing. If I judged by tonight, I would say I did not like it here, but I have come to work, and will put up with some things. I had to meet all and eat while they talked, then they asked me to sit a while and I did. The fire was good and warm. I am not going to mix much though. I guess you know that. Madame Higgins offered to go with me when the trunk comes, that is kind. She said as I did not speak French I might have some trouble.

With much love,
Anna M. Lester

September 22, 1897

Dear Mother and Father,

Madame Higgins showed me my room and took me [down] to dinner. She introduced me to about six Americans who had finished dinner and were sitting round the fire, talking for all they were worth. It is something like the place where I boarded in New York—21 Washington Square—I guess I will like it when I start to work—then I will not see them—all here studying music. There is a Mademoiselle Somebody here who tries to have all speak French—she knows Mlle Ballu and at lunch wanted to know if I was her *cousin!* I think she is employed by the house to teach the *girls!* ahem, like me, French, but I have not the slightest idea what one sound means—there is no connection between the sounds and what you want to say—as there is in German.

Tell Miss Beall I did not mean for her to drink *her funeral*—but "bier" is the German for Beer and I had seen it on so many bottles [in Germany] I forgot the difference. Anyway, I stopped drinking Beer or bier two weeks ago. I do not think it did me any good. I went to *ice* water—and ice—which is much better to my notion. I only wish I could get both here—but the Doctor said drink Port wine—and that is *nice* but costs like fury.

September 24, 1897

My dear Edith,

We have Breakfast at 8, rolls and coffee. Lunch at 12:30: two kinds of meat, beefsteak and one other, tea, bread, potatoes and salad—and fruit or preserves. Dinner at 6:30: soup, beef roast or steak, potatoes, one other kind of meat—last night it was chicken—salad, bread, and dessert. It suits me very well but the others complain. It is so much more like American eating than the German. It tastes good. They say the water is good, *all* drink it. I can't tell you about the house now, but it is in the most *healthy* part of Paris. A beautiful Avenue is just at the corner and one or two streets from Arch de Triumph. Near the "Wood" as they call it. My cough is better, but the mosquitoes torment me. I have found the Post Office nearby, a wine store is just across, but I haven't courage to go and get any.

I only wish I knew as much French as I do German. French is Greek to me. I can understand Moses [Anna's female cat at home] when she talks better. If I knew more History it would help me, but you know I do not know any. So, I am deprived of a great deal of pleasing. I only wish I had been taught how to study and then had a good teacher and not Mr. Sam Caldwell!

Letters from the Lesters in Rome did not survive, but I assume that, like all anxious parents, they wanted their children to be settled. Fleetwood struggled in business; Edith was a serious student in Berlin but was enjoying herself. Anna gave up a substantial teacher's salary to draw naked models in Paris. Her parents must have inquired about her plans for the future.

September 30, 1897

My dear Mother and Father,

Don't set your hopes on *me*. I am a drop in the ocean, much less a bucket. There are *thousands* and hundreds of thousands who do better work than I could dream of—I am going to do my best always, and that is *all* I can do—I might as well cry for the moon as a prize of *any* kind! I never expect to be rich—if I can get any *pleasure* out of my work, I will be satisfied. I am coming home after a while, but I will never be anything more than "Miss Annie" and have a few pupils.

I am too old to make a [new] start [teaching] anywhere, and I don't have any idea what I will do after this year—I am going to study in the [Académie] Julian—drawing and painting—and take private lessons after a while.

September 30, 1897
Dear Edith,

Father misses us but I cannot paint a Madonna or anything else. I am *nothing* and the sooner the family find it out the better for them. So they will not be disappointed. [Father wants a Madonna] like Raphael! My goodness. If I could paint a *cat* I would be glad.

————————————

After a short doze in the vibrating plane, I walk the aisles to combat claustrophobia. The airplane symbol on the projection screen hovers in mid-ocean. Where, please, is the coast of France? At last, overhead lights flicker, attendants pass steaming towels, and the smell of coffee filters from the galley. On the SS *Noordland*, Anna's breakfast menu listed: Cantaloupe, Bouillon, Boiled Hominy, Fried fresh Haddock, Broiled Sardines on Toast, Veal Cutlets, Dry Hash, and Buckwheat Cakes with maple syrup. For my airborne breakfast, I eat my hard-boiled egg as we make our final approach into Charles de Gaulle Aéroport.

This morning I will check into a small hotel in Montparnasse. Finding the hotel two years ago was groundwork for this current expedition. During the summer of 1996, as I browsed through Granny Harbin's Berlin scrapbook, I found a November 1898 envelope addressed to Miss Anna Lester in care of a Madame Grégoire. I didn't recognize the handwriting or the name of the street: rue Sainte-Beuve. Who sent the letter with the Topeka, Kansas, postmark and no return address? Where was rue Sainte-Beuve? Using a magnifying glass, I found the street in my 1957 *Plan de Paris*. Only one block long, the street runs between boulevard Raspail and rue Notre-Dame-des-Champs in the sixth *arrondissement*.

A few months later, in October 1996, David surprised me with an anniversary trip to France. We wanted to visit île de Ré and Normandy before spending our last nights in Montparnasse. While doing research for our trip, I found a guidebook of small Paris hotels in an Atlanta bookstore. As I searched through hotels in the sixth *arrondissement*, I stopped, astonished at one listing: Hôtel Sainte-Beuve on rue Sainte-Beuve. Sister Anna's street. I sped back to Rome, dug out Granny's scrapbook, and looked at Anna's 1898 envelope. More amazement. The addresses were identical: Hôtel Sainte-Beuve occupies 9, rue Sainte-Beuve—the building where Anna lived.

With trembling fingers, I telephoned the hotel. An impatient young woman answered, and when I inquired about our dates, she replied that the hotel was "*tout à fait complet.*" Totally booked. Click.

I had found the hotel, but there was no room in the inn. I pressed the 1898 envelope between my hands, looked up, and said, "Sister Anna, if you want us to stay at *your* hotel you will have to help." I mustered the nerve to redial the hotel number and asked if we could be on a cancellation list for the requested dates in October.

The receptionist said, "Let me look again. Oh yes, we have a room for those two nights." She may not have looked the first time, but I do not argue with gifts from the sky. I told her my story: my *grand-tante* lived at the hotel address in 1898. I had an envelope to prove it. Now she was animated. "*Incroyable!* Incredible!"

I collapsed onto the bentwood chair by the phone because my legs were limp. I knew Sister Anna's spirit from her art books, but I did not know she was a celestial travel agent. I learned an important lesson in perseverance: never take the first No as a final answer, especially in France.

David and I saw the Cuttino house on île de Ré and the Notre-Dame-Sous-Terre chapel on Mont-Saint-Michel, but at Bayeux, the treasure house containing the labyrinth was locked. Due to a *grève*, a strike of train workers, we arrived at the Hôtel Sainte-Beuve late at night in a heavy rainstorm. The lobby was bright with silk draperies and sisal carpet; our room on the fifth floor had antique porcelain and Porthault washcloths. Sister Anna's hotel was posh. Descending the spiral staircase to the lobby, I ran my hand along the railing. On what floor had Anna Lester lived?

After a day trip to Chartres to see the labyrinth, we returned to a rainy black Paris with no time to explore Anna's neighborhood. Before leaving for the airport, I gave the night clerk a gift for the hotel: a small collage copied from the envelope Anna received at 9, rue Sainte-Beuve. I returned a bit of her history to the hotel, but I left with many questions.

For this centennial trip, the Hôtel Sainte-Beuve—Anna's last residence in Paris—will be my base for nine days. At first, I had planned to stay a week, but my age demands a time cushion for fatigue, weather, or the inevitable *grève*. If I'm frugal, my money will last. I like the symmetry of nine days, beginning on the ninth day of November (the ninth month of the Roman calendar), at number 9, rue Sainte-Beuve.

Anna's address book has a tiny note beside Madame Grégoire's address: *troisième étage*. I have requested a room on that floor, the equivalent of our fourth floor. I know Anna's room faced the street because she wrote of looking out her window one morning to see Laura Berry coming to call. Laura was the sister of Martha Berry, who founded the Berry Schools near Rome. Another Rome woman, Mary Young, was studying in Paris. She and Anna saw sights together, but Anna refused to act as tour guide for peripatetic Romans; she came to Paris to work.

———◆———

My shuttle van whizzes through the morning traffic, past several *portes*, the original gates to Paris. The streets Anna saw included the boulevards sliced by Baron Haussmann in 1853 on the orders of Napoleon III. Frenchmen remembered their defeat by the Prussians just as southerners mourned their loss of the Civil War, but the Belle Époque was a time for optimistic rebuilding. Gustave Eiffel completed his tower for the 1889 World's Fair. During the poster craze of the 1890s, Henri de Toulouse-Lautrec portrayed life in Paris music halls and cafés. Alphonse Mucha painted posters for Sarah Bernhardt's plays, and Hector Guimard designed Art Nouveau entrances for the Métro, due to open for the World's Expositon in 1900.

Anna crossed the city by omnibus, double-decker tram, and horse-drawn carriage. She inhaled smoke from charcoal fires and stepped around horse manure in the streets. Eugène Atget's camera snapped the people of the era: the hurdy-gurdy man, the lampshade peddler, and the woman delivering bread. In Atget's photographs, street vendors push carts of vegetables, umbrellas, and pots and pans. On a foggy day like this, you can still see old Paris through Atget's lens; slices of the city resonate with his charcoal blacks, smudged grays, and faded sepias. As the van crosses the Seine, I see Notre-Dame Cathedral, blurred through a scrim of mist. My driver spirals into the heart of the Left Bank, to boulevard Raspail, to the front door of the Hôtel Sainte-Beuve.

Day One
Monday, November 9, 1998
Arrival at the Hôtel Sainte-Beuve

"Bonjour, Mademoiselle, je suis Susan Harvey."

"Oui, Madame Are-vay." The receptionist hands me a thick plastic key chain marked with the number 9.

"Quel étage?" I ask.

"You are on the *troisième étage*, as you requested."

The number nine seems propitious, and I am relieved that my room is ready this early. I glance around the elegant lobby where deep armchairs flank the fireplace. The striped silk draperies puddle on the floor by the windows, and Ionic columns add classic drama to the corners. I will enjoy being back in this refined space. After squeezing my bags into the elevator, I rise three floors and emerge into darkness. French halls and stairs have timed switches, so I fumble for the *minuterie* button and gain enough light to unlock the two doors of my room. Light from a tall French window illuminates the space. I go to the window and turn the oval brass knob. The hesitant scrape of the sliding bolt brings instant nostalgia for my bedroom at the Jungs. I close and open the window several times, absorbing the sound. Yes, yes, I am back in France.

A wrought-iron grille prevents me from falling when I lean out over the street to hear the taxis honking down boulevard Raspail. Across the street, the neon cross of a chemist is a pulsing green heartbeat. A woman follows her leashed dog on the sidewalk; her heels tap the pavement in a staccato city rhythm. Sanitation men wash the street. Their jocular conversation reverberates in the stone canyon of rue Sainte-Beuve.

My Paris abode has walls the color of European butter. Four historical prints hang above the quilted headboard of the bed, and square pillows top the scalloped white bedspread. The linen draperies have a pattern of intertwined red tulips and green leaves, and plaid taffeta curtains cover the lower half of the window. In the apartment across the street, a young girl plays a video game; I recognize the figure of Mario from my grandchildren's games. City dwellers become oblivious to the proximity of neighbors, exchanging modesty for light. I will adjust to the presence of strangers across the way.

In the corner of the room, a wooden desk awaits the Sister Anna Archives. I prop her photograph against the wall and spread out her letters, address book, and *Baedeker's Handbook for Paris*. Anna's journal entry for November 9, 1898, reads: Worked all day. If this was her room, I know who lived in the room next door.

Before I left Rome, I identified two of Anna's Paris friends from some cartoon sketches in the trunk. The captions did not match Anna's handwriting, but the scenes were at Madame Grégoire's pension. Who made the drawings? Rummaging through an old tin box in my basement, I found letters addressed to Anna from two Scottish women, Amy Steedman and Frances Blaikie. They wrote of good times living next to Anna at the Grégoire pension. A mystery solved: Frances Blaikie's looped handwriting matched the inscriptions on the cartoon sketches.

I found Amy Steedman on the Internet; she was the author of more than forty books, one illustrated by F. M. B. Blaikie. These Blaikie drawings could be valuable, but for me they are priceless: they depict Anna's life with her only compatible friends in Paris. The young women from Scotland arrived at 9, rue Sainte-Beuve just three weeks before Anna left. She wrote to Edith in November 1898:

> I would not have time to get lonely if these two Scotch girls were here all the time. They are just as pleasant as can be and come in any time. Invited me to tea on Saturday. Gave me a nice sketch of myself bringing my own cup, by request. One has quite a good deal of talent for all funny sketches.

Miss Lester is requested to bring her own cup.

Miss Blaikie and Miss Steedman serve tea

In my briefcase, I have copies of Miss Blaikie's drawings to give to the management of the Hôtel Sainte-Beuve. The originals waited one hundred years in Anna's trunk before returning to the place where they were drawn.

Anna described the decorations in her room to Edith:

> When I came here there were two pictures in this room—one an old man mending a clock and one a funny thing I could not make head or tail of—the people looked like idiots and I never once saw the name. Well it did not trouble me much, but when Madame Bazin came [to visit] *she* saw the name and made a great face. Then I too saw what it was—a house for crazy people. I wish you could have seen Madame Bazin! "Oh do take it down, do not keep it here, etc." So I laughed and said I would. I did that day, and put my yellow daisies up and gave Marie the "beauty" to put in some other room!

I sniff the Roger & Gallet soaps and bath oils in the gray marble bathroom and evaluate the emergency rations lurking in the minibar. My city-black Paris wardrobe fits into the built-in closet. What a luxury to have nine days in one place, unpacking only once. My utilitarian clothing is not French couture, but I will be warm and dry. Anna's preference for practical fabrics was similar to mine. When their aunt got married, Anna wrote to Edith:

> So Lutie is going to have a satin [dress]—If *I* ever get forgiven for buying mine I will not be in a hurry to get any more. Wool dresses for me

hereafter. Satins and silks are no earthly account to one. I wish *half* I have in my trunk was back at home so I could fill up on my return with what I *want*. I wonder if I ever will have what I want in this world?

After the long flight, I need fresh air and exercise, and I've waited two years to explore Anna's *quartier*. I plunk the heavy key chain on the front desk, push open the glass doors of the hotel, and walk down to the rue Notre-Dame-des-Champs. Rue Vavin and rue Bréa merge, forming a small triangular park. Adjoining shops sell fruit, pastries, vegetables, and children's toys. Motor scooters surround one of the green cast-iron water fountains given to Paris by Sir Richard Wallace—a wealthy but thirsty Englishman. After Wallace could not get a drink of water in 1872, he donated fountains to the city. Four goddesses stand in a classic temple, supporting a dome from which a trickle of water flows.

The facade of the building at 26, rue Vavin is white ceramic tile accented in royal blue. Trees and plants peek over the gradated balconies designed to admit light. Some Art Nouveau architects used ceramic tile to make buildings more hygienic after a tuberculosis epidemic. Despite the unusual material, the 1912 structure by Henri Sauvage is congruent with the surrounding buildings, part of the layered architecture in Paris. On the ground level, a paper store, Marie-Papier, displays writing instruments and handmade papers. I will come back here.

Art students stride along the streets with black portfolios under their arms. Even middle-aged American women carry art supplies to fulfill their Paris painting dreams. I whisper, "Go Ladies! May the spirit of Anna be with you."

I want to establish a café base in my neighborhood, so I walk to the corner and into the Café Vavin. The air is thick with smoke.

"Une table, non-fumeur, s'il vous plaît."

The waiter leads me to a small round table by the window. He scoops up the ashtray, making it a "nonsmoking table." My jacket adds precarious weight to the loaded coatrack in the corner. When I settle onto the wicker chair, the burden of travel anxiety melts, and a grin lifts the corners of my mouth. I'm here, sitting in a Paris café. My first meal will celebrate my safe arrival.

I am the only café patron not smoking or talking on a portable phone. Nonsmokers in France wage a futile crusade against the acrid smell of the Gauloise; restaurants are required to have smoke-free areas, but the law is rarely obeyed. Outside the café window, even young students in backpacks sabotage their lungs on the way to school.

The waiter brings my *poulet grillé* with *sauce béarnaise* and my favorite vegetable, *haricots verts*. The beans fill half the plate with their green crispness. What is the herb in the sauce? Tarragon? Do I eat my beans European-style with my knife and fork or just spear them with the fork? A classic French dessert appears on the chalkboard of daily specials. *Île Flottante*, a meringue and custard delicacy, embodies Paris to my taste buds, but the floating island will be a deferred pleasure.

Back out on the street, I take deep breaths as I stroll down rue Vavin to the massive iron gates of the jardin du Luxembourg, a verdant retreat from the boulevard Saint Michel traffic. I often came here between classes at the Sorbonne or the British Institute. The first building is the apiary of wooden pagoda beehives. A bass cello rests under the gazebo as though a cellist recently serenaded the bees. A few obstinate leaves cling to the plane trees, and a tarnished-silver mist broods over the park benches. The stones are slick with moisture, so I step off the path onto sandy gravel where my shoes leave impressions. Like a passport controller's rubber stamp, each footprint validates my presence in the city.

One of many women drawn to the freedom of expression in Paris, Isadora Duncan came to the Luxembourg at dawn to leap among the statues and trees. As she danced, her chiffon scarves fluttered in the breeze. Today, a meditative group dressed in black practices tai chi. As I traverse the *jardin*, admiring the statues of the Queens of France, a squadron of pigeons dives in my direction. I dodge the strafing birds, but they crash into an elderly lady dressed in black. She and I laugh, shake our heads, and continue our walks. Her good humor contrasts with my memory of the women who controlled chair rentals in the garden in 1957. Because of their status as widows of war, those black crows collected a few coins per chair. They pecked angrily at illegal chair-sitters who forgot to pay.

A persistent Luxembourg legend has Hemingway stealing pigeons when the *gendarmes* were not looking. After wringing a bird's neck, the hungry writer stuck it under the covers of his baby's carriage and sauntered home for a roast pigeon lunch. Leaving the gardens, I pass a statue of Pan, dancing on one foot with pipe in hand. A boastful pigeon sits on his head, safe from latter-day Hemingways.

The Café Orbital is a *cybercafé* on the rue de Médicis whose address I found on the Internet. Dozens of computer terminals line the walls, and customers pay by the minute with a thirty-five-franc minimum. The *cyberhôtesse* turns on a computer for me. The French keyboard has some letters reversed, but I ignore the unwelcome letter *q* that pops up in my words in place of an *a*. The period and comma replace each other so part of my message is one run-on sentence. My e-mail takes seconds to travel to my house in Rome, two blocks from the former Lester home. In another one hundred years, will this communication be done with thought waves? One of my great-nieces will be able to retrace my steps and simultaneously broadcast her voyage. I believe the affection of family and friends will penetrate space and time, across oceans or galaxies, regardless of the century in which we live.

In 1898 letters took eight days to reach Paris from New York, nine to reach Berlin; Anna and Edith timed their letters to catch the weekly boats leaving Europe. I also corresponded with my family by letter in 1957. Each day, I checked the entry hall for blue airmail notepaper from my family and from David. My parents never used the transatlantic telephone. By the time my college-age children spent summers in Europe, we communicated by telephone. I had the dubious pleasure of a call from my son—in a phone booth in Spain—immediately *before* he ran with the bulls in Pamplona. Some news should travel—after the fact—by sea.

When I shut down the computer, I sever connections with America and step out onto the streets of Hugo, Stein, Sand, Flanner, and Fitzgerald. The pages of their masterpieces stack themselves around me like a *pâte feuilletée*, a pastry of leaves. Compared to my nine-day project, the richness of past talent in Paris is overwhelming. I float up the street in culture-shock fog—buoyed along by the Perrier fizz of the city.

Soon I am lost in a maze of streets. Maybe I turned the wrong way when I walked back around the garden. I need to find a bank to cash travelers' checks, a post office to buy stamps, and a Métro station to purchase a weekly pass. The Métro must be near; there's no mistaking the fumes rising from a sidewalk grate. In the bowels of Métro Vavin I find only multiple exits and passages under the street. In the reverse of Sartre's *No Exit*, I am a frustrated character in the torment of *No Entrance*.

Walking down the boulevard du Montparnasse, I remember that Anna's second address in Paris was on this busy thoroughfare. Only weeks after arriving at the Lafayette Home, she had to move.

September 30, 1897

The Lafayette Home

187, rue de la Pompe

My dear Mother and Father,

Yesterday Madame Higgins told me this room I have was engaged to two girls who were here last year. She could not say I could have any other room and they were expected Oct. 15. When the time came to move she would find me another place. As you would say, Father, I was "set back." I decided however to take the matter in my own hands, so after lunch I went across the City to make arrangements for my art work. Found the Studio all right and a number of girls working. Got terms and told the man I would be down on Monday.

I then went to The Girl's Club. You remember seeing a piece about this place in the France Journal this summer? They only had one room—and I did not like that, so the lady in charge asked me if I would like to go into a French family. I told her I would like to see the rooms. And, will you believe it, she got her hat and went with me! Was just as kind as possible.

It is a pension on the 2nd floor. Nice new and clean and plenty of sun, not five minutes walk from the Studio—Académie Delécluse—where I want to work for 6 months, then I will go to [Académie] Julian for a while. Here it takes over an hour by Buss and I could not stand that all winter in bad weather. Board, room, and two French lessons a week for 160 francs. A month, service, and light 10 francs, the fire extra, that 170 and my lessons 30 makes just 200 francs—$40.

Now no use to get worried for Madame Higgins says if the lady at The Girl's Club recommends a place it is *all right*. You know at the club they only take Americans and unmarried women, so she's bound to send me to a good place. I am sure I could trust her, she had a good face. I am near to everything over there—two studios, the club, and the Franco-English Guild.

You know I think it is Providential that Madame Higgins did not want me here. I never could have stood two hours a day Buss riding and one hour walking to go to and from my work.

October 3, 1897

144 bis, boulevard du Montparnasse

My own dear Father,

Sunday. I moved yesterday and you would be surprised how much I did. In the morning first thing I packed the satchel with my books and papers and it was heavy as *lead*. Then I put on my hat, cape, and rubbers for I did not know what minute it might rain. I went up to Place Victor Hugo and took a Buss for the bank.

I am going to the studio in the morning, so will have to be up bright and early, have my breakfast and be there by 8 o'clock, work until twelve, then I will come back here to what they call second breakfast. I call it lunch. The "wonderful" first breakfast consists of a *bowl* of coffee and cold light bread. This place is stingy with its sugar and you know how much I like in my coffee, don't you dear? Well, this morning the girl brought me a bowl the size of your peach bowl and *two* lumps of sugar!! I made a sign that I wanted more and she went and brought *one!* I had to drink it not sweet and guess I'll *have* to learn to *like* it that way.

Monday afternoon. I went to the studio and worked until 12. I got there in time to draw for my place. You see, there is *one* model and about 30 girls work from the one. So they have numbers and the one who gets one, two, and three, have first choice—and so on—that is about the first time I ever got as good a number and the funny part is when the man in charge called out 3 in French I did not know myself by that funny name—"trois" for 3.

Give my love to the pets, Dickens, Danny, and Moses—at the Studio there is a jet black cat and during the rest it came and got up in my lap. I want you all to keep well and fat, so eat my share of everything, sugar, too.

With much love for you and Mother,

I am lovingly,

Anna

October 7, 1897

Dear Edith,

Monday bright and early I went to the Delécluse Studio, paid for 6 months and the entrance fee 170 francs. This 6 months is for any time; if I want to stop and rest a month I can and he lets it come off. That is good and *cheap*—3 criticisms a week—working from the Life all the time! This is just half what Julian is and we would do the same, however for the *name* of it I *have* to go to Julian's some while here, so will do so when I am in better practice. In Art one has to work out his own salvation any way, and I can do so here as well as at Julian's. The class is full now of Americans and English.

Well, Monday, Mrs. Cooley—but you do not know the household, do you? I'll tell you: three Berthier sisters, *very* ordinary French people *I* think, but I am going to do my best to like them and learn French and stay—*if* they do not *freeze* or *starve* me out. That remains to be seen.

Well, the family: one sister is the housekeeper, one teaches French, the youngest is a milliner. One widow, a boarder, Mrs. Johnson, here for French—but will leave 1st of November—she speaks well now and will move near the College and attend lectures. Mr. and Mrs. Cooley—he's an *artist* working at Julian, she's a musician studying music and French. From near London. He and I eat breakfast every morning at the same time, none of the others get up so early (7:30) He has told me quite a good deal about working from the model—and then said "It took me ten years to learn that—after you have worked hard ten years you will either go on fairly well—or give it up, *but it takes that much time to make a start!!!*" What would Father say to that? It, however, is the truth. I know that better than any one can tell me, and it makes me blush to know how little I do know. I think I did *very* well to hold my [teaching] positions.

Last night I was so sleepy, I went to bed early. Well, this morning Mr. Cooley gave me a lecture on "wasting so much time in bed." I took [it] coolly, did not tell him *why* I took more rest than he. He said, "Spend 8 hours in Art, 8 in French, 8 in bed for a day." And so it goes—for breakfast.

M. Callot criticized on Tuesday. He said I had the *action* very well but to make it more simple. Draw a new sketch every day for a while. I was dumbfounded at such a good one [criticism]. I am awfully out of practice and it is *awful* hard work to draw a *live* person with no clothes on.

Now has this week been full or not? I have been in the sun all I could. The cough is just the same—unless it has worried me a trifle more this week than before. It has been so cold and windy. I am taking the medicine still and the Wine *every* night—and have put on more clothes. There is nothing more I can do so no need to worry. It may wear off by and by. Otherwise I feel better.

With much love,

Anna M. Lester

October 9, 1897

My dear Edith,

I mailed you a letter yesterday but I have an object in this. That old *witch* of a Miss Weimar is on my track—and I want you to help me out. Get as many *different* kinds of envelopes in the house as you can without appearing strange. And get *different* people to address each one. Don't *you* address any for *she* knows your writing from last year. Have the writing as foreign as possible. Then once in a while *I* will send one in my own hand to mislead her if possible. The old hag! I tell you hanging is almost too good for that woman!! I think there are sins as great as murder—which are not punished in this world—*unless* she repents she will get her reward in the next—I am *so* furious with her.

The address is: Mlle Henriette Ballu, Mary Baldwin Seminary, Staunton, Virginia, U.S.A. Address some "Mlle" and write out the "Henriette." Some "Mademoiselle H. Ballu." You could even have one to Mary Baldwin *College* so *my friend* [Miss Weimar] will think they come from different people, if possible.

Miss Weimar is acting about me and *my* letters sent there just as she did about Miss Shattuck and the letters she sent to *her* friends after leaving. If I could just give her a *good* sound thrashing so she could not sit down or stand up for a solid week, I would be glad!

Do you think you can do this for me with *very* little trouble to yourself? I do not care if some of the envelopes are *mourning* ones—[send] *all* kinds. Get good ones and I will refund all you lay out.

October 15, 1897

Dear Mother and Father,

I am counted as a mere beginner at the studio, and truly I am in the sense I am working from Life, you know—*nude*. I never did but one sketch of that kind in New York and it is no joke to draw a full length figure from Life—models do not stand as still as [plaster] *casts*, you know, then one has the *color* to contend with and that makes it harder to see the lights and shadows correctly. I am going to do my best however—and that is all one can do.

Your loving daughter,
Anna M. Lester

At the Gare Montparnasse Métro, I descend and buy a *carte hebdomadaire*, valid for unlimited rides for seven days. Scurrying to the surface like a disoriented mole, I don't dare count how many hours I have been awake. Gloomy darkness creeps through the city as I walk down rue de Rennes to rue Littré where I find a post office, buy stamps, and exchange my travelers' checks. Many of Anna's letters are postmarked "rue Littré." By chance, I have found the post office where she mailed letters to Edith, her parents, and Mlle Ballu.

Rain spatters on the street, so I dart under a café awning, order *thé citron* and *crêpes au chocolat*, and find the *toilettes* down in the *sous-sol*. Behind a frosted glass door muddy footprints surround a hole in the floor: the infamous Turkish toilet. I had forgotten about the phallic soap jutting out on a metal rod and the unisex mingling at the sink. A large African man and I jockey for towels in the cramped space.

Ascending from the pit, I sit close to the heater on the *terrasse chauffée* and study my pocket map. Where did I take the wrong turn? With no sun in view, I can't tell which direction is north, and a chilly mist blows on the back of my neck. Taking a taxi (if available in rush-hour rain) would defeat my pioneer spirit. With the help of the waiter and a kind policeman, I relocate rue Notre-Dame-des-Champs and turn onto rue Sainte-Beuve.

Back in my warm room, I shed my damp clothing and pour bubble bath into a tub of hot water. I laugh about my first bath in Paris in 1957:

Madame Jung showed me my room, then the W.C., the handwashing place, and the salle de bain (*bath* room). Three different places! After dinner I was told I could bathe, so I did. Only problem was that I couldn't get the plug out of the tub. I realized that there was a trick to it, but being new in the land I had *no* idea how. And I certainly did not want to call Madame. So I tore up my fingernails trying to pry it out.

Tried some pieces of broken clothespins also, but no. Then another "boarder" came down the hall and I desperately asked her if she spoke English and she laughed. Seems you use the clothespin to grab hold of the thing, a center piece. I'd been working on the part connected to the pipe and all the plumbing for miles around. Oh well!

As weariness soaks away, I'm thankful for hot water. Paris has evolved since Anna lived at the Berthiers' pension:

> Since I came to Paris, I have been taking a half bath in cold water every morning. I began this at the Lafayette House because it was so hard to get hot water, and I had no stove. I think it agrees with me. Here, Ernestine brings me hot water every night so the other half of me gets a hot bath at night. That I think is good, it warms my feet up.

I crawl from the tub, dry myself with a Porthault towel, and slide between the ironed linen sheets of a comfortable bed. Lying in the dark, I'm aware of the street noises dulled by the curtains. I hear the elevator door open and close. Some voices in the hall. British? American?

I'm in Paris. Alone. Now what? I have not mapped out a specific plan for each day. I may give myself permission to wander tomorrow. The outer arcs of a labyrinth require freewheeling motion before condensing into the inner rings. My aunt and I have linear, goal-focused personalities. Can I alter that? I'd like to wake up tomorrow and just walk out into the city.

Day Two
Tuesday, November 10, 1998
Hats on the Brain

To be happy one must choose well his atmosphere.

Lamartine

I say choose Paris.

Anna Lester, April 1898

On my first morning on the *troisième étage* of the Hôtel Sainte-Beuve, I open the door to the hallway. Above me, the stairwell is a chambered nautilus circling to the top floor. The woven stair carpet is buff, bordered in red—like a pleated French dish towel fanning down to the dark ground level. In 1898, coal scuttles, breakfast trays, and Anna's trunk from Rome, Georgia, came up this spine of the building. Anna, Amy, and Frances held the wooden railing as they went out for the day; their long skirts brushed the iron balustrades as they returned from the opera. I walk down in a spiral between two centuries: Anna's stair rail on my left, taupe wallpaper with white check marks on my right.

Approaching the ground floor, I hear the hiss of milk being steamed for coffee, the clink-chink of silver spoons on china, and the rustle of morning newspapers. This morning's receptionist chants into the phone, "Hôtel Sainte-Beuve, Bonjour!" The bar area serves as the breakfast room, but a tour group occupies the tables and sofas. I climb onto a barstool and order a *petit déjeuner complet avec café au lait*. I combine streams of frothy milk and black coffee into my cup and add sugar cubes. Since my back is to the other diners, I lift the croissant and bury my nose in its underbelly. No French perfume can compete with the aroma of toasted butter. My breakfast tray also holds a glass jar of creamy French yogurt, a golden pear, toast, butter, and raspberry *confiture*.

While I eat, I show a few of Anna's letters to the woman who brought my tray. "These were written from this address in 1898. My *grand-tante* lived on the *troisième étage.*"

"*Incroyable.*" She shakes her head.

After breakfast, she lets me peek into the other rooms on my floor while they are being cleaned. Room number 10 has two windows and was probably expanded from two smaller rooms. Number 11 is about the size of my room and has one window. If I stay in each room on this floor on return trips to the hotel, I'll be assured of sleeping where Anna and the "Scotch girls" slept.

When I go back down to the lobby, I see my framed collage from 1996 propped on a shelf near the fireplace. I take it to the reception desk and introduce myself to Fabienne, an animated woman with the innate fashion sense of French females. Her gray worsted suit is perfectly tailored, her hair arranged in a stylish coif.

"I'm in Paris to research the life of my *grand-tante*, Anna Lester, who lived here in 1898."

"Oh, Madame Are-vay, *you* made *le petit collage!*"

I show her copies of Miss Blaikie's drawings, which I want to give to the hotel management. "Who is the owner of Le Sainte-Beuve?"

"Madame Bobette Compagnon, but she is at her château."

"Madame Champignon?"

"*Non, non!* Not Madame Mushroom, *Madame Compagnon!*"

When we stop laughing, Fabienne tells me that sometime after Madame Grégoire's era, this address became a *hôtel de rendezvous.* A few years ago, Madame Compagnon rescued the building and made structural and design changes. As I prepare to leave, Fabienne promises to connect me with Madame Compagnon this week.

I am wearing my Paris uniform—black sweatpants, a ribbed sweater, and a scarf. My jacket covers the valuables strapped around my waist; my pockets are lumpy with maps and gloves. My notebook lists Anna's addresses, but I have no agenda for the day. When I leave the hotel, I feel great; my sore throat is gone. I am again a twenty-year-old student, elated to be in my favorite city, with time and freedom to explore narrow streets. Paris is a treasure map spread out for my pleasure.

I've recently reread Julia Cameron's *The Artist's Way.* She asks, "What if God is a woman and She is on your side?" If God is a woman and She is on my side, this is exactly what She would do: send me to Paris. I justified the trip as a family research project; the Female God wants to give me art, music, a Métro pass, and an Île Flottante.

On the boulevard Raspail, I walk through a crowd of students smoking cigarettes. Possibly this was the student club we came to in 1957. Did Anna walk on this boulevard or the smaller streets? I hush my questions; this is my day to be seduced by the city. The pollen from flower shops tickles my nose. My fingers itch when I see inks, papers, and elegant writing paraphernalia in a bookstore window. A home furnishing store displays linen fabrics and ceramic creamware on whitewashed tables; blue gentians and purple hyacinths bulge from flats in front of a garden store.

On a side street, I find 27, rue de Fleurus, the former address of Gertrude Stein and Alice B. Toklas. In their legendary salons, these iconoclastic women entertained rising stars of twentieth-century art and literature. While Gertrude conversed with the men, Alice exchanged recipes with their wives. The flood of expatriate Americans arrived after Anna had left Paris in 1898. She represented the nineteenth century in her work and tastes, while Stein, Picasso, and Hemingway were revolutionaries of the twentieth.

Back on the boulevard Raspail, I walk down to rue du Cherche-Midi. I remember that one of Anna's studios, Académie Julian, was on this street. Julian was probably the most famous of her studios, but she didn't study there until the month before she went home. During my time in Paris, it will be impossible to reenact Anna's life chronologically. I'm sleeping in the last place she lived; today I'll walk by her third studio address.

I dissect the street name: Cherche-Midi. Does it mean search for noon or search for the south? For my answer, I see a sundial carved on the corner of a south-facing building—a noon mark etched into stone. This street was the location of the Cherche-Midi military prison, where the French army incarcerated Captain Alfred Dreyfus in 1894—before his espionage trial and imprisonment on Devil's Island. The Dreyfus affair continued into Anna's era, causing a scandal in the army and provoking Émile Zola's angry attack on anti-Semitism.

The French have a graphic term for window shopping: *faire du lèche-vitrines*, literally "to lick the shop windows." This phrase suits pastry and confection vendors, but antique jewelry, ormolu furniture, and leather-bound books also cause the shopper to salivate. One store features pendulums, astrolabes, and New Age books. When I ask the salesman the name for dowsing rods, he says they are called *baguettes*, like the rod-shaped loaves of bread. Dowsing rods are also known as divining rods, tools for getting in touch with divine energy. Last year, my sister Edith and I bought copper rods in Avebury, England, and dowsed Neolithic stones, crop circles, and turf mazes from the coast of Cornwall to the hills of northern England. When we crossed the threshold of the Merry Maidens stone circle near Penzance, we hit a wall of energy that took our breath. Those rock "maidens" had a palpable magnetic field.

I use dowsing rods to construct labyrinth designs on the ground, to help me find a potent spot for the goal. As I walk around a site, rods in outstretched hands, I feel connected to my barefoot ancestors who walked old tracks and ley lines in England. I can't walk the streets of Paris with dowsing rods as I did the moors of Devon; Sister Anna must guide me.

A red awning across the street bears the number 55. I pull out my notebook and verify that this is the address on Anna's receipt from Académie Julian. The building houses a restaurant, La Marlotte. Why not eat lunch on the street where Anna studied art? In the humid restaurant, wine and garlic fragrances assure me that I have made a good choice. The owner escorts me to a banquette and takes my bulky jacket. When I slide into my seat, my sweatpants catch on the nap of maroon velvet. I wish I were wearing silk. I dine among urbane Frenchmen in business suits and women in Hermès scarves; their conversational patter is more soothing than background music.

Boeuf bourguignon is the perfect meal for this cool day. I spread butter and ripe cheese on my bread crusts and try not to flinch when *l'addition* arrives. This is only my first full day in Paris; I must ration my francs. On the way out of the restaurant, I show the *patron* my copy of Anna's receipt from the Académie Julian.

"*Ma grand-tante* studied here in 1898."

He looks with interest at the paper bearing his address, then leans out the door and points to the right. *"Dans la cour, Madame, dans la cour."*

The courtyard is a long passageway with buildings on three sides. According to Anna's flyer from the Académie Julian, there were studios for women at 27, Galerie Montmartre; at 5, rue de Berri; and at 5, rue Fromentin. Anna's printed flyer has the 55, rue du Cherche-Midi address added in ink. I assume she chose this location because it was the closest to Madame Grégoire's pension.

The main Julian studio for men was at 31, rue Dragon. There, male students paid half the tuition charged to women for a month of drawing classes. Women also paid more to rent easels and stools. The Académie had an elaborate system of weekly and monthly awards for drawings. Since the contests were judged anonymously, men and women competed equally. The best students received cash prizes and medals, and Julian entered their work in the highly competitive Salon. Exhibiting in the annual Salon was the height of success for an artist.

Midway down the *cour*, stone columns form an entryway to what was once a *hôtel particulier*, a fine private residence. Renovation is underway but no workmen are in sight so I walk inside the building, dodging ladders and drop cloths. The sunny rooms make it easy to imagine stools, drawing pads, and a nude model posing in the light. I see a portly instructor in a frock coat stopping at Anna's easel. He mutters, *"Pas mal, Mademoiselle, pas mal."*

"Not bad" was higher praise than I received in my art classes at Hollins. I could hear my art professor sigh when he approached my easel in 1958.

All art history majors at Hollins had to take a drawing and painting course in order to graduate. Drawing was not my forte. Portraits never looked like their subjects; the reflected light on green wine bottles refused to transfer to my canvas. One day, my instructor—a master of still life painting—paused at my easel. "Miss Gilbert," he said, "why don't you stop daubing at that picture and let it die a natural death." I passed the course, but lost enthusiasm for painting.

When David and I moved to Rome in 1964, I joined civic organizations and the PTA. One day, I heard about a class in design at Shorter College. I was hungry for art, and design sounded less threatening than painting, so I resigned from clubs, found nursery schools for my daughters, and enrolled in the class. The teacher, Virginia Dudley, was a gifted sculptor who introduced me to three-dimensional design. I had loved my classes in medieval and contemporary architecture at Hollins. In Virginia Dudley's classes, I transferred this passion for interior space into assemblage and installation. I recovered from the stigma of not being able to draw or paint, and I've spent the past thirty years composing my own still life compositions.

I sit on the front steps of the neoclassical building. What have I read about the Académie Julian? Rodolphe Julian, a wrestler from the Vaucluse region of France, moved to Paris to become an artist, but he saw there was more money in management than in painting. He became an entrepreneur, opened his first art school in 1868, and formed the academy in 1873. Julian was one of the first teachers to give women the classical training men received at the state-subsidized École des Beaux-Arts. Art officials urged women to decorate fans and ceramics, thus supporting themselves and the economy of France. Men produced *le grand art* and could apply for the top art award, the Prix de Rome.

Students at the École des Beaux-Arts opposed the admission of women; females might inhibit their rowdy pranks. The men also feared competition for the medals awarded to top students. A gold medal exempted a man from military service, so competing with women was a matter of life and death. Through the efforts of the Union des Femmes Peintres et Sculpteurs and other feminist groups, women gained entrance to the École in 1897. Anna attended a lecture there in January 1898. She told Edith: "Today I found my way to the Beaux-Art to a lecture on anatomy. I could understand very little that was said, but I could *see*, and made some sketches of the bones. Then the Professor had a model to pose in the same position in which the bones were placed. I enjoyed it."

From the flyer in my hand, I see that Rodolphe Julian hired eminent painters to teach in his Right Bank ateliers: Jules Lefebvre, William Bouguereau, Jean-Paul Laurens, Benjamin-Constant, and Tony Robert-Fleury. The professors listed at 55, rue du Cherche-Midi were Marcel Baschet and François Schommer.

Anna investigated several academies for courses using a *modèle vivant*—a live nude model. She preferred Delécluse and Colarossi but wanted the cachet of Académie Julian on her résumé. In October 1897, she wrote to her parents from the Berthier pension:

> In the spring, when I begin working *all* day, I will probably go to Julian's. There are four of his [studios] for women, but I tell you Delécluse is just as good if not *better* for work, numbers have told me so. Julian has a *big* name, and of course, I *must* go there some. Julian is no artist you understand. [Anna did not know Julian studied with Cabanel and had exhibited in the Salon.] He just started these studios and has the artists to come in and criticize. I think some are over stables as the studios in New York are. No use to tell any body what my plans are, I prefer not.

The stone steps are cold. Seeing Anna and a professor in this elegant building was an embellished fantasy; the low structures lining the court were more appropriate for rental studios. I ask the receptionist in an architectural firm if she knows the former location of the Académie Julian. She shrugs. *"Je n'ai aucune idée, Madame."* I have no idea either. This courtyard was a dead end in the Anna maze. If she walked these stones in October 1898, it was only to boost her reputation.

Back out on rue de Cherche-Midi, I resume my window-licking ramble. Down a side street, I see Anna's favorite department store, Le Bon Marché. Anna purchased gloves and shirtwaists and had her umbrella recovered at this *grand magasin*. She told her father: "The Bon Marché is far ahead of Macy's because the clerks are polite and at Macy's I cannot stand the coolness of the shop girls. I do not like to trade there."

Nearing the main store, I hear music. Mechanical vignettes in the shop windows illustrate the eighteenth-century fairy tale, *Peau d'Ane* (Donkey Skin). The princess and fairy godmother twirl in froths of sequins and tulle; the goddess of weather floats in clouds, feathers, and crystal snowflakes. I whisper to her: Please, bless the Paris weather this week and keep me well.

After enjoying the window theater, I cross a side street to La Grande Épicerie. More than a grocery store, it's an epicurean art gallery. Asparagus, artichokes, and baby eggplants are still life arrangements awaiting Flemish painters; burlap sacks brim with lentils, garbanzo beans, and gourmet coffees. Glass cases hold cartwheels of cheese, while loaves of bread render praise to French bakers.

Anna's second obsession in Paris, after her art, was getting enough of the foods she liked. In fact, my family's love of eating probably dates to Bannester Lester's grocery store. In 1898, he sent Anna an advertisement:

> If you want nice healthy children get Mellin's food, Imperial granism, Ralston breakfast food, Pearl Tapioca, cornstarch, Wheaten Grist, Farina, White Wheat and Oatflakes at Lester's.
>
> Home-made preserves, sweet pickle peaches, Quince and Peach, Strawberry and Cherries, Cream and Edam cheese, Hams and Breakfast Bacon, Holland Herring and Fat Mackerel, at Lester's, Old Postoffice Corner, Rome, Ga.

Homesickness can attack through the tastebuds and nostrils, and Anna missed delicacies from Georgia. She wrote Edith: "Father makes me hungry talking about ripe tomatoes. How I would enjoy a great big dish full. I have seen them in windows all winter but have not bought any. When I get rich—which will be never until I reach Heaven, I will have all I want of every thing under the sun."

My appetite mimics Anna's as I walk past the cheese display; I could consume a round of Boursin—*toute seule.*

I leave La Grande Épicerie and enter the main store, a marvel of steel and glass. Gustave Eiffel designed Le Bon Marché in 1852; interior designer Andrée Putnam added the escalators that crisscross the domed well of the atrium. Walking through the aisles of the main floor, I touch paisley shawls and leather gloves. I didn't inherit the Lester skill with numbers, so converting the francs into dollars takes me a minute. The store is spacious and easy to navigate, but I am startled to see leashed dogs shopping with their owners. One woman picks up and carries her Labrador retriever when he refuses to mount the escalator.

I don't need appliances or furniture, but I stop when I pass the hat department. I love hats. When I joined the Episcopal church at age fifteen, all females covered their heads. My mother and I shopped at Rich's in Atlanta for Easter and wedding hats. When my mother-in-law died, I took flowered hats from her closet, but I've used them as costumes for my performance characters: Miss Verna Equinox, Miss Marigold Hibiscus, and Miss Dottie Dot Com. When I put on a hat, I assume the persona of my character.

Fashion was another obsession of the Lester sisters, after art and food. Before the Civil War, Bannester Lester sold fine fabrics in his store in Georgetown, South Carolina. After the family moved to Rome, he opened another dry goods store but, unlike the Low Country, north Georgia had no wealthy plantation wives buying fabric for ball gowns. Bannester lost his business in bankruptcy and started over in groceries, but his descendants inherited his love of clothes. Anna gave Edith detailed advice:

> I do not think the braid [should be] *all* over the skirt—18 inches is enough I think. It would make your skirt so heavy. I would not have the dress trimmed much only in black braid, made plain and stylish and so you can wear a long time. Be sure and get a *dark* color, light soils so easily. I sent you three books on Monday, you can see the styles from those. Thank goodness I will not need any. I would get one made, if I did, at the Bon Marché. Dressmakers make me too tired to live, while they are fussing with me.

Anna wrote home in the spring of 1898:

> Hats are on my brain now. So Wednesday I took the Buss and went up town to see what they really had at the Louvre [department] store. I went in the wrong door last time. Well if ever any body *saw* hats, I did that day! Only *one* suited me and I did not get it. I got a white sailor for

79 cents—3.75 francs, can be trimmed into a cool summer hat if I wish. I have that green mull [muslin] you know and with a little touch of narrow black ribbon I have and two black chicken feathers, I'll have a *Paris* hat for my little money.

The Bon Marché hat department has a vast but expensive selection. I wander through a covey of women trying on chapeaux. One family brought three generations to give advice; mother, daughter, and grandmother debate the choices. When Anna bought a hat in November 1898, she wrote Edith:

> This morning was simply too dark to see [to draw] so I did a wonderful work of art—I Bought a Hat!! Now what do you think of your sister? I had decided fully *not* to get anything but a black one trimmed in green or a green one trimmed in black—and bought a *dove* color. With purple velvet violets and white wings—whew—how young I do look in it. The color and effect is good but of course, the felt is not, but that does not matter. I shall have to wear it home to get it there—it would not go in my trunk. Don't you wish you could see me in that hat and my fur cape? One dollar and ninety-five cents is not much to spend every two years for winter hats!

Anna bought a hat in November 1898; I should buy one as a centennial celebration. The cost will stretch my budget, but how often will I go shopping with Anna in a store she loved? She chose one with violets and white wings; I try on a black derby whose rolled brim suggests the nineteenth century. In the camaraderie of shopping, the women around me nod and approve my selection. At the cash register, I ask the saleswoman to take my photograph.

She flutters her hands, as if fending off a hex. *"Interdit! La photographie est interdite*—streekly forbeeden—*au Bon Marché!"*

I counter with my Great-Aunt Anna spiel: *"Mais, ma grand-tante a acheté un chapeau.* One hundred years ago. *Je veux documenter…"*

"Oh! C'est une tradition familiale! OK, oui, bon, ça va!" She surrenders and photographs me by the hat display. Pleased with my victory, I depart with my orange Bon Marché sack. Like Anna, I will wear my hat home to America.

———※———

Fabienne reports that, *malheureusement*, Madame Compagnon arrived at the hotel while I was gone, but has now left for the day. I get a Perrier and *glaçons* (ice cubes) from the lobby bar. My dinner is the last V-8 juice from my travel pack and the pear I saved from breakfast—a strange combination, but the price is right.

I close the linen curtains against the night, put on my new hat, and stand before the antique mirror. If Anna lived in this room, did she look into a similar mirror to admire her November hat? My reflection in the crazed surface of the looking glass resembles a daguerreotype of my Lester great-grandparents. Would my connoisseur great-grandfather, his fashion-conscious daughters, and my discriminating mother approve today's purchase? Anna is probably in Heaven picking out some chicken feathers to spruce up my simple hat.

Seated on the bed, I look through *Pariscope*, a weekly listing of events in the city. I want to hear music, see art, and get out of the city for a day. I rule out movies, operas, and trips to Versailles and Fontainebleau, but I see some concerts scheduled in late afternoon. I will miss going to the theater, but I can't keep the pace I did in 1957. My schedule may resemble Anna's in 1897:

> I have never been out later than 6:30 and I am not inclined to be, but I hear the girls at the studio talk of *not being* afraid to stay out until 1 A.M. Excuse me from trying that! I am a little too old to begin, anyway I am sleepy and tired before eight, and sometimes excuse myself from the dinner table before the others get through talking and come to my room.

I pick up *Baedeker* and read the places Anna marked: Bois de Boulogne on September 25, 1897; Sainte-Chapelle on October 28, 1897; the Panthéon on November 11, 1897. As I turn the pages that Anna turned, the atmosphere in the room shifts, as if the barometric pressure is falling. At the entrance to my room, the image of a woman drifts through the locked door like an English Channel fog. She wears a short cape, maybe fur-trimmed, and since her hair is under her hat, I can't tell if she's a redhead. Standing with her back to me, she tilts her head and lifts her right hand to pull a hat pin from her hat. Then, she glides over to the desk where I left my Bon Marché hat.

Oh, dear. Anna is not decorating hats in Heaven tonight; she's here in this room. I've felt the spirits of departed people, but this is the first apparition I've seen. Did the hat, the mirror, or the *Baedeker* trigger a time vortex? No one is going to believe this.

I will my visitor to stay, but she seems unaware of my presence. I am the voyeur, trespassing in *her* space. Maybe she's not here to see me, but has returned to a place where she was happy. As she fades, the air smells as if a spring freshet had blown through.

I lie down and hug the covers to my neck. I talked about finding Anna in Paris, but I never expected a visible *fantôme*. I will sleep with the light on.

There are souls which become extinguished, after having burned for all that is beautiful and noble in the moral world, without having found the means, as without even having felt the need of manifesting themselves to others.

George Sand

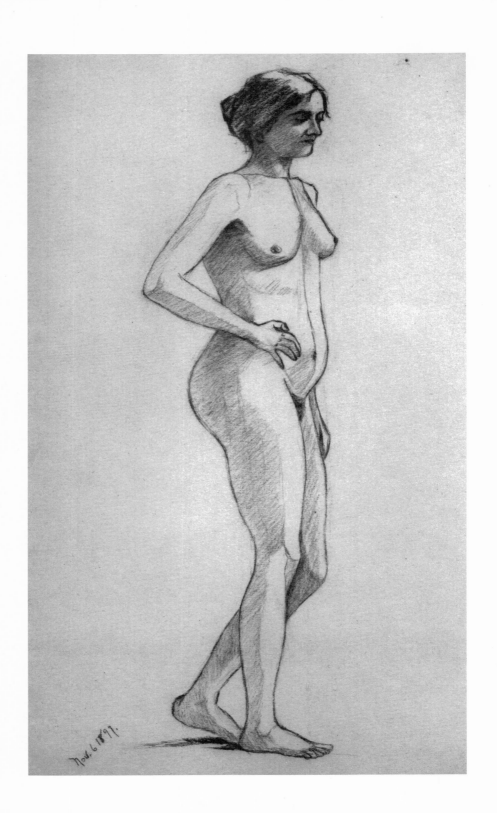

Nov. 6 1897.

Day Three

Wednesday, November 11, 1998

Chopin and Star-crossed Lovers

If not in Time, then in Eternity, there must be room for Penitence to mend Life's broken chains, Else noise of wars would unmake Heaven.

Elizabeth Barrett Browning

The sky is bright blue on November 11, the eightieth anniversary of Armistice Day 1918. At the eleventh hour of the eleventh day of the eleventh month, the remaining World War I veterans will roll out for the parade down the Champs-Elysées. Queen Elizabeth of England is in Paris to unveil a statue of Winston Churchill and to place wreaths at the Arc de Triomphe.

Queen Elizabeth also came to Paris on a state visit in 1957. We skipped classes and scuttled to various viewing points along her route in a game of *chassez la reine*. All the fountains spurted in the Place de la Concorde, a gigantic flag flew from the Arc de Triomphe, and my French family took me to an apartment on the Seine to view spectacular fireworks and an illuminated Eiffel Tower.

I will avoid the crowds on the Champs-Elysées and visit Père-Lachaise cemetery. Anna marked her *Baedeker*: October 18, 1898, Beautiful day! She wrote Edith:

> In the afternoon, I took the bus to Père-Lachaise. For the first time. I was "agreeably disappointed." [Anna and Edith used this expression when something was better than they expected.] Florence Young had told me it was ugly, but it is not one bit. It looks like a beautiful toy village. The monuments, some of them, are lovely and trees everywhere. Walked all over. And the light through the trees yesterday was a picture. Long avenues of trees in gold and the sun coming through. I got a little slip [sprig] from

Chopin's grave for you in case you do not come here again. Stayed there
until 4:30, I guess, then took the Buss, and did not have to change. It runs
from the Gare [Montparnasse] to place Gambetta, just at one of the gates.

Coming back the wind was cold and as I had on my sailor, had no
way to keep it off my head, so that gave me a headache. It was warm
enough out there not to wear my cape. I am so glad I went. Today was
simply perfect.

Although Anna went by bus, I choose the underground route. The Métro lines
are becoming familiar again, and I recall destinations such as Mairie d'Issy and Porte
de Clignancourt. On this festive morning, the Métro swarms with panhandling
musicians; I hear a violin, a saxophone, and three accordions as I hike through the
ceramic tile *correspondances*. A drummer from New York plays bongo drums in the
Métro car. He passes the hat to stone-faced passengers and says, "Smile! It won't kill
you!" I am the only one who chuckles. Several stops later a poet leaps into the car,
reads a poem, and distributes copies. I drop a franc in his hand and read the title,
Elle Vagabonde. His heroine throws caution to the wind as she travels.

The Père-Lachaise cemetery, named for the Jesuit confessor of Louis XIV, is
called the finest address in Paris because of the illustrious persons buried here. A map
shows grave locations: Bizet, Colette, Delacroix, Molière, Piaf, Proust. Like a hamlet
of streets and small castles, the tombs and statuary cover one hundred acres of
wooded hillside land. Cobblestone walkways have signposts: Chemin du Dragon,
Avenue des Acacias, Avenue de la Chapelle. The serpentine paths wind between
numbered divisions of the cemetery.

The temperature is one degree above glove weather. Dampness rises from the
graves and settles in my chest, as if lichens were taking root in my lungs. I've felt
this oppressive moisture on other burial grounds: Powhatan's mound in Virginia,
Cuttino graveyards in South Carolina, and West Kennett Longbarrow at Avebury. I
move to a brighter path where shafts of tepid light illuminate a trio of stooped
women—the Three Graces gone gray—planting memorial flowers on their family
plots. In our Rome cemetery, there are rows of Confederate graves and a
monument honoring the Women of the Confederacy. In all centuries, men devise
the wars, women mourn the dead.

My first destination is Chopin's grave because Anna came here for my
grandmother. Stone pillars and an iron fence barricade Chopin's monument, which
was erected by *ses amis*. His friends and admirers continue to mound flowers around

the shrine. A marble angel grieves on top of the gravestone, holding a clump of uprooted purple pansies in her hands.

Chopin died from tuberculosis on October 17, 1849. Anna Lester died on October 17, 1900—exactly two years after her visit to Père-Lachaise. While I sit on the stone curb—hoping Anna's spirit will find me—black crows clack about in the sky. Crows often circle our family graves in Myrtle Hill Cemetery.

About fifteen years ago, I went to the Lester lot to copy birth and death dates. Bannester and Eliza Mary Lester lie near their daughter Mary Margaret Lester Brower. Next to Sister Minnie is her son, Lafoy Brower. His birth date was his mother's death date. Sister Anna's stone is shaped like a scrolled piece of paper, very fitting for an artist. When I sat on the ground to copy her dates, I noticed a long word inscribed at the base of the stone. Our industrial air blackens all tombstones, and I thought I might need rubbing paper to decipher the word, but after I traced three letters with my finger, I understood. *Auf Wiedersehen.* My grandmother had marked her sister's grave: Until we see each other again.

Chopin's curbstone is not a piano bench, but one of his ballades seeps into my memory, and my fingers tap the melody on my numb legs. I give up on a visit from Anna and move up the pathway. I skip Jim Morrison's memorial, a shrine for another generation.

My next search is for Sarah Bernhardt's grave. The art deco design of her monument recalls one of her costume headdresses in a poster by Alphonse Mucha. On May 17, 1898, Anna watched the "Divine Sarah" die of consumption in *La Dame aux Camélias.*

> Monday, Mary Young got me a ticket to Sarah Bernhardt for Tuesday night; she was going too. I was delighted with Sarah—I had half expected to be disappointed, having heard so much of her—She is fine! And knows how to love and no mistake. She did not die quite as I expected—but that did not matter. I was *satisfied.*

I want to see the Colombarium—a burial dovecote surrounding the Moorish crematorium. Isadora Duncan has a cubbyhole here, but her file drawer eludes me. Perhaps she is off dancing among the chestnut trees in the jardin du Luxembourg. In 1927 Isadora jumped into a Bugatti shouting, *"Adieu mes amis, je vais à la gloire!"* As she announced her departure for glory, her long scarf caught in the car's wheel and strangled her.

Loosening the wool muffler around my neck, I leave this library of the dead and climb to the upper part of the cemetery where the rectilinear arrangement makes the map easier to follow. On the back row of the Avenue Circulaire, Gertrude Stein and Alice B. Toklas share a tombstone, their names inscribed in gold on either side of the white stone slab. Here, following Jewish tradition, admirers leave pebbles instead of flowers. A stein is a stone is a stein; there are no roses.

I make a detour to find the grave of Amedeo Modigliani, whose tragic story interests me. Whispering his last words, "We are pledged to everlasting joy," the artist died of tubercular meningitis in the presence of his pregnant mistress, the painter Jeanne Hébuterne. Jeanne's Roman Catholic parents, who disapproved of her relationship with the Jewish artist, allowed their daughter to return home but banished her to the maid's quarters in the attic. The desolate Jeanne jumped from the fifth-story window, killing herself and her unborn child. The family refused to accept the body and hired a workman to cart Jeanne back to Modigliani's studio in Montparnasse. There, the concierge denied responsibility; Jeanne was not a legal resident. The handcart sat all morning in front of number 8, rue de la Grande Chaumière until it was rolled to the police station. The lovers were buried separately, but after five years (when Modigliani's reputation had increased), Jeanne's parents allowed her to join Modigliani in this grave at Père Lachaise. Under Jeanne's dates are the words: *di Amedeo Modigliani compagna devota fino ali estremo sacrifizio*. The words "devoted companion" and "extreme sacrifice" could subtitle many inscriptions in this cemetery.

At the lower part of the cemetery, the most famous lovers of the Middle Ages occupy a playhouse tomb built in Flamboyant Gothic style. Around 1115, Abélard fell in love with Héloïse and arranged to be her tutor in the home of her uncle, Canon Fulbert. When Héloïse became pregnant, the pair married in secret. They named their son Astrolabe, "Star Catcher." Canon Fulbert's men castrated Abélard, and Héloïse went into a convent, but the couple corresponded until death. Buried apart, Abélard and Héloïse were reunited in Père-LaChaise in 1817. Their carved effigies rest on top of their sarcophagi.

I walk down the rue du Repos in search of lunch. Because it is well past noon, I have my choice of tables at the Café Rondpoint. I did not see Colette's grave, but I sit near a booth named for her and enjoy salad, salmon, and teeth-challenging French bread.

I've not yet been to the island heart of Paris, so I go home by way of l'île de la Cité. From the Saint-Michel Métro, I surface into mild sunshine. The humid air along the Seine warns me to enjoy the sky, as rain simmers on the horizon. Before me is Notre-Dame, the Queen Mother of Paris. An industrial plastic apron covers the cathedral from the waist down, but her clean torso is sparkling white. People walk along the passageway between the towers; their shapes mimic the gargoyles leering from the balcony. The tower bell bongs in a funereal cadence.

In 1985 David and I climbed the 286 steps of the south tower of Notre-Dame; we stopped to see the bell named Emmanuel (God with us). The bell rings only four times during the year, and Armistice Day is one of them. Our guide said that when the bell was recast in 1631, the women of Paris threw gold and silver jewelry into the melting pot. The sacrificial metal gives the bell a plaintive sound. The word *douleur* sways in my head as the mournful beat of Emmanuel follows me into the Latin Quarter.

At the church of Saint-Julien-le-Pauvre, I remember two legends. Dante may have worshipped here, and the oldest tree in Paris, a false acacia, has grown in the adjacent garden since 1601. A swinging gate opens into the square René-Viviani. From this wide-angled viewpoint, Notre-Dame is a Gothic ocean vessel tethered in the Seine. A poster on the churchyard fence announces a concert this afternoon in Saint-Julien-le-Pauvre. At four o'clock, the pianist Nicolas Boyer will perform *Les Belles Pages de Chopin*. With the memory of the composer's grave fresh in my mind— and his damp curbstone still imprinted on my derrière—I decide to attend.

The cashier informs me of a bonus of old age—reduced-price tickets for seniors. After forty years, I have returned to the "reduced" status of my student days. I'm delighted to find the afternoon concert, but in my fatigue I envy the *clochard* snoring behind the church door in a tattered sleeping bag.

At the first note of music, my tired feet are forgotten, and the rush seat of the straight chair is endurable. Chords from the Steinway ricochet from the twelfth-century stones, and tears stream down my cheeks, shaken loose by harmonic vibrations and a wave of remorse. Edith Lester Harbin deserved a concert pianist descendent. I could not fulfill that role, and neither could my mother. Before my mother's senior piano recital at Shorter College, she practiced all day then went out at night with her friends. She collapsed from exhaustion. Music demands solitary sacrifice; my extroverted mother loved people.

I played the piano through high school, but my math-phobic mind never learned to count properly; I finessed the timing with a good ear. When I followed Sister Anna's path into art, music returned to a listening pleasure, as it had been in my childhood home. During dinner, we asked our dad to play "side seven" of the *La Bohème* album or the Bruch violin concerto. Ten years ago, when my mother's mind began to slip, she still played love songs for my dad. She forgot who we were, but Mamie's arthritic fingers could pick out the Lehar waltz, "Vilia, the Witch of the Wood."

I stare out a grilled window at the spire of Notre-Dame, tinted coral by the setting sun. My forgiving ancestors are beside me in this small church on a day for remembering the dead. I lift my face to the arched vault and let Chopin—and absolution—pour down on me.

———

At five o'clock, I emerge from my Chopin shower into twilight. The early winter night stabs between my shoulder blades as I plow through Left Bank tourists and take the Métro back to Vavin. Saluting Rodin's statue of Balzac—my landmark on the boulevard Raspail—I walk down rue Bréa to the intersection with rue Vavin. After my cemetery tour and the cathartic concert, I need the restorative comfort of food. Tonight I will have a hot supper, instead of eating the breakfast yogurt I left in the minibar. I go into the Café Vavin where crowds of coffee-drinking students chatter and smoke.

Malheureusement, my appetite does not coincide with the dining hours in France. I am in culinary limbo, searching for food at five-thirty—far past lunch and too early for dinner. When I ask a distracted waiter if I can order a bowl of soup, he does the hand-waving expression of disbelief, *"Mais non, Madame!"* Why would I want food at this hour? I persist. He relents, goes to the kitchen, and returns with a bowl of vegetable soup and a crust of bread. I don't dare ask for water or butter, as I have exceeded café protocol limits.

I gnaw on my bread and muse on my family's love of butter. My grandmother served creamery butter with cornbread; my mother's graham biscuits dripped with melted butter. Anna was furious about scarce butter at the Berthier pension:

> The whole breakfast is enough to make anybody leave (who had not
> paid a month in advance—that is the rule here in pensions.) Hard cold
> bread and scarcely any butter and weak coffee is *all* I have until 12:30.
> Now think of putting a little thin piece of butter on bread hard enough
> to make Dickens turn his head one side to chew! On a table covered with
> *oil cloth!*

During World War II, my mother, brother, and I traveled with my father to three army bases before he went overseas. In one hotel restaurant in Carlisle, Pennsylvania, we each had one small pat of butter on a tiny butter plate. When I asked for some more butter, the waitress scolded me: "Young lady, don't you know there's a *war* on?"

During the years of war rationing, Pete and I begged for the privilege of mixing oleomargarine. The greasy white lard came sealed in a plastic sack with a pellet of yellow-orange coloring. The trick was to explode the capsule, then squeeze and massage the coloring into the lard, without bursting the sack. The mixture turned into a sticky yellow substance: ersatz butter.

When we found World War II ration books in my mother's attic, the one with my name on it still had coupons inside. As a six-year-old, I could have claimed more butter and sugar. I don't want to lie in a nursing home with unused coupons in my life ration book; I want to come out even. By coming to Paris and, except for tonight, eating real butter, I've used some of my coupons.

I sip my soup of puréed vegetables and watch two young women at the next table. They are doing homework, drinking coffee, and puffing on cigarettes—more in tune with the Paris digestive regime than I. Their French is proficient, but the USA sweatshirt and the DKNY wallet scream: Americans in Paris. They could be students on this year's Hollins Abroad program.

If I had known in 1958 that I would not return to Paris for twenty years, I might have refused to board the *Mauretania*. The next year, my new husband took me to Okinawa where I studied Dr. Spock instead of French idioms. As I drove kindergarten carpools back in the States, I daydreamed of careening through the Loire Valley in a *deux-chevaux*. I want to whisper to these young women: Stay as long as you can. Don't go home. Stay. Stay. They will have to learn this on their own, not from a wistful older woman.

I ask the harried waiter about dessert. *"Une Île Flottante?"*

"Impossible, Madame! Impossible!" he shouts over the din.

As I leave the café, noisy patrons spill in. They will order beverages appropriate for this hour of the apéritif. Across the street at the Pâtisserie Montaudouin, the metal shutters are clattering down, but I duck under the rolled louvers and point to the last *mousse au chocolat*. My purchase empties the refrigerated case, and the shutters bang onto the sidewalk behind me.

Back in my room, I watch CNN for war news and eat bites of dark chocolate mousse with a two-inch plastic spoon. When I see a map of France on the televison screen, I visualize my body placed on the dot named Paris, but the diagram is mere geography, unrelated to me. Should I worry about being so far from home if we decide to bomb Baghdad? I resent the fact that politicians might interrupt my research before I've found Anna's pensions and studios.

Build upon resolve and not upon regret the structure of thy future.

Ella Wheeler Wilcox

Day Four

Thursday, November 12, 1998

Lost in the Louvre

The morning rain is a gutter-cleansing deluge. I could have breakfast delivered to my room, but hungry for a conversation in English, I go downstairs. My breakfast companions are speaking Japanese, so I enjoy my *petit déjeuner*—a large cup of steamed cocoa and a croissant slick with butter. The weather report suggests that the rain and lowering temperatures will incite us to stay by the fireplace corner this weekend. I cannot afford such luxury. This soggy weather has *museum* written all over it.

The Musée d'Orsay is on my master list for the week. Housed in a converted train station, the dazzling museum specializes in turn-of-the-century art. Some of the academic works that Anna saw at the Luxembourg Museum are probably now at the Musée d'Orsay. In the nineteenth century, the members of the French Academy were the tastemakers. They determined the subject matter of paintings and sculpture as well as the curriculum at the École des Beaux-Arts. The Impressionist revolution swirled around the Paris art world years before Anna arrived, but she had little interest in experimental art. I would love to discover that my great-aunt knew Mary Cassatt or visited Rosa Bonheur at Fontainebleau, but she was a small-town art teacher, learning new skills. Anna did, however, have a fine reputation among women's colleges in the South. When she directed the School of Art at Shorter College, the catalog stated: "The mere announcement that Miss Lester has charge of this important school is a guarantee of its unsurpassed advantages."

Three of Anna's Shorter students won honors and studied abroad. Anna awarded a gold medal to Mollie Boyd who, unlike her teacher, embraced Impressionism and studied with the American Impressionist William Merritt Chase.

She was the first woman to receive the Silver Elliot Medal at the National Academy of Design. When Anna left Shorter to teach at Mary Baldwin in 1893, Mollie became head of the art department. She and her sister came to Paris in the fall of 1897. Anna wrote home:

> Mollie and Alice Boyd will be here in a few weeks. They will live on less perhaps than I, *one* can. Get a room and cook their own meals. If I was young I might try this—but I am an old dog now. I suppose I will see them but I haven't time to keep up with anybody.

Imogene Coulter lived in Paris and exhibited in the 1903 Salon, but Anna never knew of her pupil's success. Celeste Ayers toured Europe before she became head of the Shorter art department in 1898. She reported her experiences to the Lesters. Anna disputed Celeste's opinion of art as well as the views of Mrs. Johnson of the Berthier pension:

> October 10, 1897
> 144 bis, boulevard du Montparnasse
> Dear Mother and Father,
>
> Celeste don't know what she is talking about if she says they pay attention to impressionest [*sic*] over here. They do not! Only two small rooms have I seen in all the Galleries I have visited and you know I am taking things slower and more thoroughly than she did. Mollie Boyd is the student I count on in Rome.
>
> Mrs. Johnson appeared and I was real sorry, for I am getting tired of her. I really do not know *why* she came to Paris, for she is always saying if ever she gets home she will stay there, and she despises the French people, nothing in Paris is as *artistic* as in New York, etc. She shows her ignorance for N.Y. is not one *bit* artistic and in Paris everything is sacrificed to Art! I asked her why under the sun she did not *go back*. Or, go to *Italy* if she wanted to be warm—or keep a fire in her room. She's a goose!
>
> How I wish you both could come, there is a world of beautiful things in Paris—I want to stay a long time—but I know my money will not let me. If only I had more talent and had come ten years ago! How happy I would be if I could paint *one* decent picture. There are thousands you know here studying, and I *see* where I stand—and it is right at the

foot of the ladder, though you need not say I have said so—I hope Mollie Boyd will succeed. I take pleasure in *her* progress because I think I helped her along a little.

Do keep well and happy and I will work hard and try to be able to *do* something worth looking at when I come back. Paris is a *beautiful* city.

Paris *is* beautiful, but today's weather is foul. Outside the hotel lobby window, black umbrellas shelter pedestrians, and automobile tires smack on the wet street. In spite of the weather, museums are calling. Going down into the subway, I recall my fast-paced student days; I clipped down Métro steps like Audrey Hepburn in *Funny Face* and sprinted for trains as the doors were closing. A sprained ankle would thwart my current mission, so I hold the wet handrail and step around trash on the stairs. There will be other trains if I miss the first one.

Instead of long lines outside the Musée d'Orsay, I find groups of gesticulating people. A notice on the ticket window states that the museum is closed due to *une grève*. Our lives in 1957 were often disrupted by strikes. During one *grève* we had no heat or electricity. During another, no water. Without elevator service, we hiked up the stairs to the sixth floor; after supper, we gathered in the kitchen to get our *bougies* (candles). I could not walk to school from the sixteenth *arrondissement*, but bus number 63 ran when the Métro did not. After a two-hour wait for a place on the bus, I often arrived late for classes or found the professor and students on the sidewalk, locked out by a striking functionary.

What can I do but imitate the gestures of other disappointed museum patrons? *Of course* there's a strike. What did we expect? On my way to the Métro station, I see a number 63 bus, one of the new claustrophobic ones. I miss the classic rattly vehicles with metal side panels and a standing platform on the back. The conductor droned *"Odéon, Section"* as we approached the designated stop. Maybe, on a fair day, I'll ride the route back to the sixteenth *arrondissement* and find the Lafayette Home address.

My Plan B for this morning is the Musée du Louvre, where Anna spent many hours viewing painting and sculpture.

September 24, 1897 [Edith's 21st birthday]

187, rue de la Pompe

The Lafayette Home

My dear Edith,

Many, many, happy returns of the day. I hope you are having it as bright and beautiful in Berlin as it is here. I went to the Louvre yesterday afternoon—all by myself—and saw *three* things. The *Venus de Milo*—she is beautiful, *The Immaculate Conception* by Murillo, and *La Source* by Ingres. That last is beautiful and no mistake—I never saw such natural flesh. These were all I went to see that day but you would have been amused if you could have seen how long it took me to find them. I did not go in the door that led to them direct, not knowing, you see, so I walked all round *creation* and finally came out and started over, then found them at once. It is a *big* place and no mistake.

October 10, 1897

144 bis, boulevard du Montparnasse

My dear Mother and Father,

Last week I went to the Louvre one afternoon. It will take a "month of Sundays" to see all there. I only take a part of one room at a time, so I can remember them. You may know, or you may have forgotten, that I have *no memory* at all. Everything slips away from me.

There are miles and miles of such beauties. How *anyone* has the cheek to copy those old masters is what *I cannot* understand. I have found out where I can get permission [to copy] but I doubt if I ever go there. You know the fresh paint never looks like the old work that has dried in for several hundred years—and then it is almost impossible to catch the *exact* expression. Of all the copying I have seen only a few looked well.

I feel like giving Celeste [Ayers] a good whipping! To think she came over here and did not appreciate what she saw is provoking.

On the Métro, I sit near an American woman with a cane. Her silver-blonde hair and erect posture remind me of Miss Frances Niederer, whose Hollins courses inspired my love of Greek statues, medieval cathedrals, and the architecture of Frank

Lloyd Wright. Hearing her New Jersey accent in my head, I pretend that she is here for one last trip to the Louvre. How pleasant to have her company.

I must, like Anna, choose from the bounty of this treasure house, so I select three works to find: a Greek Cycladean figure for Miss Niederer, the *Venus de Milo* for Anna, and the *Winged Victory of Samothrace* for me. My choices are all from the Mediterranean, the seat of goddess culture.

The Cycladean statuettes are small stone carvings dating from about 2500 B.C. Contemporary in their simplicity, they could have been sculpted by Brancusi. An Aegean artist reduced the female form to a violin-shaped body with folded arms; shorthand markings indicate breasts and genitals. These goddess figures are stunning in their self-contained presence. Some nearby pottery has scroll designs representing the eye of the goddess as well as the spiral nucleus of the labyrinth.

Using the museum signs for direction, I locate *Venus de Milo* in her vaulted hallway. Compared to the rigid symmetry of the Cycladean goddesses, Venus is jaunty. She stands in a sexy slouch with drapery sliding off her backside. Tourists cluster at her feet for photos, but she is as patient as a kindergarten teacher, unperturbed by the chattering brood. Anna's plaster statue of *Venus de Milo* is a family heirloom, retained from her drawing courses at Mary Baldwin Seminary. One of my uncles inherited the charcoal drawing of Venus that hung over my grandmother's piano; the plaster statue came to my mother and then to me. I have used Anna's Venus in some of my sculpture installations, and the statue sits in a corner of my living room inside a golden obelisk frame. Painters and window washers at our house linger outside the window beside Venus, entranced by her Grecian goddess breasts.

My next destination is the *Winged Victory of Samothrace*. When I came to the Louvre as a student, I saw the statue at the top of the entry hall staircase. I climbed to her shrine like a penitent at Delphi. This morning I approach the *Winged Victory* from a side hall. Even without head or arms, her thrusting body commands respect.

In my debut show in 1979, I exhibited a work titled *Winged Victory*. White dove wings escaped from ammunition crates topped with saltshakers, which signified the hope for peace during the SALT treaty talks. At the time, the work was a commentary on war and peace, but if art is autobiographical, I portrayed my own escape from patriarchal boxes: I was testing my wings as an artist and as a woman. Standing before the *Nike of Samothrace*, I'm thankful that I took flight to Paris in spite of rumbles of war. I ask the statue if she represents peace or the thundering flap of unfettered female wings.

My watch says one o'clock—past time for lunch. On the lowest level of the museum there are quick service tables where David and I shared a *croque-monsieur* in 1996. On that visit, I peeked into an elegant restaurant and read the menu. I was the hungry "Little Match Girl" with my nose pressed against the glass. This afternoon, Little Match Girl and I walk into Le Grand Louvre.

The plush restaurant has maroon walls. Halogen spotlights illuminate vases of freesia on the white tablecloths. Seated on leather banquettes, self-absorbed couples complete their meals, encircled by black-and-white photos of nude torsos. The restaurant is a padded cloister, peaceful after the food court clatter.

"La soupe du jour?"

"Potiron avec langoustines, Madame."

"Le potiron?" I don't know the word.

"Hallowe'en," explains the waiter, drawing a big circle in the air.

Unfortunately, prior patrons have eaten all the pumpkin and crayfish soup. He brings me a *salade frisée*, a striped vegetable terrine, and lamb stew in a red wine sauce. I resist dessert.

I could leave the Louvre now, but I want to see art made while Anna was in Paris. The French painting gallery is easy to find on the map, but many steps separate me from the nineteenth century. At the top of a gargantuan staircase, a sign announces that the galleries are closed for reinstallation. My muttered exclamation is unprintable—in English or French. I sit on a stone window seat to regain my breath. Looking out the window, I discover a striking vista: a pigeon's-eye view of the glass pyramid in the courtyard below. I see how well the twentieth-century structure anchors the classical wings of the Louvre. The Tuileries gardens stretch to the Champs-Elysées, which leads to the Arc de Triomphe. The sun escapes from behind clouds, burnishing the golden horses on the Arc du Carousel. The top of the Eiffel Tower peeks over the Louvre roof. Gustave Eiffel's steel monument pierced the sky in 1889 and caused as much controversy as I. M. Pei's glass pyramid did in the 1980s. Both structures are now icons in the Paris cityscape. I am content gazing from my aerie. All museums should have windows to the outside to rest the eyes and the mind.

On the opposite side of the Cour Carrée, I look down onto St-Germain-l'Auxerrois. When the bells rang in the church tower on August 24, 1572, they launched the Saint Bartholomew's Day Massacre of French Protestants. The blood of slaughtered Huguenots stained the streets of Paris and dyed the river Seine a fatal crimson. I stroke the Huguenot cross on a chain around my neck. The French-

Protestant insignia is a Maltese cross with a descending dove symbolizing the Holy Spirit. During times of persecution, faithful Protestants substituted a golden teardrop for the dove.

Sunshine calls me out of the Louvre and into fresh air, but the *sortie* directions are confusing and perversely circuitous. I must go up steps and down again to get to an adjoining room. I tromp through immense galleries past monumental paintings Anna saw on her visits. Delacroix's *Liberty Leading the People* is appropriate, as some guidance to freedom would be welcome. On our first visit to the Louvre, we Hollins students wore dress shoes to traverse these galleries. One of my high heels penetrated a ventilation grate on the floor, and by the time a museum guard extricated my shoe, my group had disappeared.

How did I end up in the dark crypt within the original walls of the Louvre's moat? Passing mummies, sarcophagi, and the *Seated Scribe*, I go around bends and climb more steps on a labyrinthine forced march. I must put one throbbing foot in front of the other until I emerge intact or the Minotaur eats me for supper.

Back in the entrance hall, I find the shop that sells photographs and slides. Do they sell single slides of artworks?

"*Mais non, Madame.*" The salesman squints. "You must be a *professeur.* They always want to buy just *one.*"

To use Anna's word, I am provoked. I refuse his prepackaged selections and buy postcards of my three destinations: the *Venus de Milo*, the *Winged Victory of Samothrace*, and the Cycladean figures. Then I discover a long line at the *vestiaire*. After forty minutes, I retrieve my jacket and, *enfin*, escape from the Louvre into the sun.

Out of Anna's three selections on her first trip to the Louvre, I saw one, the *Venus de Milo*. The other two, *The Immaculate Conception* and *La Source*, may be in other museums. *Baedeker* says Murillo's painting represents the Virgin Mary as the "woman clothed with the sun, and the moon under her feet, and upon her head a crown of twelve stars." Ingre's *La Source* is "perhaps the most perfect specimen of the treatment of the nude among modern paintings."

Baedeker describes the *Venus de Milo* as the "only statue of Aphrodite handed down to us which represents her not merely as a beautiful woman, but as a goddess. The form is powerful and majestic, and yet instinct with an indescribable charm of youth and beauty, while the pure and noble expression of the head denotes the goddess's independence of all human requirements and the calm self-sufficiency of her divine character."

What better description of the power of woman could I find? Anna Lester was an example of the "independence" and "self-sufficiency" attributes of Venus. I crave them for myself.

———◆———

Now that the weather is pleasant, and I'm back in Anna's neighborhood, I find the pension of the Berthier sisters at 144 bis, boulevard du Montparnasse. The three Berthier sisters went in this door with meager rations for their boarders. Upstairs, Mr. Cooley and Anna discussed their art classes at breakfast. Anna tolerated Mrs. Johnson on sightseeing trips, but until Mary Young arrived from Rome, Anna's principal friends were cats.

October 9, 1897
144 bis, boulevard du Montparnasse
Dear Edith,

There is a little black pussy cat that belongs to the studio and it has made friends with me, comes each day for a little piece of bread. You know I am usually liked, and like, by all animals. Have you ever read "Shirley" by Charlotte Brontë? If you have you will remember she says *that* is a good way to judge character. If I had the same feeling towards all people now I might do, but I *have not* because I see so much deceit and unkindness. An animal does not *forget* its friends.

I started to tell you how stingy they are here I think in my last letter and got off the track. For lunch they put little dabs of cheese on each plate and the same way at dinner. Every thing is proportioned out in that way. I have had enough though except one day—so when I came in just before six after having been up to the Lafayette [Home], I asked Mrs. Johnson what to say for "I am as hungry as a wolf." She told me and I told Mlle, so she laughed and got some bread and butter.

Mrs. Johnson asked if she could have tea for lunch, when she was making her arrangements to come and they said "yes" then *after* she got here, they told her if she did have tea, "*she* would have to furnish her own sugar." I'll be bound I will do without it before I will do that and pay board too. I do have sugar *in* my room but they shall not see it! And I gave the maid a cup and expect to have tea when I like. I call them *stingy old maids*. I am an old maid but if I had boarders they should have good sugar and plenty of it too!

They told me two down right lies, and if you could see the whole set of them, you would wonder why I came.

First, Mlle Berthier said the *sun* passed into this room *all* the morning, but the sun *never* gets to this room! I am on the 1st Etage and the sun cannot get down so far in the court. It was afternoon when I came to look at the room, and I did not calculate the height of my opposite wall.

Second, she said there was a warm chimney to one side. The kitchen *is* next to the room, *but* the chimney is on the other side next to the dining room!

Truthful, eh? Little things count with me. Now I am sure they would tell these pretty little anecdotes just as fast as a horse would trot about any subject they choose. I hate to move for I *do* think I will learn more French here than I would anywhere else I boarded. I do not wish to be with Americans—or English anymore than I can help.

Mrs. Johnson and I have been looking at one or two places. One place on the next corner from here and *nearer still* to the studio has a room with a balcony and into this room the sun does go until 12:30, *when it shines*, for I have looked each day I passed coming home to lunch.

I hate to move, but tell me what you think and if I could save money. Or had I better stay here and study French. What a nuisance it all is any way.

I was tired out yesterday because I could not sleep Thursday night. Miss Weimar was on my brain. Mlle Ballu *had* to tell me [about the letters] you know, so I would be careful—and I'm glad she did.

October 10, 1897
Dear Mother and Father,

I had a fire made in my room after lunch and settled myself to write a number of leters. When there was a knock at the door, I said "entrez" and in walked Mary Young! Well, you can imagine my surprise and pleasure to see her and she looked so well and happy, it did me good to look at her. Mary thinks this place is "palatial." She gets along on less than I am paying but she gets one meal herself every day. I do not want to do that.

Anna's room faced an interior courtyard; I need to get into the building. When a man rings the bell, I follow him into the tiled entry hall. I go out into the courtyard, but there's no way to tell which was Anna's sunless room on the second floor. As I leave the building, I think about Anna's life in October: she was struggling to adjust to pension life and was learning new skills in the studio. To keep her letters to Mlle Ballu from getting into Miss Weimar's hands, she continued her postal subterfuge.

October 13, 1897

My dear Edith,

I am so much obliged to you for fixing the envelopes [for Mlle Ballu]. It must have been a great deal of trouble to you dear, but I do *hope* it will miss lead that being [Miss Weimar]. (I will not call her a cat for I like cats.) I am going to use one of the mourning ones first and I'll wager it will fool Mlle Ballu at first, for I do not think she will think of my doing that. I'll put on some black sealing wax. I am glad you told me not to mail on my Avenue, for I had not thought of that.

Yesterday, Mary came here and I had told her of my doubts [about the Berthier sisters]. She went with me to the balcony house and we saw one room. The one I saw before is taken. This one is just as good and goes out on the balcony too, all her rooms seem to. The windows get the morning sun—I have seen that and no hearsay!

Of course, I know nothing of the fare, only what she says—and Mary and I both like her looks—tall and round. Her name is Madame Bazin. She said I could have *all* the bread and *butter* I wanted for breakfast.

I am going to have my new place 20 francs cheaper—a front room only two stories up—so in case of fire I would have some chance of getting out—tie a sheet to the Balcony railing.

I have turned over a new leaf, Edith. I think it a good plan to be more affectionate if you do not mind. It may do us both good. I do not see any use in being so cold and undemonstrative, as our family has been. Life is too short, and we better get more out of it while we live. Death comes soon anyway and then we regret.

October 16, 1897

My dear Mother and Father,

This house is all right as far as respectability and cleanness goes but they are too intolerably stingy to suit me. Last Sunday night a Scotch girl came to stay—the first time she appeared at breakfast the girl brought the same little pitcher of coffee *I* had been having, put it down between the Scotch girl and me and said "that is for two." I was so provoked but could not answer, not knowing French. However, I told Mary Young of it in the afternoon and she told me what to say and said we would write it out. I learned my little speech and on my way to breakfast next morning I passed the kitchen and *said in French*, mind you, "Mademoiselle, one pot of coffee is not enough for two, give me more if you please." And I got it!

Old sinner, I wonder if she thinks this is any way to keep or get boarders! The little pots, they are really pitchers, hold a little more than one of our after dinner cups—and you pour this coffee into a great bowl of boiled milk! *Fine*, I tell you. When we have pears for dessert, they are cut in 8 pieces! I felt like throwing a piece at Mlle Berthier's head. I am not storming, don't think that, I am only telling you this to show *how* stingy they can be. Little things show the character of people I think.

Anna's outburst recalls my frustration when things did not go as I thought they should in my French home. I tried to predict the correct thing to do when I did not know the rules. In March 1957, I wrote home:

I wish I could tell you all about how this place is. But it's impossible. It's thousands of little things constantly going awry that get me down. Like always thinking the toilet will overflow and flood the whole house. For a small example. Nothing great big is different as it would be if I'd gone to the North Pole, but it's the little things that count and they're so different and unexpected and important. Nina and I have had some terrible experiences, which only seem terrible to us. We seem accident prone, or something. Some people breeze thru without a bit of trouble. But I can't help thinking that this adjustment period is taking a little too long. Probably just me. Mainly, it's starting out to do the right thing, with the right attitude and being completely misunderstood, and put in the wrong and not being able to explain that you were right. Rather confusing, n'est-ce-que pas?

When I accepted the fact that one young American was not going to change a household or a nation, I was happier. This lesson served me well as a new bride on a Pacific atoll. The Navy owned David, Mother Nature sent typhoons, and slow ships from the States determined when the commissary would have iceberg lettuce.

October 23, 1897

My dear Mother and Father,

This old sinner, Mlle Berthier Senior, will not give me any French lessons now since I told her I was not going to stay. Oh, if I could only speak French I would tell her a thing or two that she would remember and make her ears burn! I ache to tell them how stingy they are and that that is the reason I will not stay. But my goodness, if you could see one or both of them you would say *don't* tell them anything, for such eyes and such mouths as they have! And voices! I am going to church in a little while so I must not get on this subject too much, I will spoil my frame of mind.

October 28, 1897

Dear Edith,

No use for Mlle Ballu to *tell* the Post Master anything about keeping letters. That has failed over and over again even when the teachers had a private *locked* box at the P.O. There is absolutely *no* way but through Miss Weimar's hands. I am trying now not to think of her at all. I want to forget it all and forgive if I can for I believe that is the only way to be happy.

October 29, 1897

Dear Edith,

Your letter came today at noon, dear, and it was such a nice one—I enjoyed it all—I am afraid though you are trying to do too much—don't go so often at night. You need more rest, it will tell on *you* and your work, too.

I am thinking of going to the Berlitz school on Léopold Robert but have not quite decided yet. I wish I knew if Mlle Ballu thought this a good place. She *knows*, and in this last letter of hers said not to let *these* people [the Berthiers] impose on me about French—but to ask her—if I got into difficulty about French. She has told me so many things—in fact more than anyone else would have dreamed of that is a wonder we had not brought up *this* subject.

I asked Mary Young if she would to the Drugstore with me—I happened to think of cod liver oil and malt for my cold—*why* I have not done so before is more than I can tell. Going to that Park Sunday used me up. I am forever doing something I ought not to—but it was such a *lovely* day and I had on my warm dress and took my cape "like an old lady" but for all that I have not felt quite as well since. So yesterday I took Glycerine, sugar and Rhum and began on the Oil this morning. And already I feel much better *inside*. No use to worry about me, I am doing *all* I can to get well and I hope by the time you come Christmas to be "fat." I really *look* better now, for I happened to see myself in a good light in the glass a few days ago suddenly and was *struck* by the fullness of my cheeks!!!

I have told the home folks I am considered a beginner at the studio, and so I am, at drawing from the nude. I do hope they will not expect *me* to bring home anything but *myself* somewhat improved in *health* and *ability*. If I do that, dear, I will have accomplished a good deal.

An American family came yesterday. The Mlles Berthier are doing things up in style for *them*; at the same time I do not get a *clean* napkin *today* because I am to leave on Tuesday—neither did I have clean towels yesterday. And by the way, I found out by accident that I am paying *ten* francs more than *anybody* in the house! That is pleasant!

I simply dread moving, no one knows how I dislike to change about, but I could not stand it here, no more of this for me, if you please.

Lovingly,

Anna M. Lester

———⊰⊱———

Madame Bazin's balcony house at 2, rue Léopold-Robert also faces boulevard du Montparnasse. The doorway is a two-story stone horseshoe studded with carved rosettes. The concierge is cleaning the foyer; she is too young to know anything about Madame Bazin. Anna moved her trunk to her third Paris address on November 2, 1897.

November 3, 1897

2, rue Léopold-Robert

My dear Edith,

Well, Edith dear, here I am in my new quarters, a fire and my lamp burning. I really think I am going to like it here so I will not have to move again. Madame Bazin has hominy and rice! What do you think of that? Today for lunch for dessert, she had hominy fritters and maple syrup. Am *much* pleased with the fare and the room. Madame is a harum scarum, wholesome person, I do not think she is quite as neat as one could be, but I would *much* rather have her around than those fussy old maids. They ran me crazy.

Madame Bazin made my fire herself and has been in a number of times to see if it was doing all right, then insisted that I should go in the dining room until this one was warm. I am going to stay here whether I like it or not, I simply cannot move any more.

I paid 2 francs for moving trunk and valise, my goodness they are heavy—and full too. I brought my two shawls, cushion, cape, and steamer rug in the strap, wore my jacket, then after leaving the strap and umbrella here I went to the coal man to bring the trunk and on my second trip I brought the lamp. Then Madame Bazin ordered my coal, which came in five minutes, then I paid 3.55 francs for that and went across the street and got a gallon of oil and brought that myself, filled the lamp and unpacked a few things.

I hope your good work with Barth will go on. At the same time I want you to tell me just how many hours you practice for you *must not* over 4 and a half any day. If you do *I* will work eight hours and then you know I might get sick. I wonder you do not take me for an example and not do so much for you see the results of too much *steady* going day in and day out with me, don't you dear? Slow up *while* you are strong, don't wait until you are tired out. Of course, I know you include your Harmony, and that is a change and rest, but you *must* go to walk while it is warmest every day, just after dinner is a good time. Don't wait until it gets cold and dark. I do wish Berlin could afford weather like *Paris!* Get plenty of sleep.

With as much love and as many kisses as you want.

Your loving sister,

Anna M. Lester

November 7, 1897

Dear Edith,

You know I never could spell anyway and now I am getting it all mixed with German and French—so I am in a pretty fix. I have to look up everything as I go along—will forget my name next. When I want to think of anything in French, it comes to me in German. Then too, I have made a list of words by the *sound* as they are pronounced in French and if I *see* them written I am at sea again—it is fun and fine, too! But let me tell you I get along as well as Mary Young does even if she does speak. I do not have that faraway absent look that Mary and Miss Ellie Lou have—and people *think* I know—but how mistaken they are to be sure.

November 7, 1897

My dear Mother and Father,

I promised to tell you what I have to eat, did I not? In the morning, I have a cup of coffee, the size of Father's largest one and two rolls—with butter all I want now—at least three times as much as at Mlle Berthier's. I then come in here and take a wine glass of Porte Wine and am off to the Studio at 8 A.M.

At twelve we stop work, and I come back, just have time to wash my face and hands, and we have lunch at 12:30. That really is the second breakfast. First, some kind of meat, Beefsteak or Mutton, Potatoes, rice—or some other vegetable—then sometimes beet salad or spinach. Plenty of Bread—and wine, not the sweet wine, you know. Then some kind of dessert—stewed pears or baked apples—or Prunes and crackers and sometimes tea after that. Madame Bazin always asks if we will have more, and things are not *counted out*, so that there would be *no more* to have if we said yes. That made me so mad at Mlle Bertier's that I did not enjoy what I did eat.

For dinner at 7 P.M.: First soup, then meat and vegetables—bread—always two and sometimes three'kinds of vegetables counting in Rice. At Mlle B's only *one* [kind] and Potatoes—until I nearly turned into a potato. Then salad, lettuce, or something else they have to take its place. Wine all along and then dessert. I really feel stuffed tonight because we had chestnuts and crackers fixed some way that was nice. You know they stuff their geese when baking, with chestnuts! I never heard of such a thing, but it is nice.

And my goodness, I have been meaning to tell you all along—they have Pumpkin Soup!! I have to pile in the salt to be able to eat that. Nearly *all* the soups are thickened with tapioca.

I want to learn a little French—I must have it—but I think considering I am dull, old, tired, and a number of other things, I am getting on very well. I can count now and know the days of the week and can get along very well at the table and ask for nearly all I want for my room. When I go out to buy I usually write out what I want but cannot pronounce some of the words. Mlle Ballu gave me a *very* useful little book, you remember my pockets were made to fit that.

I see *no* difference in Paris—as far as safety is concerned, and any other city except it is better, the men do not stare as in New York—and they have sense to get out of the way and let a lady pass and that is what they do *not* do in Berlin. German *men* think they are better than women, you know.

November 17, 1897

My dear Edith,

I washed my hair this afternoon, had a good fire and have been as warm as toast, so do not see *how* it could give me cold. And do you know, in some way Mother has gotten hold [news] of this cough. Did you tell her? I have not said Jack Robinson, except that I did not want them to give my address to *anybody* to write to or to see after in Paris, because I wanted to rest. I meant to rest from everything I did *not like to do*. Surely not my *work* for that is *pleasure*, the very kind I have wanted for years! *Auf Wiedersehen.*

Lovingly,

Anna M. Lester

P.S. *Auf Wiedersehen* is so much prettier to my notion than *au revoir*. I found a lovely piece of poetry once about the goodbyes of different languages and *Auf Wiedersehen* was heard—but that I cannot find. I have spent hours looking. I put it away over three years ago. If you know it tell me.

November 20, 1897

My dear Mother and Father,

I have taken a raw egg with a little sugar and two teaspoons full of Jamaican Rhum every morning this week *before* my coffee and roll. Don't you think I am good? I do not like it much, however, it can do no harm and I think will do a great deal of good.

I believe I am forgetting how to write since I have stopped Penmanship teaching. My hand feels helpless and weak. I need practice but it is holding something I like better than a pen these days. *Charcoal*— and I hope after Christmas it will be brushes. I must paint! I am anxious to see color!

December 5, 1897

Dear Edith,

If you [want to] see *all* the pictures in Paris [at Christmas], you better bring your large trunk and stay longer than three weeks. You have no *idea* how large the Louvre is. Then while you are here I want to visit a number of the studios, I mean like Julian's and Madame Vitti's—to see what kind of work they do and if I will wish to make a change when my six months is out at the Delécluse.

Bring your muff unless you have warm mittens like mine. Nearly half the people here have muffs. I do not think you will need the tights, especially if you have not worn them in Berlin.

I only hope it will be good weather, if like today we will see absolutely nothing—for I must not go round in the rain, eh? I am trusting it will be cold and clear—if not you will just *have* to come again, for Paris must be seen.

December 8th: I will be 35 tomorrow and I feel 55 tonight. I did not intend to do so much today, but it rained and I got awfully tired.

I hope Madame will have some cornbread when you come. I am going to *tell* her to be sure to have *fritters* and syrup.

I must say good night. I really am tired out—pleasant dreams and sweet repose. *Auf Wiedersehen.*

Before Christmas, Anna gave her parents instructions for sending Mlle Ballu's gift to Staunton:

Enclosed you will find a letter to Boston. I want Mother to add on that blank line with the little "x" the author of "Prince of the House of David." Get it from Edith's [copy at home]. And send my letter and card with Draft for $3.00 to Boston. That will be *all* and I will be so much obliged if you will do this *exactly* this way. I have a *good* reason for *not* buying the book and mailing from Rome. I want it to go from this [publishing] house in *Boston*. I could have written to Mrs. Shultz in Staunton and had the bill sent home, but I did not want to do that. This way I have thought of is the *only* way practicable—and I want a *nice* one, that is why I send $3.00. That is my only Xmas present outside of home. I expect to treat Edith to her stay here for hers, and we will not give each other anything else. Love will fill up the space.

It does not matter if the Book does not get to Staunton until afterwards, it will be enjoyed more. No use for any word to be sent from *Rome* to Staunton, I'll see about that, in time. Mlle Ballu is a *very* dear friend of mine and has been *so good* to me always. I do hope she will like the Book. I tried to think of the *purest* and *best* to send her and I hope it will be *new* to her—she has read everything in all languages it seems to me. Thank you so much for doing this.

During their Christmas break, Anna and Edith went to the Louvre and ate "splendid beefsteak" at Duval's on the rue de Rivoli. They attended the American Cathedral at place d'Alma, where I worshipped in 1957. Anna said: "The church is pretty and all that, but I prefer the chapel to the mother church." Edith saw all the sights of Paris but concluded: "Two weeks vacation is enough. Paris is very nice to visit, but give me Berlin to live in, unless I was very wealthy and had a horse and carriage."

From across rue Léopold-Robert, I can see lamps in the third floor room where Anna lived for eight months. Up there, she and my grandmother celebrated Christmas. They stepped onto the balcony after eating hominy fritters. At the dining table, Mr. and Mrs. Hunter shared bulletins from the *Herald Tribune*. A Creole restaurant has covered the ground floor facade with white lattice trim. Palm trees sit on the awning roof, but Anna's balcony above the restaurant is undecorated. Anna crossed the boulevard to buy a gallon of lamp oil. When I step off the curb, car horns startle me into alertness. I remember Anna's traffic reports to her parents:

I have been trying to remember to tell you how funny it sounds here on the street. The trams have horns and such a tooting one never heard only in the South at Christmas time. Coming home the other evening, it was a gay scene down boulevard St. Michel, and I thought if you were here you would think you had dropped down on Christmas Eve night.

The carriages they have here run by Electricity—no horses—and they are all sizes and shapes—go whizzing along, I tell you. And something funny, it is the law in France and in Germany if a person gets run over, *he* has to pay damages if any are due. So you see everyone's on the looking [out] for number one.

One of these carriages has a great Cat tiptoeing from a ledge in the back and looking over in front—it is too funny—I have met it several times and it makes me laugh each time I see it.

I have just found out what it is they toot on these cars for I never *saw* the horns though I heard them all the time. It is a bellows and the driver pushes a lever with his foot! But my, how they go. Over on the Ave St. Michel on the way to Mary Young's there is a certain wagon that makes the most unearthly noise. I always jump and look to see how many poor dogs and cats are being murdered—before it dawns on me what I am hearing.

—◦———◊———◦—

Back at the hotel, I settle in for the night with Anna's journal. Was she more candid in the journal than in her letters? My 1957 diary contained facts I did not write home. I never told my parents about the sleazy men who pinched and groped us on packed Métros. My revenge was to lift one foot—the only moveable body part—and grind my pointed heel into the offender's shoe while maintaining an innocent schoolgirl demeanor. I hope I broke some French toes. Pete and Edith read my letters, but he was in high school, and she was only ten years old. Like Anna, I waited decades before my sister became my confidante and traveling companion.

January 1, 1898

Went with Edith and Mary Young to the theater. I liked it but it did not stir me as I wanted to be. Bought pickles.

January 2, 1898

Today, Edith and I went to St. Luke's church, then took the boat at Pont Royal and went as far as the boat goes. Edith left on the 9:25 train.

January 3, 1898

I was glad to get back to the studio today. Miss Regalle said, "Well, Miss Lester, you still have your cold."

January 3, 1898

My dear Mother and Father,

I wish I could come in [home] and eat some raw ground nuts and oysters with plenty of lemon and *red* pepper. I was simply *starving* for something sour so at dinner I asked for the vinegar and you should have heard them exclaim. Madame said I could have two drops but when I did get the cruet I *poured* it on my beef—had nothing else to put it on. They said I was a bad girl, etc.

So the very next day, Edith and I stopped and got two small bottles of Pickles, one chow chow, and one plain, and some crackers. We came in here and *went* for them! Edith began to laugh, said she never saw such an expression on anybody's face as I had. It was the best thing I have tasted since I left home! And I ate *all* I wanted, and I expect to do the same if I get hungry for sour things again. They *never* have any thing of the kind on the table. The salad has plenty of oil but very little vinegar.

Madame knows *not* what *I* have in my cupboard. They think anything acid would kill a person almost, so to tease her I say, "I do not like *sweet* things, only sour like vinegar!" And they say, "Oh! You must not, etc."

On the feast of the Epiphany, Madame Bazin served her boarders the traditional *galette des rois*; the pie contained a small token predicting good luck or forthcoming marriage.

January 6, 1898

Mr. Hunter gave me *his* little King out of the Pie. Much good that will do me!

January 9, 1898

After lunch I got a letter from Bubber. The first in over a *year*. We had that Pie again and this time *I* got the little King for myself, much to the delight of Madame Bazin. She said I would be married the very month I set foot in America! Likely, eh?

January 12, 1898

2, rue Léopold-Robert

My dear Edith,

The difference in my staying [over here] and yours is this. I have had experience and you have not so it may be easier for me to find a place [to teach]. I am waiting to see how I like the other studio before I decide, but I *expect* you to remain a year longer no matter *what* I do.

I am going to tell Miss Douglas I haven't an idea where I will be in the summer and if I should stay next winter I shall be in *Paris*. She is restless, and wants people to do *exactly* as she says. No, I thank you. I am independent until I marry that handsome man.

Yesterday afternoon as my medicine had given out, I decided to *make* a cough syrup, an old fashioned kind—vinegar, honey, liquor, and red pepper. So I went to my little corner store and got the things. Came back and boiled them together. Madame was horrified at my buying vinegar so at dinner I told her what I made and now she wants to *taste* it. She will *wish* she hadn't for it is *hot!* The cough is about the same I think. I can't see that the doctor did any good.

You know if I go home in August it will be because I *want* to and not because I cannot stay, so rest easy on that point. If I make as much headway in French the next three months as I have the last, why I will astonish the natives when I travel in the summer.

Your delightful letter came last night a day early, and was so welcome. If you think I know "hard" I might as well keep on, eh? To tell you the truth, dearie, I am tired of the cold heartless way we have always had at home. I want plenty of warmth and love sprinkled in between the every day affairs. Life is too short to avoid such things.

I do pay so much for Cod Liver Oil. I really believe though it is putting a little flesh on my bones—Oh, I tried to make a composition this afternoon, and you should see it if you want a good laugh. It is a blacksmith's shop. I did my best to recall the one back of Mr. Wilkerson's store, put in a horse and then a little dog with a sharp nose. This is the *rough* sketch. I am going to see if I can color it in watercolors tomorrow. I may as well *try* even if I do not send it in. I am afraid the one thing needfull is lacking in me.

You are fortunate in having bright company to keep up your spirits. What do you suppose you would do in my place? Not a soul to talk to except at meals and the ten minute rests at the studio. No one even to go out with. Mary Young doesn't count because I see her so seldom.

You know I am not expecting you to feel you are to pay me back for the money you use—unless I am old and decrepit and really need help. I hope to be well by summer and able to work with some spirit and really get some benefit of my trip over here.

January 17, 1898
Such a charming letter! And the Poem!

January 19, 1898
That dear little poem sings in my ear and keeps the charcoal point cheerful! "Sing them over again to me, wonderful words of Love."

January 20, 1898
I have not been back to the Dr. but I *may* go tomorrow. I am taking Cod Liver Oil and malt—and Mr. Hunter's cough medicine. I do wish *something* would *cure* the cough *now.*

January 21, 1898
Of all days this has been the *best* as far as Art is concerned. M. Delance gave me such a good criticism it took my breath and voice quite away! He is a dear old fellow anyway!

January 23, 1898

Went to the little chapel. Coughed so I did not dare stay to communion. Real cold and Madame kept lunch waiting as she had company.

January 25, 1898

Went to see the pictures at 7 rue Volney by the French artists of the day. Some were lovely. One by Bouguereau and a portrait [by] Benjamin-Constant were *fine*. Also one by Lefebvre. The hair was wonderfully well painted. Miss Holden, an English girl, went with me and we walked back! Such nonsense. It was clear and bright and I saw the new moon.

January 25, 1898

Dear Edith,

After lunch Madame went with me to the Doctor. The old goose says I am better but I do not believe him for I have not felt so by any means. But I will try this medicine and if I do not feel decidedly better I will go to Mr. Hunter's doctor and see what he can do. I told him of the expectoration mornings and other times. And he coolly said "but never any blood?"—which quite shocked me for the time. I said no, but yellow and I want it stopped, also the *cough*. I am *not* going to him again.

January 28, 1898

Got a pretty good criticism considering. Could not work much, my eye gave out.

January 30, 1898

An exhibition of the drawings of the concours at Julian's today. I was too sick to go and am so sorry to miss seeing the work.

January 31, 1898

The last day of the first month. Stayed away from the Studio because my eye was not well. And I wanted to try rest and see if *that* would cure this pain in my side. No letters and it is almost two o'clock. How I am to get through with the afternoon if they do not come is more than I know. About nine this morning I heard Madame Bazin at my door, "Are you sick, my dear? I was worried about you, my darling." She *is* good to me.

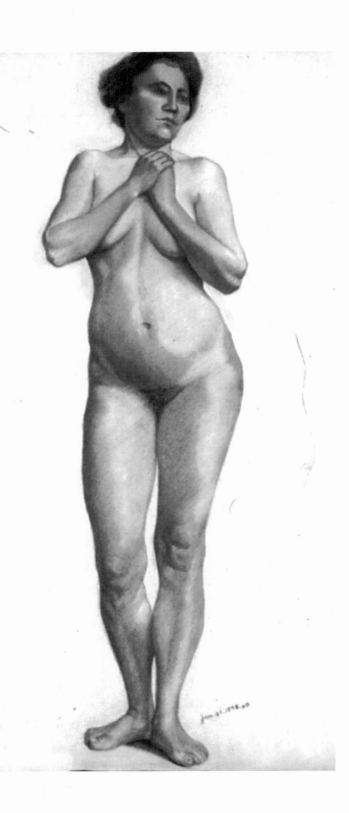

Day Five
Friday, November 13, 1998
Frissons on rue de la Grande Chaumière

Anna's *Baedeker's Handbook for Paris* has been a pontoon bridge linking me to her era. These guides were indispensable for all travelers in the nineteenth century. Anna told Edith in October 1898: "What *Baedeker* does not tell—when one knows where to look—is not worth knowing about a place. You know I have seen pretty near all of Paris—by *Baedeker*—though very few of the places roundabout—those I cannot do now."

I won't be able to see the "places roundabout" either. When I flip the pages of the guidebook, an aged newspaper photograph floats to the floor—a self-portrait of Eugène Delacroix. I want to visit the painter's museum in Saint-Germain-des-Prés; Anna's clipping prompts me to go today.

The front page of *France-Soir* features "Beel Cleenton" in a shadow profile. A cartoon shows Saddam Hussein on a pedestal inscribed "My favorite enemy." The Iraqi leader sticks out his tongue at Clinton, who hits the pedestal with boxing gloves. The paper says the danger of an air strike on Iraq increases and that Saddam Hussein appears to have the power to resist American force.

The taskmaster in my head says to get up from breakfast and do something, since I do not know what the political situation will be in the next few days. The laggard in my body remains seated as I read the weather report. Morning clouds will multiply, rain will begin toward midday, and the temperature will be around ten degrees Celsius. I laugh when I translate my horoscope for Friday the thirteenth: Always touched by myths, consciously or not, you oscillate all day long. Good? Not good? So, charge toward your wishes. I acknowledge my vacillation, drop the paper, and charge from the hotel.

In the middle of the jardin du Luxembourg, I face north on the garden axis. Marie de Médicis's palace is before me; the avenue de l'Observatoire runs behind me. When Louis XIV authorized the Paris Observatory in 1667, each facade of the building faced a cardinal point of the compass. The line of longitude running through the observatory became the official Paris Meridian. Even after Greenwich became the Prime Meridian for navigators in 1884, the French continued to recognize the Paris Meridian for timekeeping until 1911 and for navigation until 1914.

In 1994 I straddled the Greenwich Prime Meridian. This morning I may be standing on the Paris Meridian. Although meridians are imaginary lines on the earth's surface, they give stability to a location. In 1990 I designed the Harvey Prime Meridian in the courtyard behind my house. A line of bricks forms the north-south axis of a *cadran solaire*—a twenty-foot analemmatic sundial. On bright days the sun hits the vertical gnomon and casts a shadow on marble triangles marking the hours. I move the gnomon along the meridian from winter solstice to summer solstice. At night I stand on the line and look north to Polaris, aligning myself with the axis of the earth.

The Palais du Luxembourg is now the French Senate. Where is the Musée du Luxembourg, one of Anna's favorite museums? A guard directs me outside the garden gate to the rue Vaugirard. En route I pass a wall fountain dedicated to Eugène Delacroix. *Baedeker* describes the monument in terms any artist would envy: "a fountain with a bronze bust, and bronze figures of Time bringing fame to the artist and the Genius of Art applauding him."

I could be walking on Anna's daily route:

After being in the sun an hour I went into the Luxembourg Gallery—the pictures there are beautiful—and I am so glad it is near where I go to walk. I can drop in anytime for a little while.

Anna walked up the steps to the Musée du Luxembourg to see work by master artists of her day. When she saw Rosa Bonheur's *Husbandry in Nivernais* and *The Meeting* by Marie Bashkirtseff, did she know these women's stories? Bonheur had government permission to wear men's clothing to paint in the stockyards and horse markets; Bashkirtseff studied at the Académie Julian and authored scandalous journals before dying of tuberculosis. The Luxembourg museum is now used for temporary exhibits, but today it is closed for reinstallation.

A cold rain falls as I turn downhill to the church of Saint-Sulpice. Anna marked her *Baedeker* for a visit on October 3, 1897. She wrote Edith:

> Sunday morning I had planned to go near here to church back of the
> Girl's Club but Mrs. Johnson said she was going to St. Sulpice to a special
> musical service and wanted to know if I would go too. So I did, but the
> music was not good, and I am afraid I took a little more cold. It was damp
> in there and rained a little before I could get back here. The church is
> lovely. We will go there to see that when you come. I looked all I could
> but I expected to be sent out every minute.

The Delacroix murals are in a chapel on the right side of the church. When Anna stood in front of this painting of Jacob wrestling with an angel, did she dream of working on such a large scale? I notice a line of metal recessed in the floor of the south transept. Because of my interest in labyrinths on church floors, I often look down for designs on stone pavement as well as up at stained glass windows. The copper line runs to the base of a marble obelisk—a gnomon—in a corner of the north transept. The line must be a meridian marker.

In a side office, a gentleman sells me a Saint-Sulpice guidebook. He comes out into the nave and points to a window high in the south transept. A circular opening in one of the gray grilles admits a beam of sunlight; each day at noon, the sunbeam hits the metal line on the floor. The disc of light travels across the church from summer solstice to winter solstice and back. My guide opens the balustrade gate to the altar and points to a copper oval sunk into the floor.

"*Les équinoxes.*"

"*A midi?*" I ask.

"*Exactement.*" He shuts the gate.

The sun hits the oval at noon on the equinoxes. Even while denouncing solar science, church fathers depended on these noon marks to determine the date of Easter—the first Sunday after the first full moon after the spring equinox.

The egg-shaped equinox marker delights me. About thirteen years ago, friends and I started a festival to celebrate the first day of spring. Romans gather at noon on the steps near our town clock to stand eggs on end. The event, called "Standing Ovation," is a balancing act; participants feel a sense of accomplishment when their eggs are upright.

I circuit the ambulatory to see a colossal golden statue by Jean-Baptiste Pigalle. The Virgin Mary, holding a young Jesus, stands in rays of light on top of an immense sphere emerging from clouds. Does the orb represent the earth or the moon? I'd like to think it's a golden egg standing on end.

At the western end of the church are two fluted shells from the South Seas. I run my fingers along the brass borders of these gigantic holy water fonts. The carved marble supports—signed by Pigalle—have underwater foliage and sea creatures. The scalloped shells incarnate the word *rococo*. Near the exit, art students with sketchpads huddle around their professor. I eavesdrop on his lecture. He says that Delacroix, fighting illness, moved to this neighborhood in 1857 to work on the chapel murals. I go back out into the gunmetal weather and aim for the Delacroix museum.

The church of Saint-Germain-des-Prés offers refuge from a downpour. The famous Benedictine abbey complex replaced an earlier temple of Isis on this spot. Saint Germanus was the bishop of Paris in 576 when this area was the countryside south of the Seine, so the area became known as Saint Germanus in the Fields. Sitting on the edge of a straw-bottomed pew chair, I hold my hands near the votive candles for a hint of warmth. The ceiling of the church is Virgin Mary blue with gold stars punctuating the painted sky. The stone arches form a warm gray visual blanket, but my wet feet are cold. Leaving the church, I walk into the back streets of the Saint-Germain-des-Prés *quartier*.

Anna wrote to her parents in November 1897:

No use to worry about me, Paris is not any colder than Rome, I suppose—of course the houses are not heated by steam and they do not have Elevators—but I have a room on the second story with a good outlook—a balcony—and always a fire when needed. Then Madame Bazin has a self-feeder [stove] in the dining room and I leave my door open when I am not in and the room gets the warmth from the dining room and kitchen. That is one reason I wanted this room. I am bundled up in clothes—union suit and stockings and drawers, too—heavy flannel skirt—winter dress—jacket, mittens and fur collar—veil always. The only white things I wear are that petticoat and waist and my gown. If it gets any colder I will put on my other flannel shirt over the union suit as I have done with the drawers, then I will not wear the white shirt. I brought just *twice* too many things. I wish *all* the white ones were safe at home— and the silk and the muslin wrappers too.

Having been alone for days, I am beginning to have punch-drunk conversations in my head.

"Whatever possessed you to come to Paris in November," I mutter.

"Sois brave! If Anna could do it, so can we," I reply.

"Bon! Allons enfants de la patrie!"

We march on past trendy shop windows flaunting cashmere cardigans and pashmina shawls. More alluring are the wafts of sautéed garlic that float from doorways. The menus posted on restaurant facades have humorous English translations: herring fillets to the tepid potatoes oiled, thigh of young rabbit to the old fashion mustard, apples leafed to the Armagnac.

On the rue des Beaux-Arts, I pause in an entryway to get out of a deluge. A plaque says Oscar Wilde died here in November 1900—two weeks after Anna Lester died in Georgia. Wilde claimed, "I am dying as I have lived…beyond my means." This would certainly be true today because the former Hôtel d'Alsace is now the swank L'Hôtel. The rose marble columns of the rotunda glow with reflected light; I would not dare put my wet shoes on the polished floor. On his deathbed some floors above me, Wilde said, "My wallpaper and I are fighting a duel to the death. One or the other of us has to go." I have known such belligerent wallpaper.

The rain is approaching cat and dog velocity, so I go into a cozy restaurant named l'Echaudé St-Germain. I ask for *non-fumeur*; the waiter smiles. I can have my choice of any table. I take a window seat—even though the view resembles the underside of a waterfall. The *plat du jour* is pork roast with mustard sauce and potatoes. As I eat an ethereal *crème brûlée*, some Frenchmen sit down at the next table, about one foot away. An elderly gentleman leans over to me.

"Je peux fumer, Madame?"

Our tables are two boats in a sea of white tablecloths. He's not going to push me out of mine.

"Très allergique, monsieur." I cough. *"Un moment, s'il vous plaît."* I finish my dessert. He twirls his cigarette lighter in his fingers then taps it on the table until I pay my bill.

Feeling warm, fortified, and assertive, I splash my way to the place Fürstenberg, once part of the cloister of Saint-Germain-des-Prés abbey. I remember the soft glow of the lamp globes at twilight and the quiet of the square after plays or concerts. When a motor scooter roars from a side street, I jump onto the platform of cement in the middle of the square. Not the day for quiet reminiscing. The concrete pad is bare except for four paulownia trees in iron collars. What have they done with the benches? How do Paris lovers survive without benches in the place Fürstenberg?

The Delacroix Museum entrance is in a corner of the square. Anna's clipping of the self-portrait of Delacroix is tucked in my guidebook. When I walk into the museum, the original painting greets me, so I buy a postcard to accompany Anna's souvenir. In the spacious studio, Delacroix's sketchbooks, paint boxes, and tobacco pot are on display. Many of the paintings reflect the artist's 1832 visit to Morocco. One portrait of a man in a headdress reminds me of Anna's portrait of a bearded man in a yellow turban. When I see it in my living room, I'll remember my visit with Delacroix. Looking out the window onto the drenched garden, I recall that the artist said his lodgings were "indeed charming." I agree.

Headed for the Métro near Saint-Germain-de-Prés church, I walk down rue de l'Abbaye. In 1957 we came to drink cognac in a smoky club at number 6 bis. In passing I snap my fingers, the approved method of applauding Lee Payant and Gordon Heath for a rendition of "Lord Randall" or "Auprès de Ma Blonde." They warned that loud clapping would disturb the neighbors; we felt very sophisticated instructing newcomers in the rituals of l'Abbaye.

———⊜———

When I get back to Montparnasse, the rain has subsided. Clouds float upward and so do my spirits. I can search for Anna's studios. On rue Notre-Dame-des-Champs I look for the address of Académie Déléluse. The street number is missing, but a stock boy in the basement grocery store confirms that this charcoal gray building is number 84. The building is a fortress with curved buttresses below the fourth floor. Did it exist in 1898? Was Académie Délécluse in an interior courtyard like the Académie Julian studio on rue du Cherche-Midi? I ring at a side door, but no one answers.

This was Anna's first studio. She studied with Professeur Délécluse, Paul Delance, and G. Callot for six months, her longest period of study. Most of the nudes in her trunk were drawn at this address. She gave Edith a weekly account of her classes:

October 9, 1897

One week's work is done! The model poses five days in the same position, then on Saturday a change is made every half-hour! My goodness that is hard. I only got two out of the seven [poses] to look at all right.

The man got into such awfully hard positions, it was out of the question for me to draw him. He takes any pose he likes, you see. It is a mystery to me *how* he keeps still—and I should think he would be cold, but he does not seem to mind so I guess I need not.

I got a pretty good criticism yesterday, Callot said taking it as a whole it was good but needed more strength. I had the action very well. On Tuesday he told me to make a new sketch every day, yesterday he said I should "block" in the shadows next week. The girl who sat next to me translated for me. The criticism is in French. After he left, she said that was good, he made her work three weeks without shading. I only wish I could work fast and well too.

October 13, 1897

On Monday morning when we went in the room, the model looked so much like that Christ of Monkatsky (I cannot spell his name) in the Modern Gallery at Dresden. You remember with the striking white drapery? It gave me quite a shock. Thought at first I could not look at him long enough to draw.

I went down stairs to look at the model there; we could take our choice; and a Gipsy Girl slipped off every *rag* of her clothes and stepped on the platform! She was too fat. Of the two, I took the man. He is awful hard [to draw], all the bones show, and I can see his heart beat. What a life to have to lead! I really am sorry for them.

October 28, 1897

On Tuesday, when Delance came, he simply took the charcoal, drew two lines, one from the head to the shoulder, one from the chin to the waist, said, "action is not good, better start a new sketch." Dropped the charcoal on the easel, shrugged his shoulders, put out his hands palms up—very expressive, but the expression is one I do not fancy!

On Friday, he gave me a better criticism—that was when Miss Braun interpreted. Today I dreaded to have him come, for I knew the feet were not good—and was not at all sure of the rest—but he said the action was "pas mal" and showed careful study. Then he showed me *how* to fix the feet, so I feel better. He is much more severe than Callot. They take a turn about coming here, two weeks at a time. The change is good for us.

November 12, 1897

Tuesday, you know, the Professor comes and I could not afford to sleep late. M. Callot almost took my breath away—you see he has been away two weeks now—and Delance had his turn. Well, Callot really *looked* pleased and *said* he was at my improvement, made a few corrections, then said it was not bad at all! I have tried and no mistake but I never expected him to say so much.

On Friday Delance said I had worked carefully and very painstakingly, if there is such a word, and the whole was not bad—but I put in too many details and needed to make things more solid and simple. Well, I was satisfied with *that* from him, I tell you. I may get drenched in cold water on Friday. There is no telling. For really I do not understand *how* they make the charcoal look so much like flesh—and no two work alike. My men look often as if they had on tights. But I am going to do all I can this week to get the hang of it.

December 9, 1897

Now about this criticism today. I do not like *two* men to criticize *one* drawing—for nearly always when Delécluse comes in the middle of the week he will say just the opposite to what has been said on Tuesday. Then if I go by what *he* says when Friday comes, the first man says it needs undoing, just what the second had done. It puts me in a bad humor and hereafter I shall either leave when Delécluse comes or start a new sketch. Several times I have been upset as I am now and I am tired of it. I don't like to get angry—it is bad for the wrinkles in my forehead—Callot said it was good and now Delécluse says the drawing is *bad* and he hopes I will do better next week—*Which shall I believe?* I would like to know!

January 14, 1898

On Friday when M. Delance came to mine he said, after showing me how to make a few changes in the shading, *"Beaucoup mieux, beaucoup mieux!"* That was good wasn't it? I like him you know better than M. Callot. He draws so much better—really beautifully. Then today when Delécluse came he said I made improvement always. I do try hard, I know that, but I am afraid I shall never do what I want.

Oh, you ought to hear the criticism *I* got today!! A woman is the model and do what I would, she would look straight when she was leaning. Delance said *too* straight, it looks like a *stick*. Then he began by flapping off the charcoal with the chamois, then he began to take the points and bless you the old gentleman found them *right* with a plumb line and *said so* but said I did not have the swing right between the main points. You know we always go by the ankle and neck with a line. So after all said and done, not much change was made. It *amused* me and I did not care if he did rub it out. I knew it did not look right before he came.

My goodness but today is dark and foggy! I could scarcely see how to work. My girl does not look so much like a *stick* now.

Delance came by early and got to me fourth. So I had time to make the corrections he pointed out before noon. He says I get the outline right and action good and it is a *pity* I do not see the forms of the lights and shades better. It is a "pity" and one I have been working to overcome, but I see too much and that upsets affairs.

What if Anna's letters had survived and the sketches had been lost? Together they bring me into her world. She studied with master teachers. After my design classes with Virginia Dudley, I have had no formal instruction. My sculpture is an intuitive reaction to materials appropriate for my subject matter. I alone decide if a construction works or not.

When I began writing poetry in the mid-eighties, I was surprised at the collaborative nature of the writing process. No one ever suggested that I rearrange my sculpture; now fellow poets had their fingers all over my gerunds and participles. I like the camaraderie of poetry as a team sport, but not the lack of closure. Once an art piece is welded or glued, it's finished. A poem is never completed; it lies on the page waiting for one more word to be changed. As I've moved from visual art to performance and writing, I miss the finality of the welder's torch.

I leave the Delécluse address and turn onto the rue de la Grande Chaumière to look for Académie Colarossi. Rue de la Grande Chaumière got its name from the thatched (*chaume*) roof of a dance hall on the bouvelard du Montparnasse. At La Grande Chaumière, the polka was popular along with the erotic *chahut*, later named the cancan. I've read that during the height of the Montparnasse art era, the upper end of rue de la Grande Chaumière was the site of a model market. Every Monday morning, men and women posed in doorways and on the street to compete for jobs in the academies. At Colarossi, women drew alongside men, but modest women could choose from draped or undraped models.

The Colarossi flyer lists studio addresses at numbers 10 and 16, so I walk up the right side of the street. Sennelier, a well-known art supplier, is at number 4. Students with drawing portfolios bump past me as I look in the window at seductive boxes of pastels and colored pencils. The undampened watercolor ovals demand the touch of a virgin paintbrush. The jointed wooden mannequins would look great sitting on my studio worktable.

At number 6, the Maison Gaudin is a stained glass factory whose artisans restored the rose windows in Chartres Cathedral. Next door a plaque marks the ateliers of Modigliani and Gauguin. When Modigliani died, his cat jumped to its death from the studio window, sharing the fate of the artist's mistress. Remembering the macabre story of Jeanne Hébuterne, I step around an imaginary cart holding her body on the doorstep of number 8.

A Polish restaurant and an antique bookstore are on either side of a locked wooden door at number 10. A man and woman exit, slamming the door before I can look inside. When I ask them about the Académie Colarossi, they direct me up the hill to number 14 where a sign marks the Académie de la Grande Chaumière. Since no one is in the director's office, I walk down the silent hall. A classroom door is opened about five inches, allowing me to see students seated on stools. They hold large drawing pads on their knees and must be sketching a model at the other end of the room.

A man tiptoes out and escorts me to the sidewalk. He is French but now lives in California. He has studied here and at the Académie Julian on rue Dragon.

"What are you looking for?" he asks.

"Académie Colarossi. My great aunt studied there in 1898."

He points to a plaque beside the entrance door. Antoine Bourdelle, R. X. Prinet, and others founded the Académie de la Grande Chaumière in 1904.

"*Dommage.* Too bad. Too late for your aunt."

The director walks up the street to where we stand.

"Académie Colarossi?" I ask.

He thinks that it was around here somewhere, but he doesn't know where. The men go back into the academy, and I cross the street to view the two buildings at numbers 10 and 16. They are similar in style—Mediterranean plaster with white metal shutters. Anna's Colarossi card states that the "ancient Swiss academy" was founded in 1815. Professors included Cartier, Giradot, Injalbert, and Prinet. The academy offered classes in sculpture, watercolor, *modèles vivants*, and ancient and modern costumes. On this side of the street, at number 9, I am next to the Hôtel La Villa des Artistes, the former Hôtel Liberia where Nathanael West, Samuel Beckett, and Alphonse Mucha lived. Given the history of the legendary hotel, the Best Western logo seems incongruous.

I amble down the sidewalk to a cement wall with brick corner posts. A blue enamel sign, etched with rust, bears the number 5 in white. Over the tall black gate I see an interior garden bordered by cream-colored buildings on the sides and end. I turn around and press my back to the wall, staring up the street at the door of number 10. Was Académie Colarossi in a courtyard behind the locked brown door? It seems more likely than the building at number 16.

Without warning, a damp chill transfers from the wall onto the back of my neck. From ancestor searches in England and Virginia, I know this frisson means I am close to a significant location. With my feet grounded on the sidewalk, I raise my antennae. Are the nineteenth-century models bustling to the studios to expose their bodies? Maybe Modigliani is en route to Madame Charlotte's Crèmerie at number 11. Perhaps Jeanne Hébuterne's body is, *enfin*, on its way to the morgue. Or—a few years before their time—Anna Lester may be arriving for a class at Colarossi. Sometimes I feel as if Anna is one step ahead of me, her black skirt and cape disappearing around a corner as I approach. Does she want to be found, or am I losing my mind in a circuitous chase?

After a few minutes by the wall at number 5, my watchful spirit yields to my weary body. My search for Académie Colarossi has been inconclusive, but rue de la Grande Chaumière is steeped in the ghosts of artists.

February 2, 1898
What weather and how sick I do feel. I am sure I do not know just what *is* the matter.

February 4, 1898
Letters must be mailed no matter *how* hard it rains.

February 7, 1898

Went to work again. Got a place next to Miss Holden. A very good model. A woman came in and went through several poses in a pale green chemise. She had red hair. Miss Rigall keeps on telling me to go away south somewhere.

February 8, 1898

Mr. Delance was very pleasant today and gave each one a good deal of time. He wants all to make the compositions. Today the subject was "Christ in the Temple." *Hard* and the work poor. But it *is* better to try.

February 9, 1898

I went to the bank this afternoon. It is such a long way and I did not feel able to walk—or ride outside the Buss and I do not *enjoy* the inside. The air is so bad. An entire stranger asked me how I was today. It quite took my breath away.

February 11, 1898

Today has been so beautiful all day. I went and mailed my letters then took a walk, coming back by the Luxembourg Gardens. Delance tried to give me some encouragement but I knew the drawing was not so good.

February 12, 1898

Pleasant. I got a little calendar. Happened to find one just like Mlle's so got it for company. Took a walk, then a nap, and balanced my accounts.

On rue Vavin I go into Marie-Papier and buy handmade letter sheets and envelopes. My attraction to paper is primal; I want to touch it, fold it, and hoard it. These tactile treasures will join my cache of fine papers "too good to use." I stockpile beautiful blank books, but I write in spiral-bound notebooks from Kmart. For what am I saving the handmade books—the mourners' registry at my funeral? As I fondle leather journals with the year 1999 marked in gold, I see Anna dipping a quill pen in ink to write entries by lamplight at the turn of the last century. Did she dream that her Bon Marché diary would be valued two generations later? My diary from 1957 will be a challenge to read. I wrote half in English, half in French, with a few encoded entries about a man I met in Coimbra.

At Le Marché Franprix, the self-service market, I buy a small quiche and an orange for dinner. A man stands by the door, distributing printed announcements. I don't make eye contact, but I think he raises one eyebrow as I pass. He whispers a suggestive *Bonsoir, Madame.* In 1957, Paris workmen muttered comments as we students walked by. I must have outgrown the old street greeting: *Allo, Mignonne.*

———————

February 15, 1898
Letters came while I was at breakfast and of course I read them, then took them to the Studio. M. Callot came today and *he* says I am making progress, but I want to do more.

February 17, 1898
2, rue Léopold-Robert
Dear Mother and Father,

After dinner, Mrs. Hunter asked me in her room a while. I suppose you have heard all about the blowing up of the war ship [USS *Maine*] at Havana? Mrs. H. says *she* thinks if it was done by the Spanish there will be war between Spain and the United States and wants to know if *I* would go home to help the soldiers. I said *no*, not unless it affected my own family. I guess she thinks I am not as good a citizen as she is but I cannot help that. I do not wish to see *any* war and I hope it was an accident, don't you?

February 17, 1898
My dearest Edith,

Yesterday I went to the Louvre for the first time since the day we were there—This time I went up on the third floor to see the drawings of Raphael and they were lovely—and kept so carefully—in frames that have fronts to cover them. They are only on exhibition on Wednesday. I did not know that until I got back—so it was fortunate I happened to go that day—for my trip was expressly to see these. Then I went to pay the Salon Carrée a visit with all of its treasures and came down and gave Venus my final call—I love her.

I have been worried with bed bugs for two weeks—so I informed [Madame Bazin] that I wanted something done at once. So while I was at the Louvre they brushed down the walls, took my bed out, gave me the one you had—and sunned my mattress, etc. I came back, took a nap, and finished off Mlle Ballu's letter and went to bed and slept like a top until 3 A.M. I *will* wake at that hour and stay awake 2 hours or so. I *must* find some way to stop that, for it is a nuisance.

I do wish I knew how to sketch and make pretty little things like this Russian friend of Mlle Bartenoff's. She asked me in their room the other day to see a book on anatomy and then showed me a lot of her own things in watercolor, pen and ink, and pencil. I always have to plod along for I suppose it is not in me. However, M. Callot told me Tuesday my figure was much better and I made progress, but I want *more*. I will have so little to show for my time over here.

February 18, 1898
M. Callot came today and now *he* says I have made progress—good for that—but I want to sketch all sorts of things. So I have begun by trying the Studio cat.

February 22, 1898
M. Callot came and gave me a criticism while the others were downstairs seeing the compositions. I went down but it was too cold to stay. Letters came today! I made Tea for the second time!

February 23, 1898
Dear Edith,

Mrs. Hunter is going to get a paper for me with all the [Émile Zola] trial in it. And I will send it. They *say* the trial is to end today but I do not know if it did.

February 23, 1898
I feel better but the weather is not good. M. Delécluse came to us today. He is a very careful critic.

February 24, 1898
This is an off day again. I do *wish* I could get well! The steamer Champagne that left Le Havre Feb 12th has not reached New York. Anxious hearts await her I know. Weather bad. I have nothing new *ever* to put in here.

February 24, 1898
Dear Edith,

Oh, the trial is over. Zola pays 3 thousand francs and goes to prison for a year. Mrs. Hunter said she would get a paper for me this afternoon. They are higher as the whole trial is in there I believe.

February 25, 1898
I really was ashamed of my work this week. When will I learn not to put too much *middle tint?* Miss Stamm came to tell me what M. Callot said. I prefer Miss Holden for Miss Stamm will laugh and I do not think M. Callot understands why.

February 26, 1898
Rain, cold, miserable.

February 27, 1898
A beautiful morning. Mary and I went to the Beaux-Arts. I liked the small chapel, contains copies of Michael Angelo's work at Florence. News from the Champagne. I am so *glad*.

February 28, 1898
I went uptown to 5, rue Boissy-D'Anglais to see the pictures. Some were very pretty—the Portraits I thought were best. Bouguereau always has something pretty. How I wish I could paint like him and like Rosa Bonheur! But no use for beggars to wish, it does not come to them.

February 28, 1898
My dear Mother and Father,

Of course, you have heard of the Steamer Champagne—that left Le Havre on Feb 12—it got disabled and could not go any further off the Banks of Newfoundland. They sent a small boat out with a few men to try and signal help and these men were found after *six* days by the Rotterdam and taken on board almost frozen. Then of course the Champagne got help. It should have gotten into New York the 20th. Two friends of Mrs. Hunters were on board—That *is* a big old river to cross, isn't it? I am so glad the Steamer has been found—she had not been sighted before—One of the young ladies on board had been sent for, her mother was ill—so there must have been anxious hearts on land and sea.

Today when I came from the Studio I met Madame Bazin in the hall—and she was all excitement and told me she was making something *nice* for lunch. I asked, "What?" "Floating Island," and she rushed in the dining room where I was looking at the latest news of the Champagne—beating the egg whites, as pleased as a child. Well, when the time came to *eat it* I found it was Floating Island without the *Island*, no cake! And we had to eat it with some of the same little crackers we have had everyday for months. I could hardly keep my face straight and did say in an undertone that some *ladyfingers* would be nice put in.

They haven't the most remote idea how to make or serve any little dessert. If they do have it, in all probability it will be brought and set before you *first* thing before the meat. I *wish* they could sit down to a good old-fashioned dinner and have *coffee* after. This thing we have mornings is not coffee. But it is all we can have, so no use to grumble—she is good to me, says I eat like a little queen—and am dainty—because Mrs. Hunter likes cabbage and *I* do not.

Propped up in bed, I nibble cold quiche and thumb through a guidebook about literary Paris in Hemingway's time. He lived over a sawmill at the far end of rue Notre-Dame-des-Champs and often visited the Musée du Luxembourg to study the Cézannes. I read that, along with other expatriates, he attended an Anglo-American chapel in Montparnasse. In 1924 Gertrude Stein was a godmother at the christening of the Hemingways' son, Bumby, at the Chapel of Saint Luke's-in-the-Garden.

I sit up straight, spilling quiche crumbs in the sheets. Anna also worshipped at Saint Luke's Chapel. The address surprises me: number 5, rue de la Grande Chaumière. Anna's church address was the cement wall where I stood mesmerized this afternoon. Was the historic chapel behind the gate? The book says that the chapel no longer exists. Anna described Saint Luke's Chapel for her parents on October 10, 1897:

It is only plain boards, no paint, but has stained glass windows and back of the altar a *lovely* piece of Tapestry, so soft and beautiful in color. If I can find a photo, I will make one when I come home. *Now* I am working from Life and want to do that alone while here. I never will have a better chance and you know *that* is what I need.

During their short friendship in November 1898, Amy Steedman, Frances Blaikie, and Anna walked to Saint Luke's Chapel from rue Sainte-Beuve. Now that I know the location, I can hear the trio giggling on their way home after services. A piece of Anna's Paris topography has snapped into place.

I turn on the television and peel my orange. Juice dribbles down my fingers while a French channel presents a film on Delacroix's life, a synchronistic coda to my visit to the artist's studio. CNN airs a segment about the Reverend Howard Finster, a folk artist who lives twenty-five miles from my home. He and I share a passion for assemblage, although his collection of found objects far surpasses mine. Here in my hotel room, I bridged the distance between Delacroix's studio in Paris and Finster's Paradise Garden in north Georgia with one click of the remote control.

CNN newscasters discuss a possible bombing attack on Iraq. I understand Anna's hope that war with Spain would not affect her studies, because no one willingly gives up Paris. Some writers and artists disregarded the portents of World War II and became trapped in the Nazi occupation. Gertrude Stein and Alice B. Toklas retreated to the country near Annecy; Sylvia Beach and Adrienne Monnier hid themselves and their books in Paris before the Nazis interned Beach. I am much closer to Iraq than I would be in Rome, Georgia. Am I being cautious enough?

On trips to Europe, I never wear white tennis shoes or valuable jewelry. I hope that, in my simple black attire, I'm less conspicuous than the shrill American women in fur coats on the Métro. My passport, credit cards, and extra money stay buried around my waist. Do I need an escape plan? In an emergency, would I rush to the airport, abandoning Anna's papers and my Bon Marché hat? The television counters my anxiety with a bit of humor: a clip of Prince Charles at his fiftieth birthday bash—dancing in a lineup with the cast of *The Full Monty.*

In the middle of the night, a posse of police cars goose-honks down boulevard Raspail. I bound from bed and peek through the curtains. Below my window, students quarrel on the corner. I cannot understand what they are excited about, so I switch on CNN to see if we are at war. The hour is 3:30 A.M. in Paris. In America, Larry King interviews Dee Dee Myers and Lucianne Goldberg. Paula Jones has settled her case against President Clinton, and the jabbering continues about the presidential scandal. There are no bombs in Iraq.

Day Six
Saturday, November 14, 1998
Ten Dollars in Kisses

March 2, 1898

Such weather I never did see—I verily believe! I cannot get well while it lasts.

March 4, 1898

Weather! Yes it is and no mistake. I put those letters in the [post] office and came back quick but I felt in my bones what the consequence was to be to *me*. I am so sick. I really wish I was at home where I would have someone to nurse me. I do not know *what* to do.

March 5, 1898

2, rue Léopold-Robert

My dear Mother and Father,

    I do not care to dispose of any of my stock and when *all* my ready cash is out we will decide what to use. I do not care to sell my 5th Ward place. I am thinking of living over there in my *old* age when I am all alone, with Moses if she lives that long and *no* cat if she dies. I think my heart's best love, for cats, has been given to Moses and I do not want any one in her place. Father does amuse me so, he wants people to marry, that is the boys, but does not see that *some* women think it is the main object in life to get up some entertainment to bring young people together. How could they marry, pray, if they do not get acquainted? The more the merrier, to those who like it, *if* the husband is able to support the wife and all the children who come. Otherwise, stay single forever.

The Hunters have not gone yet, much to my pleasure. Don't imagine I am pining for friends here. I only see them at the table and she is the only one who talks to me, as I do not speak French. The only time I speak to a soul is at the table and three ten-minute rests mornings at the Studio and when Mary comes. She has told me long ago of the Warmsleys coming, and I have been dreading the visit. I do not care to tramp around with them and I do not like to meet strangers, so that is the long and the short of it. Nevertheless, I suppose I will *have* to see them. The older I get you see the worse I am. I'll be *polite* never fear. I do not think there will be war. I *hope* not, I am sure.

March 5, 1898
Stayed in bed until nearly twelve it hurts so to breathe. I am actually frightened. I would not budge out today for a pretty.

March 6, 1898
Letters for Breakfast! They were delicious, too. I am too ill to do anything but worry and write bad letters. If I could only get well!

March 8, 1898
Snow! And very cold. I have stayed in and done nothing, slept late then took a nap this P.M. I see everybody going out, old ladies and all, and *I* have to stay in. It goes against the grain. But I am trying to be good.

———◆———

21 mars, 1957
15 bis, boulevard Jules Sandeau
Dear Family,

Well, I was wondering how long my throat would let me have fun in peace. Several times when the weather has changed suddenly I could almost feel the respiratory vaccine fighting. Good feeling. Well, Monday the throat won. It had become very wet and rainy and cold. Guess that was why. Monday I told Mme J. I thought I had a touch of flu. She threw me in bed with a centigrade thermometer, a pill that's guaranteed to kill the "grippe" in 2 days, tea every hour all afternoon. Almost *too* much attention. I don't think she has enuf to do and was just waiting for a chance to mother (or smother) me. Well, it worked and I'm up today. Took a little walk in the sun this morn and am going to visit Nina this afternoon. Flu completely gone. Am being VERY CAREFUL.

Much love to all,

TuTu

—————————

Wonder of wonders, this morning's sky is blue. When I lean out the window, I catch a whiff of sea air from the Atlantic. This is a good day to visit the Picasso Museum in the Marais district.

After Picasso's death in 1973, his heirs gave the French government an enormous collection of art in place of estate taxes. These works fill L'Hôtel Salé, the former manor house of a rich salt tax collector. The Salty Mansion suits modern museum usage with apertures in walls to see from one gallery into another. Diego Giacometti designed the wrought-iron chairs used by the uniformed guards; the curved metal echoes the stair railing and chandelier in the entrance hall.

When Anna arrived in Paris, Picasso was studying at the Royal Academy in Madrid. He moved to Paris in 1900, exhibited in the Paris Universal Exposition, and met Gertrude Stein in 1905. The museum displays are chronological, from Picasso's academic work to his Minotaurs and cubist portraits. As an assemblage artist, I admire his collages and sculpture. I think of my own portraits constructed from junk metal: *Guinevere*, made from a plow part and a castellated nut; *Sir Lancelot*, armed with a jousting chisel; and *Admiral Farragut,* straddling a torpedo.

Picasso's disfigurement of the human form would have appalled Anna, and, with her academic training, she would not have understood my sculpture. My installations about religious persecution and military power are closer to Picasso's *Guernica* than to Anna's precisely plumbed nude drawings.

—————————

March 9, 1898

2, rue Léopold-Robert

Dear Edith,

I was amused this A.M. Delécluse came to criticize and said always begin at the head—or you will get it out of plumb, don't put the foot in until last. I let him talk, then said, I began at the head and the foot was the last thing I did—old sinner—it was not so much out [of line] after all—considering I had only worked one hour on the sketch and from the knee to the foot of *one* leg. I had not had time to put in the other at all. That fact ought to have told him where I began. He is a very careful critic though, and I was glad to see him this morning.

March 14, 1898

Got up early and went to the studio, then drew 19! It is a *concours* [competition] this week and I have entered—just to try. A *good* model— weather pleasant, went to Napoleon's Tomb—it is so beautiful there! Letters today.

March 16, 1898

I decided today that I had no business in that *concours* and would go upstairs [to the other studio]. My woman is a failure!

March 16, 1898

Dear Edith,

Mother writes that she thinks I have started a *life work*. And for her part she would prefer Tapestry and Flowers! Don't refer to this at home. I suppose it is a life work—but drawing is doing. And I did not know how to draw a figure and nearly *all* pictures have them. I am so glad you came over here young, before you taught.

Speaking of my drawing from Life. How can Tapestry be pretty without figures and ought not one to know how to draw those figures? Artists come here and sit down beside *me* beginning and peg away for dear life—in charcoal. I do not think I have wasted my time. I have done my very best and worked all I could. Now I want to paint and sketch. I want to be able to make *one* picture before I die—a real picture I mean.

March 16, 1898

Dear Mother and Father,

Yes, drawing from Life *is* a life work—but I needed to learn *how*— for in all pictures figures will appear, you know—and I must learn *how* to draw. I want to paint and will this summer and *perhaps*, I do not know yet, stay in Florence next winter and paint, then come here next spring again. I am doing my best you may be sure but if one can draw and paint figures he ought to be able to do anything else for *that* is the hardest. I have improved but have not done half what I wanted to. What it all is going to amount to I am sure I do not know. I am getting so old and rusty now—If I had been able to come at 18 when I first started, *then*—well, no use to think of that, *then* I could not come—so I will do all I can now.

Eliza and Bannester Lester shared Anna's accomplishments with interested townspeople. They saved an article written in the spring of 1898 by Mrs. J. A. Rounseville, art editor of *The Rome Georgian*:

Since the days of her infancy, Rome has been known as a city of intelligence and culture, but that so many of her daughters possess in such marked degree, a talent for art, in the special branches of painting and drawing was never suspected until the coming of Miss Helen Fairchild to the Rome Female College. One member of that first free hand class, who has followed most worthily in the footsteps of the instructor who inspired her early efforts, is Miss Anna Lester, who, after winning many honors in the finest Metropolitan Art Schools of this country, and presiding with notable success over the art departments of Shorter College in Rome, and the Mary Baldwin Seminary of Virginia, is now sojourning in Europe, reveling in the art treasures of the famous galleries of Paris, drawing from life in its celebrated schools, and attending lectures on the Anatomy of Art.

Within the past year, Miss Lester has viewed the masterpieces of many of the celebrated artists of the old world in the churches and galleries of Antwerp, Brussels, Cologne, and Dresden. During the coming summer months she hopes to go leisurely through Switzerland and the Black Forest, sketching and painting from nature, and spend next winter in Italy, at the painting schools of Rome and Florence.

Eliza Lester wanted Anna to bring home "Tapestry and Flowers." How could she display Anna's charcoal nudes? When I first exhibited my gritty, political sculpture in 1979, my mother-in-law pleaded with me to "make some pretty little watercolors of magnolia blossoms." To her, art was a painting to hang over a Chippendale sofa. My sculpture is not lady-like art.

March 18, 1898

I have been *burning* letters this afternoon. M. Callot came today, my man was almost right, but they voted for quick sketches upstairs this week and I will not be able to finish him.

March 19, 1898

Our model did not give us very good quick poses—we all stopped at 11:30. Still bad weather. When will spring come? I read *all* my letters, then burned them!

March 20, 1898

I got up in time today, to go to church as a Christian would. I could not have stayed away from service after reading my letter.

March 21, 1898

I got a good number this week–3–and found the place I wanted but, oh my, what an odor there is. I believe a dead cat or rat is under the floor. A good man this week. A magnificent day. Went to the bank and then walked to the Arc de Triomphe.

March 22, 1898

M. Delance came and my, how he gave it to them about the compositions. Mine was about right, my figure I mean, but he does not want the shadows sketched and I thought that was just what Delance did want. A beautiful day. Went to the Louvre and enjoyed the pictures so much and my Venus, too!

March 24, 1898

Delécluse came today and found very little fault, but I want it *right* and to look like flesh. A little snow today and very cold.

March 25, 1898

Snow! Snow! Cold! Delance came early. He gave me a most careful criticism and is very kind. The dead cat or rat has not been found yet!

March 28, 1898

Such a time at the studio. The stove pipe came down and the room was so cold I had to go upstairs. I hate to begin the week this way.

March 30, 1898

A charming day! Saw the hats at the Louvre [department store] and got a sailor. A white one! Now I will be a beauty.

———⊷⊶———

Outside the Picasso Museum, rain startles me; the bright sky of morning is gone. I lower my head and run to the covered walkways of the place des Vosges. The arcades around the square were an urban-renewal project by Henri IV, a novel experiment to protect shoppers from the elements. This twentieth-century visitor is grateful for their shelter. Strolling by galleries and map shops, I read the restaurant luncheon menus. A very pink establishment advertises lobster bisque, which is reason enough to choose La Guirlande de Julie. Garlands of ivy and flowers hang from trellises around the restaurant interior. I hum "La Vie en Rose" as my steaming soup arrives in a white porcelain tureen, accompanied by grated cheese and buttery croutons. The dessert menu lists *Île Flottante*. The meringue islands are good but the sauce is runny. Anna would have added a few ladyfingers.

Back out under the arcades, I study the architecture. It's too wet to venture into the garden to guess which of the bricks are *trompe-l'oeil* paintings. I've read that the colors of the roofs, stones, and bricks symbolize the *bleu, blanc, et rouge* of the French flag. Number 6, place des Vosges, was the residence of Victor Hugo from 1832 to 1848. His house museum is a convenient place to wait for the rain to let up. The displays span Hugo's life from his dressing table and writing desk to his deathbed and death mask. Hugo designed the dining room for his mistress, Juliette Drouet. The wooden panels are Chinese style with porcelain plates in shallow niches as part of the design. Looking from a window, I think about the duels fought at dawn in the square. Wasn't there a secret exit in the rear of the apartment, from which Hugo left for his clandestine affairs? I want to learn more about life, death, and amour in the place des Vosges.

I have no shield against the rain when I leave the covered archways. The early morning sunshine seduced me, and I did not bring my umbrella. I could buy another, but, like my penny-pinching great-aunt, I hate to spend redundant money. The name of this area, Le Marais, referred to the marsh caused by flooding from the Seine, and today the word *swamp* is apt. Jumping puddles and darting in and out of doorways, I make my way to the Métro, I remember the French saying about the daily routine of Métro, work, and sleep: *Métro, Boulot, DoDo*. This week, I am doing my own version: *Métro, Musée, Dodo*. At the hotel, I hang up my soaked jacket and take a short nap.

April 1, 1898

A most dreadful day! My criticism was discouraging. M. Delance said my woman had "Transatlantic legs and was sick beyond cure." The news after lunch was so sad. Oh dear, what a life this is.

April 2, 1898

The model was too sick to pose nude and was not at all attractive dressed, so we all left early. I went to the Bon Marché in the afternoon.

April 2, 1898

2, rue Léopold-Robert

Dear Edith,

I got a *beautiful* criticism this week past. The legs of my figure were too long and Delance said she was a "Trans Atlantic Woman"! I had to laugh— but the dear old fellow ought to have said so on Tuesday—and instead of saying they were too long then, he said make them longer, which I did, but I thought all the time she would be a "stopper" when I got her finished.

When I looked through Anna's charcoal drawings, I noticed some writing on the sketch of April first: "D. transa." Either Anna or professor Delance wrote this abbreviation for *transatlantique*. I thought he meant the model had long American legs until I looked up the word. *Le transatlantique* means ocean liner and *le transat* means deck chair. In fact, the way the model's legs fold up does look like she has deck chair legs. Monsieur Delance's words, "sick beyond cure," echo my Hollins professor's comment, "let it die a natural death."

April 3, 1898

Dear Edith,

I have just three weeks left to make out my six months at the Studio. That seems a long time to have done so little. I really am ashamed to look at what I have. I *want* to do so much—but guess it is not born in me and I cannot make myself over—God must have known best when he gave me no more than I have.

April 3, 1898

Went to service at the Chapel and as I came in my letters were handed to me. Of all things to distress me was the account I heard of that book "Prince of the House of David." The very idea of their sending for another and tormenting Mlle Ballu so—was too much—I would not have had that done for a whole jug full of nice sweet cider! Oh, I *am* so sorry—what on earth *will* she think?

April 8, 1898 [Good Friday]

This morning I went to my own little chapel to service. After lunch mailed my letters. I trust God will go with both I sent to Staunton. I met Mrs. Hunter at the [Post] Office and she asked me to go with her uptown so I went. I was so *lonely*. Have been homesick all the week.

April 9, 1898 [Easter Eve]

Went to St. Etienne du Mont and to the Panthéon. The church was as beautiful as ever—they were fixing the flowers for tomorrow. One year ago tonight! Do I remember that?

April 10, 1898

Easter! And do I remember last Easter? Would to God I had that day to live over! I went this morning to our little chapel to early communion then up to the Madeleine to hear the music.

April 16, 1898

Miss Holden, a Mrs. Somebody, and I went to St. Germain. Had a lovely time after reaching there, walking on the Terrace and in the Wood. Got wildflowers and then came back. The air is delicious! How I wanted a horse.

April 17, 1898

Went to our little chapel. I am glad I went. "I *know* that *my* redeemer liveth." How comforting that is. Then the lesson Isaiah 1.2.43. That too is comforting. Beautiful weather for two weeks! Charming!

What mixup occurred with *The Prince of the House of David*, Anna's Christmas gift to Mlle Ballu? What happened on Easter Eve and Easter Day to make those days memorable? Anna's diary entries are tantalizing but enigmatic. I wish I could read between the lines. Instead I read the Bon Marché promotional pages giving directions to the store by tram, train, or boat. Engravings picture the store interior with grand staircases, bulbous light fixtures, and throngs of shoppers in feathered hats and ruffled capes. One page lists sales events during 1898, the best times to buy rugs, gloves, lace, and confections. A map of Paris shows plans for the universal exposition of 1900. Each month has a menu of restaurant dishes, including recipes. The November menu featured *langue de boeuf au gratin* (beef tongue with cheese), *soufflé de marrons* (chestnut soufflé), and *omelette au sucre* (sugar omelet). Thinking about a sugar omelet makes me hungry. Bon Marché has a restaurant designed by Andrée Putnam. I'll go down for a cup of tea.

At the restaurant, the waiters are stacking chairs and cleaning floors, but I persuade a stressed young waitress to bring me a cup of tea. The tray arrives with a pot of tea but only one cube of sugar. I'm annoyed but must laugh when I remember Anna and the stingy Berthier sisters. I like my tea very hot with sugar and a slice of lemon— never the milk of English tradition. My mother added spice by studding the lemon slice with cloves. This afternoon I am grateful for this simple, slightly tart, cup of tea. I reach in my jacket pocket for my notebook and feel two small lumps—of sugar. I took them from a restaurant several days ago because the wrapping paper has portraits of poets and musicians. I unwrap Paul Verlaine and Alfred de Musset and plop the cubes in my teacup. The steam rises to fog my glasses. "To your health, Sister Anna."

From Madame Bazin's pension, Anna told her parents about assembling tea paraphernalia:

> I went up on rue de Rivoli by the Louvre, to get a little French book, then to the English Tea Store for a little Tea, after that to the Louvre for a while. It amuses me how I make *preparations* for having tea. Over two weeks ago I got a cup and saucer for 4 cents, I had the sugar here. Yesterday, I got a little boiler, now maybe in the course of a month I will get the stove, one only costs 13 cents or 29 cents and I have not decided whether to invest in the cheap one or not. I have the little bottle ready to buy the *Alcohol*—so will get that soon and maybe by Christmas I will get a cup of tea! I like it you know and have had none since I left the Lafayette House, but it is kinder pokey having it alone.

Later, she reported:

> I have at last gotten my [alcohol] stove. I split the difference and got
> one for 19 cents, a teapot for 13 cents, and alcohol to last a month. Then
> this afternoon I got ten cents worth of nice crackers like our 5 o'clock teas
> at home. If Mary comes to see me, as she says she will tomorrow
> afternoon, I will christen the whole outfit. Cup was 4 cents and I got a
> wine glass for the same, all extra fine quality, *of course*.
>
> Before I leave Paris for good, however, when ever that is, I am going
> to invest in a teapot and cups I saw at the Bon Marché. They are beauties
> and cost, I think, for cup, 2.50 francs, Tea Pot 5 francs. I cannot afford
> them now. But I will not forget to have it for my old maid room when I
> *settle* down.

After paying for my tea, I look at china teapots in the antique department of
Bon Marché. The Lesters sent Anna money for a Paris keepsake; she chose the blue
china teapot and two cups she had seen at this store.

A glass bridge spans the street from the Bon Marché main building to La
Grande Épicerie where zucchini and apples glisten like emeralds and rubies.
Cooking with these jewels would be a pleasure, but as I have no kitchen, I buy
jambon and Boursin to go with the yogurt and pear in the minibar. On the way
back to the hotel, I turn onto the rue du Cherche-Midi, in the opposite direction
from Tuesday's exploration. In a carved medallion on the facade of number 19, a
Greek scholar instructs a cherub in the making of a sundial. The inscription reads:
Au Cherche Midi. As I thought, this street is associated with the "search for midi,"
the meridian noon mark of a *cadran solaire*. At number 8, baking smells drift from
the legendary Poilâne bakery, where they offer samples of their trademark sugar
cookies. In a Proustian nanosecond, the sandy texture transports me to my
grandmother's front porch.

Back in my room, I eat my take-out supper and learn something from a Paris
guidebook. The rue du Cherche-Midi may refer to an old French saying, *Chercher
midi à quatorze heures*: to search for a noon meal at two o'clock—after the lunch
hour has past. This has been a leitmotif of my trip. I ask for a meal before the proper
hour or arrive for food after the service has stopped.

April 17, 1898

2, rue Léopold-Robert

Dear Mother and Father,

War seems to be almost here I am too sorry—how I hope yet it will all end in talk. I hear Atlanta is the headquarters of the U.S. Army. I do hope there will be no war, don't you?

April 20, 1898

Dear Edith,

The United States gives Spain until Saturday to decide what she will do. I am afraid if war begins other countries over here will help Spain and we will be in a muddle. Oh, I am so sorry! Why don't they settle some way without war I wonder.

April 21, 1898

I thought this morning I was in for something. I could not breathe and when I found it raining went back to bed, so was two hours late at the studio. A shame! I feel a little better now, but this cough!

April 22, 1898

M. Delance says he always has to tell *me* the same thing. That is pleasant I must say. Dear old fellow—I do try but he forgets I am old and tired.

April 23, 1898

After dinner paid Mrs. Hunter a visit and she told me about miniature painting. I think I will try it. War has begun! I am too sorry.

April 24, 1898

Went to St. Roch, then stopped in the Luxembourg Gallery to see a miniature by Hortense Richard—it *is* fine. I have admired it before but did not know she taught.

April 24, 1898

Dear Mother and Father

It looks as if War has begun sure enough. I am too sorry, I think some way could have been managed to settle matters without fighting. You are not getting excited about it, are you? The French papers say we did not have any right to take that boat with the mules because war had not been declared—but the Spanish were pretty quick to stop one of our boats coming into Antwerp, eh? Mr. Hunter says there will be no trouble about crossing—for we go under the Dutch flag if we go by Antwerp. When I come home I want to go by way of London—if England does not join Spain—just now she is for America—but one cannot depend on anything in time of war.

Be sure and tell me if the war is worrying you any. It cannot affect us here or you there can it? Surely the United States will not allow any Spanish to land and fight our men over land will it? Unless somebody over here helps Spain, I do not see how she will stand *any* chance on land—but our Navy is poor. It should have been reinforced long ago.

I think for the month of May I will change places—I have one more week at Delécluse—If I should come home now I would have absolutely nothing to show for my winter except these charcoals and I suppose Rome people would be too modest to look at them—but *All* studios here have them *framed* and hung around the walls to show that the pupils *can* draw from Life. I am not sorry I have taken the course I have but if I could have worked *all day* I would have had something in color. But I could not do that this winter, perhaps I can now a while.

If Anna thought that modest Romans would not look at her nudes, perhaps she was looking for more acceptable art forms. I've not found any outdoor sketches she made in Paris, but we do have yellow daisies, forget-me-nots, and many miniature portraits.

April 25, 1898
Went to the Luxembourg Gardens to sketch.

April 26, 1898
My dear ones at Home,

I do hate so for you to be alone while this war is going on—but as Edith's letter, which has just come, says she does not know what *we* would do if we went home. We could not work, and we could not do any good unless we went to nurse—and we have no experience in that. It would spoil her life work to stop now and as for me—I better stay here and do all I can. If I was only *sure* you would not worry. I am all right and so is Edith—and if you are safe—we better go on a while longer and see how matters turn. I wish now I had been here earlier—but no use to wish for lost opportunities.

Don't worry about my not hearing the news. I hear all every day. Telegraphed from New York—"the Herald of Paris"—the Hunters take that—so I am posted. I am thankful I have enough clothes to last me a while and not buy any. Old England is on our side I am glad of that—but what is the matter with France? Is Cuba worth all this anyway? I hardly think so—still they are souls and we must try and save them.

April 27, 1898
Nothing new—only I am trying a miniature. If my eyes will stand such small work. I would like to learn.

April 30, 1898
My last day at Delécluse's for this summer. I hate to stop for I like it there, but feel I *must* be out of doors more.

———— ◦◦◦ ————

The tea at Bon Marché must have been strong. At midnight my mind spins on a gerbil wheel powered by caffeine. I pull out the 1898 envelope from Kansas. If Anna had burned this envelope, as she did letters in March, would I be in Rome, Georgia, tonight instead of on rue Sainte-Beuve? On the front of the envelope, the Topeka postmark is November first. The Paris arrival postmark is November 14, 1898—one hundred years ago today. On that day, Anna wrote "Letters!!" in her journal. She was happy to receive this envelope, but who sent it?

In Anna's steamship book, I turn to the red-inked travel advice, which I attribute to the worldly Mlle Ballu, and compare the handwriting to the Topeka envelope. On both, the lowercase letter *r* is distinctive, resembling a *v* or a seagull in flight. The letter *a* is like a typographic symbol, not the smooth-topped *a* in cursive script. I lean back against the quilted headboard. If Mlle Ballu wrote the advice, she also addressed the envelope. She is responsible for my finding 9, rue Sainte-Beuve, but what was she doing in Kansas? Perhaps Miss Weimar fired her after the 1897-98 session at Mary Baldwin.

Anna's address book has no listing for Ballu under the letter *B*. Under *K* I find four street addresses for Kansas City, Missouri. The only address with a name is Miss Barstow's School at 15 Westport Avenue. Did Mlle Ballu teach there?

Under the letter *T* there are notes on Tremezzo and Territet. For Topeka, Kansas, there is one address—621 Harrison Street—with no name listed. A business card, stained with age, is stuck in the address book pages. It gives another address:

Mlle Henriette Ballu,
Conversational French
1116 Main Street, Room 30
Kansas City, MO

"Room 30" sounds familiar; I have seen numbered rooms on a floor plan folded up in Anna's journal. I thought it might be a plan of one of her pensions. The pencil drawing is faint because the paper has been bleached by a century of light. I see that the handwriting matches the envelope and the travel advice; the lowercase *r* and *a* are unmistakable. The diagram shows a floor on which three rooms, numbered 28, 29, and 30, open onto a corridor with an elevator and a lighted court. Room 30, the "Reception Room," has a desk, chairs, and bookcases. The words written on rooms 28 and 29 are confusing: ozone bath, treatment table, static machine, dressing case. If this is Mlle Ballu's Room 30, was she renting space in a health facility to teach French? Mlle Ballu's business card exactly matches a less-faded rectangle on the paper. The floor plan and the card were once stored together.

I now have three possible examples of Mlle Ballu's handwriting: the steamship book, the Topeka envelope, and the Kansas City floor plan. Before I left home, I photocopied a crumbling scrap of brown wrapping paper addressed to Anna at Madame Bazin's. Same handwriting. Postmarked April 21, 1898, in Staunton, Virginia, the package says "Photo—No Writing." There are dozens of unidentified photographs in my basement; one of them could be Henriette Ballu.

Before I left, I also found another brown wrapper addressed to Anna with a May 6 Staunton postmark. The inscription says "Book—No Writing." If my maternal ancestors kept the wrapping paper, perhaps they saved the book. I looked through a stack of Anna's books on my studio shelf: *Le Petit Parisien, Roman and Medieval Art, The Standard-Operaglass*. One slim volume, *Deutsche Liebe*, was the approximate size of the wrapper. The flyleaf inscription matched the arrival time frame: Anna M. Lester, Paris, June 4, 1898. When I placed *Deutsche Liebe* into the fragile paper wrapper, the creases dovetailed with discoloration on the inside covers of the book; Anna had made a protective jacket from the wrapping paper. After crossing the Atlantic together in Anna's trunk, the book and cover were separated. They sat in my studio—three feet away from each other—until I put the clues together.

Deustche Liebe is written in German script with a foreword by Max Müller. A few pressed forget-me-nots rest next to a poem by Goethe. Other passages about German love are from various authors. Two poems are in English: "Sweet Highland Girl" and "The Buried Life":

> *Alas, is even Love too weak*
> *To unlock the heart, and let it speak?*
> *Are even lovers powerless to reveal*
> *To one another what indeed they feel?*

Check marks in the page margins indicate passages set off by penciled parentheses. Because the old-style typeface was difficult to read, my former German teacher and I scanned a few marked passages. I brought my scribbled translations to Paris:

> It was as if we always had lived together and with each other because it was not a feeling that she started to say which had not found a resonance in my soul, and no thought I had to which she did not nod as if to say, I think so, too.

> We learn to stand and go and speak and read; but no one teaches us love.

> She had become my good angel, my other "I" (alter-ego) to whom I spoke instead of talking to myself.

> My whole thinking had unwillingly become a dialogue with her and everything that was good in me, everything I strove for, all I believed in, my whole better self, belonged to her, that I gave her, that came out of her mouth, out of the mouth of my good angel.

> Human beings from youth are used to living in a cage and even in free air they don't dare move their wings, afraid they'll knock against everything if they try to fly.

How familiar this last quotation sounds, especially if I substitute the word *women* for *human beings*. In 1983 I continued my wing motif in an exhibit about women's lives (*Silver Shackles and Gilded Cages*, CVAA, LaGrange, Georgia). I placed winged, high-heeled shoes in birdcages to symbolize women's entrapment by traditional roles and footwear. A wire dress form with vestigial wings represented the constrictions of fashion. Later, in performance pieces, I created winged personae. "Dotty Matrix" of the "Dotty Birds" starred in a protest spoof aimed at the DOT (Department of Transportation). The pink-winged "Lunatic Moth" appeared on the top of Rome's Old Town Clock on the spring equinox.

Anna's German book comes from the Victorian era, but in my generation, after several waves of feminism, many women choose to clip their wings. Anna left the rigid expectations of small town society to chase her dreams in Paris. By marking this passage, her correspondent urged her to fly. Thank God for friends who help celebrate our flying muscles. I get up from the bed and prance around the hotel room, flapping my wings and chirping like a "Dotty Bird." Action feels good. Fortunately the curtains are closed.

Refreshed by crazy pantomime, I settle down onto the bed, surrounded by letters and books. Before tonight I've concentrated on the logistics of Anna's life and my schedule in Paris. While I've shuffled Anna's collected papers like playing cards, their significant patterns have hovered on the fringe of my consciousness. It's time to think like a detective. The red ink handwriting in the steamship manual matches the Topeka envelope, the Kansas City floor plan, and the package wrappings from Staunton. The check marks in *Deutsche Liebe* are like the ones in the steamship book. I knew Mlle Ballu tutored Anna in German, French, and European customs, but from the German book excerpts, I see she also gave advice about love. Was their relationship more than mentor to neophyte?

In Anna's papers I also found a hand-printed playful "bank note." The handwriting is now familiar; the seagull *r* is used in "Heart-Centre."

> Davidtown May 30, 1898 No. 1
> The Heart-Centre Bank
> Pay to self   on order $10.00
> (In Kisses) Ten Dollars
> Jonathan

More mystery. Was there really a place named Davidtown? And who in the world is Jonathan?

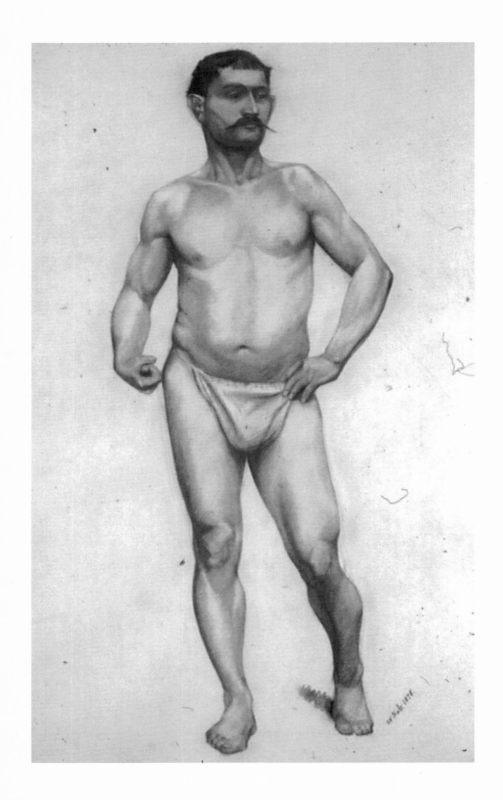

Day Seven
Sunday, November 15, 1998
Lost Letter from Geneva

CNN announces that Iraq has agreed to resume site inspections. A pause in the war rumblings may allow me to complete my mission by Wednesday. Before I came to Paris, I thought I'd meet other hotel guests at breakfast. Perhaps visitors from Scotland would know of Amy Steedman and Frances Blaikie; I could tell stories about my great-aunt and her friends and find leads to follow in Edinburgh or London. This morning the men in the breakfast area have bald pates bordered by fringes of hair. Monks? I think not, because they are smoking cigarettes and eating boiled eggs. They are English actors on location in Paris to film a movie about Saint Joan of Arc. One smoking "monk" may occupy room number 10. His cigarette smoke penetrates my wall at night, and his hacking cough reminds me of Anna's. Should I offer him some of her remedies? On April 28, 1898, she wrote Edith:

> I think sometimes I may be like old Mrs. Hardin—go barking around all my life, I was almost well I thought two weeks ago, but with last night at the Opera and the next day used me up. I think I got overheated and really felt sick the rest of the week and of course, the cough came back, blooming. I have never stopped a day since September taking all sorts of things and I lived on cod liver oil, now I am taking an Emulsion of Petroleum oil for the lungs and throat etc. etc. Raw eggs know how to slip down and I am so tired doctoring.

Tuberculosis, known as "the white plague," was a major killer in the late nineteenth century. Anna's letters and journal never mention the word, but Edith had a doctor examine Anna in Berlin in 1897. Anna also consulted doctors in Paris, but none gave a diagnosis. My grandmother always regretted that she did not know of the sanitaria in Switzerland where many tubercular patients were cured.

Standard treatments included bleeding with leeches, blistering the skin, and secluding the patient in dark rooms with no ventilation. In *Tuberculosis and Genius*, Dr. Lewis J. Moorman lists artists, writers, and musicians who had TB, including Beardsley, Chopin, Emerson, Milton, and Molière. He quotes D. G. Macleod Munro: "The patient has an insatiable craving for a full and active life. He lives in an atmosphere of feverish eagerness to seize the fleeting moments before they pass." Some experts thought that tuberculosis spores invaded the brain and drove creative people to hyperactivity followed by fever, coughing, and despair.

Dr. Moorman describes the "hopeful optimism" of tubercular patients, but I see this trait in myself and in other artists. The next painting will hang in the Whitney, the new poetry collection will win a Pulitzer, and the sculpture will go to the Venice Biennale. We feel deflated when our work doesn't measure up to our conception.

"Great show!" I said to a friend at her opening.

"Yes, but…if I'd only had another week…."

"Just smile and say thank you," I advised. "You alone know your original concept."

We looked around the gallery. "Yeah," she said. "Ninety-five percent of my dream looks pretty darn good."

An architect taught me the word *charrette*—a two-wheeled cart pulled by handles, like Marie Antoinette's transport to the guillotine. Students at the École des Beaux-Arts put their architectural maquettes on these wagons, then, adding last touches, they raced through the streets to meet competition deadlines. To be *en charrette* means to be engaged in an all-night plunge to the finish line. In our perfectionism, we artists believe that if we only had one more day, we could produce a true masterpiece. I've learned to write down the unrealized ideas of a show, because the unmade work of one exhibition contains the nucleus of the next. New seeds crop up as the old field is harvested.

Anna advised Edith not to practice too many hours and not to go out so much at night. My mother often told me, "Now, honey, don't try to do too much. Don't overdo!" My family recognized the connection between exhaustion and disease, probably because of Sister Anna's illness and death, but how does one gauge the "exhaustion meter" when one is *en charrette* to a gallery opening deadline?

After hauling a truckload of metal gears, piano crates, and old furniture to a gallery, I asked the weary truck driver, "Willie, how did we manage to move all that stuff?"

"Mrs. Harvey," he said, "you was *determined.*"

He was right. The Lester determination has propelled me through strenuous exhibitions, usually accompanied by sore throats and anger that my body couldn't keep pace with my mind. Sometimes I question my sanity, but the work provides affirmation. For one exhibit I spray-painted the piano crates that I had salvaged three years earlier from the Edith Lester Harbin Department of Music at Shorter College. I hauled the black crates back to the same building for a theatrical exhibit about music and art (*Leitmotifs*, 1983). Feverish with a violent infection, I locked myself in the gallery to assess my work.

March 22, 1983

Went to Shorter to *see* my show for the first time. No one was in the building. It was quiet and dark. I turned on different combinations of track lights and sat and lay on the floor and took it in. I really think it's neat. I felt a sense of presence, power, and weight (yeah). The best view is on the floor. Really moved by the whole thing. Very high morning. I keep asking myself if it's worth it. I guess it is, *damn it!* I can't quit.

It's strange to be really knocked out by my own work, like I have been by other people's—Nevelson and Rauschenberg, etc. Felt like I did after having trudged to Brooklyn to see "The Dinner Party" or the night we spent in Frank Lloyd Wright's Imperial Hotel in Tokyo in 1962. This show is very much related to my love of architecture.

I guess what I learned this morning was that it was worth doing just so *I* could *see it myself.* Others see it with different eyes. Only I can see it both as creator and viewer.

Part of being an artist is gauging where one fits on the art world yardstick: somewhere on a vertical scale between Olympus and oblivion. Because I was forty-two when I had my first solo show, I set my sights high. After several years of exhibiting in Washington and Atlanta, I aimed for New York City. Why not? Museum curators occasionally requested slides; I had some good reviews. What if I had major talent and never made the leap to the Big Apple because of timidity?

One winter I took my slides to galleries in Soho. In an icy rain, I walked the cobblestone streets in my suede boots. Some gallery owners were encouraging; one was sadistically rude: Who did I think I was to waste his time with this junk? I shivered in a phone booth, tears freezing on my cheeks, and called Noreene Wells, a photographer friend in Washington. "Tell me *again*," I said. "*Why* did I want to be an artist?" After that, Noreene and I repeated this catchphrase as we hauled more boxes up the Gallery 10 steps. After delivering a sold work of art to a castle in Georgetown at midnight, she and I drove to North Carolina, where I backed the rental truck off a muddy mountainside.

For my largest installation (*Monumental Erections*, Nexus Gallery, Atlanta, 1985), I unloaded two trucks and, with ropes and pulleys, hoisted an iron bed, wooden crates, a mantelpiece, and a golden metal obelisk through the third floor gallery window. With the help of five people, I pushed and pulled into shape an exhibit about male power symbols. In adjoining galleries, two artists hung photographs and small paintings on the wall. A hammer and nails were all they needed. I asked myself: What's wrong with this picture? Why indeed did I want to be an artist? I had constructed walk-in theater, but had I gone over the Brink of Overdo?

Eventually, I had the fun of seeing one of my boxes displayed next to Andy Warhol's work in a group show in New York, but I revised my ambition and scale. My smaller exhibits have given me great pleasure in research and interaction with viewers. Did Great-Aunt Anna give up her dreams of Paris success, just as I've tempered my aspirations?

After the Nexus show, I traveled and began to write poetry—a portable art. Writing about Anna may be another reduction in scale. In cooking, reduction means simmering stock to the essential fused flavors. Perhaps I'm making soup, or a multilayered Dagwood sandwich, from the leftovers of my family's life. I still feel the Lester passion to see and do everything. How can I visit all of Anna's Paris in nine days? Writing about my great-aunt may be easier than driving trucks and pushing handcarts of junk, but the universe is probably chortling at my naiveté. Dr. Moorman might compare me to a fixated tubercular patient. I must strive for balance.

My coffee cup rattles as one of the monks has a coughing spasm and shakes the table. After they leave, I look at the weather diagrams in *France-Soir*. Clouds drip with rain across the map of France, and centigrade temperature is in the ten-degree range. The forecast calls for *averses*—downpours—throughout the day. I rule out trips to Amiens or the basilica at Saint-Denis. It's Sunday—perhaps I'll follow the family advice and not overdo. I order a second cup of hot chocolate to go with the last slice of nut bread in the breadbasket. I wipe my sticky fingers on my napkin before opening Anna's *Catalogue Illustré de la Société Nationale des Beaux-Arts*.

The Paris Salon was an artistic and social event. Paintings covered entire walls of the galleries, and having work in the Paris Salon solidified an artist's career. Even though she was a beginner in life drawing and was about to learn a new medium, Anna's ambition to exhibit in the Salon comes through in her writings.

April 28, 1898
2, rue Léopold-Robert
My own dear Edith,

The Salon opens Monday and I am so anxious to see what they have. Two or three of Delécluse pupils got in on miniatures—those who have been here several years—three at least are required before one need *try*.

I am going to make a change of studios on Monday and go to Colarossi for the afternoon painting class and paint heads in watercolor from life. Then I have started by myself, but I do not want anybody here or at home to know, miniature painting. I am going to take some lessons in the mornings of a Mrs. Reynolds, but I prefer the style of Miss Hortense Richards. She painted that old woman in the Luxembourg lighting candles, a small picture, do you remember it? I thought it was oil but it is watercolor on ivory. Mrs. Hunter took a few lessons of her and she has told me exactly how Mrs. Richards does, so I am trying and after a while may go to her for a few private lessons.

This weather is lovely. I would very much like to be out of doors all day long but that cannot be yet. I am on a new track for May. I thought an entire change might wake me up.

You ought to see these dear kittens. I take the little mother out a small bottle of milk every morning. And she is so glad to see me and the little dears know me, I believe. I would like to send you the grey one. The girls have named them Queen Victoria and the Prince of Wales! They are just as fat as butterballs. Home made butterballs!

Mrs. Hunter told me the news at lunch—we have bombarded Montezuma. Where that is—is more than I know. A whole lot of soldier boys passed here a few minutes ago.

Who do you think applied for a place at Shorter? Your dear little friend Joy. Could she fill it do you think? I like Joy more I suppose than any girl in Rome or elsewhere but for an only daughter to have to teach is a shame. Now *why* does not Joy come and study French here?

Friday. Today is Varnishing Day at the Salon and the pupils who have pictures there have gone—they go free—but we poor things would have to pay 10 francs, so I do not indulge this year.

Take good care of your dear little self and don't work too hard or too long. With much love from your sister,

Anna M. Lester

I'm curious about Varnishing Day. My French dictionary gives the word for *varnish* as *vernis* along with the word *vernissage*—the day preceding the opening of an exhibition. In France a gallery opening is called a *vernissage*, but I never knew that the etymology dated to Varnishing Day. Did artists varnish their work in public to prove the work was complete? From preparing my exhibits, I know that artistic ideas accelerate as a show opening approaches. Paint and glue are often tacky as my work travels to the gallery by truck. Only the gallery opening—or a final coat of varnish—declares the work finished.

The Salon catalog lists celebrated artists: Rodin, Sisley, Sargeant, Carolus-Duran, Saint-Gaudens, Puvis de Chavannes. For the third time, I see the name Prinet. Was R. X. Prinet kin to our Hollins Abroad lecturer, Mademoiselle Marguerite Prinet? The catalog includes society portraits and earthy scenes of plowing and harvest, as well as paintings of nudes. Anna checked paintings by Delance and Callot, her teachers at the Académie Delécluse. Callot exhibited a nude woman standing by a stream with spring flowers in her hair. Her knobby knees and awkward feet resemble those in Anna's drawings.

The Salon catalog gives the marital status of women, while men are listed by only their last names. I see the name of Mlle C. Claudel, Rodin's protégée, whose fight for critical recognition ended in "madness." Female artists' struggle for parity continued far past Anna's time. In 1959 my art history textbook at Hollins contained no female artists, not even Mary Cassatt or Rosa Bonheur.

Painting and sculpture fill the front of the catalog. A back section lists smaller work: drawings, watercolors, pastels, and miniature portraits. Miniatures on ivory were popular, portable mementos in the late nineteenth century. I see that Mme V. Reynolds exhibited six miniatures. She was Mrs. Virginia Reynolds of the Chicago Art Institute, with whom Anna studied.

I inherited Anna's miniature portrait of my grandmother, a baby, and some French women. Other family members possess a man in Scottish regalia and an Arab in robes. The miniatures measure about two by three inches; working on this small scale must have aggravated Anna's eye problem. The facial features are so detailed that I assume she used a magnifying glass and miniscule brushes. Her notes describe technique:

> Put a light sketch on the ivory in pencil, then outline in color, Burnt Sienna and Blue, rub down with pumice stone.
>
> Put on the Cobalt blue then mix yellow and red. Do not try and get the color by mixing all three, it comes out muddy.
>
> Always put a little color of the face and surrounding in the background to bring things together and make them swim.
>
> To cut Ivory, let it soak in water until wet through, then cut with scissors, while *wet*, against the grain.

I lean outside the hotel door to check the weather. Bone chilling. I step back inside and go up to my room. If Anna's chapel still existed, I'd go there for church. I could go to the American Cathedral on the Right Bank, but I prefer to spend May in Paris with Anna. She is happy and in better health. I'm sure her parents were pleased that she was getting "fat," as thinness was linked to tuberculosis.

May 1, 1898
Went to the chapel this morning. This afternoon Mary and I went to the Bois de Boulogne to a concert. It was fine. I enjoyed every minute.

May 2, 1898
Took my first lesson in miniature painting. I do not like the class. Such nice letters! And the dear little Photo. How beautiful it is! I really am happy today.

May 2, 1898

2, rue Léopold-Robert

My own dear Mother and Father,

It does my heart good to hear the news from Bubber, dear precious boy, he has done just what I have asked God everyday for months, that He would put it into his heart to do. To be a Christian and write home and gladden the hearts of his dear parents by telling them of the change. God *does* hear prayers and often answers just as we ask. When He does not, the answer is a way that is better for us. I do not believe *any* prayer from the heart is wasted, no not one. Don't worry one minute over anything for we know "all things happen for the best," and then too, "Not the slightest thing can happen to us unless God wills it." The war has come but I do not think it is going to affect *us* personally in the least.

I finished my six months at the Studio Saturday and this month I am going to spend painting mostly out of doors. It is just too lovely to stay inside. Last week, as soon as the model would begin to pose for the hand I would begin to wish for the ten-minute rest so I could step outside. You see the poor nude things have to be in a warm room and that makes my clothes too warm. I wanted to *undress* too!

One of the Studio girls from Australia gave me a copy of a letter in French that I am to have put on a special paper—which costs 60 centimes—and send to the Prefect of the Seine to get permission to go sketching. This lady—girl I call her—but she is I suppose 45 or so—is going with me. So you can picture me down by the lovely river and out in the Parks making little sketches this beautiful month.

And you should see how well I am now, and I am getting fat! I put on the black silk waist that Miss Allen fixed over and I nearly suffocated—it was so tight—and as for the black satin! The only hook that will fasten at all is the top one and the bottom one and then I am almost squeezed to death. The consequence is I never wear it if I can get out of it. You know it has a vest of green satin loose with lace on it. I draw that together and so make out—I tried the night I went to the Opera to fasten two hooks at the waist and the second one flew off! What do you think of that?

Mary says I look like another person from last fall and I do feel so much better and more like work. I am going to make up for last year if I

possibly can. My work in the studio has helped me so much and all who
know me tell me I am "improving" and "getting on."

I have not at all decided if I shall stay in Florence next winter. *Paris* is
the place for art and if I get a variety I will gain by staying here. If I do
that I can go to Italy for April and May next spring. That will be charming!

I am in the notion now of working and I do trust the Good Lord
will give me the ability to really do something. Friday I went way over
beyond where Mary lives to get—what do you suppose? A bottle of Rhum!
I take still the raw egg every morning in a tablespoon of Rhum. I am sick
and tired of it but think it does good. I was so tired by the time I got back
I could hardly get my shoes off and put on the Calesthenics shoes.

Sunday, Mary and I went to the Bois de Boulogne to hear the music.
It was a paradise out there and the music was out doors! But my goodness,
the crowds of people. It is a lovely garden, beds and beds of magnificent
pansies and forget-me-nots. In the Palais they have the music in winter
and bad weather—well that was too pretty for words. Fairyland—lakes,
ferns, falls and beautiful flowers. I want to live right there—lie down on
that moss and bed of ferns and press the flowers up close to my face. I am
going again, you may be sure. I drank in all the delicious air I could. The
pine woods made me think of home. Why don't our people appreciate our
woods so near town and run [street] cars out? These people do—and
whole families go out in the afternoon and lie down and sit down on the
pine straw. We Americans *need* fresh air outdoors. Then we would not be
so nervous. Oh, it was so *sweet!* Smelt like *Georgia!*

Minmine appreciated Moses' message and sends a love letter.
Madame held her paw and wrote it. She thought of doing it, I did not. It
says "Minmine sends the many best love greetings to Moses." Then as she
finished, her tail (a bushy one) brushed over it. Tell my darling Moses no
cat on earth could take her place in my heart. Give her my share of beef
and chicken and Cream!

Inside the letter is a small messy note. Wavering black ink marks cover the
paper, as if a Japanese Sumi-e master had fallen asleep in midstroke. Here is the love
letter from Madame Bazin's cat to Anna's cat: *Paris 2 mai 1898. Minmine envoie ses
meilleures amitiés à Moïse.*

Anna continues:

I am glad the meetings are a success and I hope the barrooms will be closed. Whiskey does so much harm. War is going on—but it is way off from you. I feel perfectly safe and I don't want you to worry one minute about me or Edith or about our getting out of funds. I am sure the good Lord will take care of us and of you. "Goodness and mercy shall follow you *all* the days of your life"—we must believe that. Also "I, the Lord thy God will hold thy right hand saying unto thee. Fear not, for I will help you."

Keep well and happy all of you for my sake.

May 4, 1898

Got up early and went for canvas and the Paris Daisies. Fixed my study, then worked and sang all day!

May 5, 1898

My Dear Edith,

You make me laugh, what did I say about not going to the Salon, for mercy sake? Such an idea never entered my head or heart. I said I was not flush enough to pay the francs and go on *Varnishing Day!* Students do not go that day unless they are rich or have a card of admittance, and as I was in neither position, *I* stayed away. But it is to be open *all* of May and June and I can go any day in the week, except Friday for 1 franc and on Sunday afternoon for 50c. If I do not mind being crowded to death, which I most seriously do, so I will pay my little franc and go weekdays. On Varnishing Day all the elite of Paris go and most people who do go, go to see the costumes and the crowd. Now I want none of that, so really did not mind not having a ticket.

I got my ticket of permission from the Prefect of the Seine to sketch any place in Paris I wanted to out doors. So now I can go.

I am afraid Joy's father's gold mine is like my ship coming in—will never turn up—until I reach the other shore, perhaps. When you and Joy keep house, you will let me come and see you sometimes, will you not? For *I* will be all alone, you know.

I have been painting a study of Paris Daisies, you know those yellow petal ones, and I want to finish those in the morning. They have not come out as well as I wanted them to. I have no easel and you would be amused if you could see how I managed. I took the cushion chair and turned the other chair to its back, then tied them together, stuck my stretcher on the back of the straight chair and myself I sat on the coal scuttle with the ottoman for a cushion and then took the *plush* cover I have had on my coal all winter for my background and drapery! The real study is pretty but mine is not.

My cough has almost gone now and on that account I stayed away from the studio this afternoon, because it rained *all* day and I was afraid I might start it up again if I got damp and sat in the studio three hours. I hated to miss but I knew I could not get there and not be wet, so grinned and bore it.

I got a dear little photo of Mlle Ballu on Monday. I'll show it to you this summer.

Lovingly—and kisses,
Anna M. Lester

May 7, 1898
Went to the Salon and saw everything! Was simply tired to death—could hardly get back here.

May 8, 1898
My dear Mother and Father
Changed my dress and went to the Salon! My goodness *so many* pictures. I got so very tired because I tried to see all, and get a general idea of what was there so I would know next time just where to go and see what I wanted. Have to pay a franc each time there but if we can stand it—could go at 8 A.M. and stay until 6 P.M. and have lunch inside. But one afternoon is all I can take in. I can't see after three hours of *looking*. Some things are beautiful—others not good at all. I can judge, you know! But I would be thankful to have something with my name on it in there. If I stay and succeed, next winter I will try.

I wish you could see how they have things arranged at the Salon. All the middle part is a garden—ground floor—and the Statues are out there—and palms and flowers mixed in between. I like that. Could have stayed out there *all* day—it is under shelter—a glass roof way up high. There are two societies, one on each side in rooms—The Champs-Elysées have the two front rooms, the Champs de Mars the two in the rear. They used to be all one but about eight years ago they quarreled and divided. Mrs. Hunter tells me they were at a dinner party and got into a dispute as to whether foreigners should have the same rights as the French. One thought one way, one the other. So since then they have had a separate building for their exhibitions—until this year—they are in one place—and one fee allows visitors to both. I will have to go a number of times to see all, for Saturday I only got a general idea, and there are four thousand pictures!

May 9, 1898

Worked morning and afternoon and it was too much. I never will learn how much to use my eyes. Liked the miniature work better today.

May 11, 1898

Rain all day! Tried to paint a few Forget-me-nots. They are harder than they look to be. Am not satisfied with the study.

May 16, 1898

Dear Mother and Father,

I thought this morning I would sleep a little late, as I cannot work, I find, but half the day with any comfort to my eyes, then perhaps my mail would come by the time I had finished my *nice* coffee. Won't I be glad to have some *real* coffee though when I get home! If I were French now I would add "Mon Dieu!!" to that. It comes in so easy and smooth with them and I really do not think they mean any more than we do when we say "oh my" or "my goodness." Or a boy saying "you bet." If anything surprises them or they think what you say a little extravagant, out comes "Mon Dieu" and no one thinks anything of it. It means My God but does not sound like it to me, so is very expressive. Such liberties cannot be taken in German for "Mein Gott" is too much like English to set well. These people here seem to be happy and free whether they go to church or not.

The letters did not come and I think the reason they are a day later now going and coming, all boats have to be conducted in and out of New York, I hear, on account of the mines we have put down to keep the Spanish out. Don't worry one bit because I have plenty of money to last me at least two months.

I went to Cook's to ask about round trip ticket [for summer]. I cannot tell [with] the war, just what to do. If France should go against us, which I do not think she will do, I would stay in Germany next winter. I am skittish about Italy. Riots go on there so much. I might not like the whole winter at once, though I would hate to come back to America without seeing as much of Italy as possible. All the pictures. They are lovely.

I'm so glad the lilies of the valley are doing well. Love to "my little darling." Kiss her and squeeze her for me. Don't let old Dick and Dan die before I come home. Poor old Dick. I am so sorry he is getting stiff. He is so fat though it makes it hard for him to get along even when he was young. If I learn enough I will paint his picture with Moses and Dan when I come back home. That is a *big* if, though, for I am so old and stiff myself. I see how hard it is to teach old dogs new tricks.

How glad I am Mother is better and Father is so well and all dressed up in his spring suit and straw hat! What wouldn't I give to step in and see you this very evening and kiss you with all my heart. Funny isn't it that Edith has never been homesick, but then she is young, cheerful, handsome, intelligent and no mortal knows what else, and I am old, tired, and need some one to pet me now.

With much love, a whole heart full for each and plenty of kisses, as many as you will take.

Your loving child,

Anna M. Lester

May 22, 1898

Dear Mother and Father,

The first year over here one has to learn a lot how to do afterwards. Me, for instance—next winter if I am well and strong I want to work *all* day and really paint some. This winter I have had much to contend with and have done my best at drawing from life. I do not regret one day in that—for I needed just *that* if I expect to *do* anything in Art. If I had to go home tomorrow, I would not feel as if I had done wrong—but would be thankful for the practice and training.

I am always saying though what I am *going* to do—and somehow never get to the point. Maybe some day it will come if I live *long* enough—for Art is long and no mistake.

Anna says she had "much to contend with" during the past winter. She thought Paris would be restful after teaching in a girls' school, but she changed pensions twice and learned a new language. Virginia Woolf said a woman needs "money and a room of her own." Anna had earned those for herself. I add that a female artist also needs a secretary, a chauffeur, a cook, a yard service, a nanny, voice mail, and a Do Not Disturb sign on the front door. Uninterrupted time is gold. Women who insist on it are seen as selfish or unsociable. When I return from solo travel or retreats, there is a price to pay: stacks of mail, an empty refrigerator, and a husband hunched before the television. It's a challenge to keep the home fires burning and also stoke the creative flames.

Spinster daughters ususally cared for their aging parents, but society's rules did not keep Anna from her life work; she resisted the homeward tug from her father as long as she could. I've continued to make art during my mother's illness, and this week I'm enjoying the harvest from her attic, but a call about Mamie's death could come at any time.

May 22, 1898
Went to service this morning and when I came back I suddenly discovered I did not know one word the minister had said on his text. My thoughts were *in* my *heart*, it seems.

May 23, 1898
Letters! Nice ones!!

May 24, 1898
Madame Bazin asked me to go to the Salon but it rained so we stayed in. My throat hurts so I cannot sleep nights.

May 27, 1898
This afternoon I went to the Salon instead of going to my own, or my successor's exhibition at the M.B.S. [Mary Baldwin Seminary] one year ago—and one year from now? I do wonder what will happen by then. Cold. Have on all my winter things.

May 27, 1898

My dear Mother and Father,

A studio girl wanted to know if I would make one of a party to go to Fontainebleau on Friday. I was only too glad to say yes, then she told me two of the party had backed out! I really am unfortunate, everybody else has some special friend here and they go out and have a nice time. I cannot push myself for you know the old saying that two is company. I go by myself but half the time it is pokey. This German girl who is here somehow knows lots of artists and when *she* went to Fontainebleau she paid a visit to Rosa Bonheur. She said it was difficult to obtain a call. Now dear Rosa is sick and cannot see anyone, even if I had the chance, which I never would have. I cannot worry over that though. For I could not talk to her and it must be a nuisance to her seeing those people. I'll spare her the trouble and not try to call. I have seen some of her best work. If she were younger and I could take lessons of her now, how charming that would be.

When Anna visited the Metropolitan Museum in New York in 1887, she wrote home: "One large picture by Rosa Bonheur—the Horse Fair—is prettier than anything I ever saw. Such a feast I am afraid my eyes will not behold again for many a long day after I leave N.Y. City."

What would Anna have said to "dear Rosa" if they had been able to converse? I had a chance meeting with the artist I most admire, Louise Nevelson. When I saw an imposing figure in an exotic robe walking across a museum courtyard, I introduced myself. In a brief conversation, I thanked her for what her art had meant to me. I quoted something I'd read about not assuming a tree is dead just because there are no leaves on it. She said it sounded like something she might have said. Those words have sustained me in bleak times when I thought I had no leaves or branches. The work continued in the roots, underground.

———⊷⊷⊷———

Anna began to talk of coming home, the date to be determined by God. Mlle Ballu must have left Mary Baldwin Seminary because Anna asked her father to forward letters. The May 27 letter continues:

The *only* consolation I have is that I let Edith come over here before she was worn out—and I do not wish to burden her with the debt. When I am too old to take care of myself she will help me then, if she is living I know. I would like her to stay longer if she can. A year in Paris would go a long way with her, but you will see me coming home next summer, I am sure, if not before. I am setting no time. When God sees fit to send me I will know what He wants me to do.

In a separate envelope I send a letter to Mlle Ballu, she will write Father a note soon and tell him *where to address* it. So please just add that and mail for me. She did not know when she wrote where she was going so asked me to do this. How I wish you knew *her* and I hope you will some day. I hope you are all quite well now. Go out all you can. Dear little Moses. I would kiss her and no mistake! Love and kisses from your own little daughter. Still it rains! Will it ever stop?

May 30, 1898
After dinner my letters came—and I was overjoyed—such dear letters!!

May 31, 1898
Worked in the morning and after lunch went to the Bon Marché. Got Black Pantaloons for Switzerland. Rained hard on my way back but I stopped in the art store.

After Anna got her permit to draw and paint outdoors, she wrote home about the Parisians in the jardin du Luxembourg:

> This afternoon I went to the Luxembourg garden and sat on a bench quite a while and sketched the groups I saw in front of me. How free and happy these people seem. Everyday the gardens are full—Men go and play too. Babies of all ages and sizes are out sleeping in the sun—or fog—sometimes rain—they go *every day, it seems, no matter what the state of the weather.*

— ⊰ ⊱ —

Like Anna, I enjoyed my spring in Europe. A group of us rented a car in London and drove up into Scotland. I wrote to David:

le 1er mai 1957
15 bis, boulevard Jules Sandeau
My darling,

How goes it stateside? I hope your spring is as beautiful as ours. We were so very lucky with England weather for spring break. I think

Edinburgh was my favorite place. Our excursion into the foothills of the Highlands was the best part of the trip. Most of the girls stayed in town to buy cashmeres, but I wouldn't take 10 or 20 sweaters for the country we saw that day. Sorry we didn't get to Coventry in England so I couldn't get your Jag. Forgive me?

Today is a holiday because it's the first of May. There's a wonderful custom, everybody buys lilies of the valley and takes them to their friends. I think I'll buy some for myself, I love them so.

I got a letter from Emma telling about her engagement. From the looks of things, pretty soon there aren't gonna be many of us old maids left!

Thee I love.
Tu

Samedi, le 4 mai 1957

Up and off to the Panthéon, visited the crypt and the tombeaux, etc. Rushed home for lunch with Cornelia Haley at the restaurant George Sand. Ate *premier escargot!* Had grand time. Afterwards went in a little hat shop and tried on but nothing suited us. Home, changed shoes, walked length of Boul' Mich' trying to rent a radio, street numbers all confused, felt like in a bad dream. Finally gave up, bought some daisies and stumbled home. Amazing what flowers will do for the spirit.

Before my family came to Europe in June, I sent requests. In spite of walking miles a day, I had gained weight. I bought too many of the sugar beignets called Krapfens from a street vendor near the Seine.

I'm almost out of hose, would love about 10 pair, they're exorbitant over here. Would love a couple of drip-dry blouses (not too sheer). Blouses take a terrible beating. Maybe a dressy one, maybe a yellow or pale blue, I'm sick of my clothes and am trying every thing I can for variety. I'm beginning to think maybe I shouldn't have stuck so close to the first year's list. Nobody else did, except Nina. One girl brought seven coats! Dread when we wear cottons, it's still too cold. Need desperately another pair of summer pajamas. If those gold flats that I had last year are in *any* shape, please bring them. And the white linen beret (Does it still exist?) would be good for this summer if I cut my hair. It's almost a necessity that I buy a hat. The little black velvet I love, but not for summer. All the little Hollins girls are bursting forth in their spring clothes. I'm scared to try on mine, I've gained so much weight. Put on the black wool sheath last night and it's a little snug. Did I have any summer shoes last summer besides the black patent heels? Cannot remember *what* I had at all. And if you see a pleated washable summer skirt, bring it. This summer tour has me all panicked. I wish I could finesse the whole group and just go [on tour] with y'all.

When I met my family's boat train, my mother and Edith had on hats and gloves. Pete's first words were, "TuTu, you're fat!" We had a lovely luncheon with the Jungs and toured Paris in between my exams. Aunt Joy was also in Paris to visit her French relatives. She was 81 and I was 20. We celebrated our June birthdays with tea at a sidewalk café. Aunt Joy knew four generations of my family: my great-grandparents, Granny and Sister Anna, my mother, and me. I wish I could return to that balmy afternoon in Paris and ask her questions about the Lesters.

On the day of my twentieth birthday, I went to Notre-Dame to give thanks for my year in Paris.

Mercredi, le 26 juin, 1957
A glorious, symbolic and joyful day, completely happy and completely mine. Took the bus to the British Institute—in fact, I took the bus *all day* to celebrate—24 sections worth. Paris never looked lovelier, brilliant sparkly blue, and at Place de la Concorde one of the fountains was playing for me. Took an exam and walked to Notre Dame, stepping gingerly over the Americans. Went in and thanked God for letting me have 20 such wonderful years. I have so much to be grateful for, and the heart of this city was the place to be—I felt so little, alongside the stones centuries old and such a communion with the past as it blends into the present and future. At lunch the Jung family gave me yellow roses and handkerchiefs from Franck et Fils. They all sang Happy Birthday while we ate cherry tart for dessert. Dear Nina gave me a small silver pencil with a garnet stone on top. We had seen it in a shop window on l'Ile de la Cité and I knew she wanted it herself. A treasured gift.

Forward Day by Day, June 26, 1957
"The Heart knoweth its own bitterness: and a stranger doth not intermeddle with his joy."

I'm restless and my eyes are tired. I open the hotel window and lean out into weather more moderate than this morning. I think I'll go to Notre-Dame for the Sunday afternoon organ concert. By the time I get near the cathedral, the sun is setting in a sky the color of Georgia peaches; the Seine nudges the buildings on l'île Saint-Louis. The mother and daughter islands rest in the cupped hands of the Seine, protected by the river, but linked to the rest of the city. Inside the cathedral, I hear bad news: No organ concert today. Anna wrote Edith in the spring of 1898:

> My dear little girl,
>
> I say let the Organ rest until fall. So little time is left now before vacation you would hardly get started on the Organ. Anyway, it is too heavy work to mix in with everything else. That needs *all* of one's strength and time. That [the organ] is what I love, but I will have to wait until I get to Heaven and start a new life, with a few more brains to study, as I cannot learn the notes now.
>
> I wonder what we will do in Heaven? Just what we wish most and could not do here, you guess? Or will we just be satisfied with all things as they are? I would like to take a peep in *now*, so I could *begin* to be satisfied here. That is not allowed however.

Maybe I've extended Anna's earthly life by coming to Paris. I can't rewrite her story with a healthy conclusion, but her time here may have been her happy ending. With our shared addiction for Paris, she and I may never be satiated, may always pop down to Paris from Heaven. Where would Anna come first? If my ghost returns, I'll come to Notre-Dame.

Sitting in a stiff pew chair, I inhale centuries of incense and recall my mystic connections to this place. For several years I have had a recurrent dream: I am in Paris—always on my last day—and I have not yet been to Notre-Dame. The hour is late and I am unprepared. I travel around the city, overcoming classic dream obstacles of time and transportation, in an attempt to get to the temple of Our Lady. In one dream I entered the cathedral and walked down a spiral stone staircase into the crypt. Descending the concave steps, I passed a row of Greek goddesses similar to the *Venus de Milo*.

My dreams of Notre-Dame paralleled my search for female divinity in history and nature. As I visited earth mounds, long barrows, and healing wells, the night escapades became less frequent. This afternoon I'm putting flesh on my Notre-

Dame dreams. My cells feel at home in the spiritual womb of this feminine city, and this is not even my last day.

In the margin of her *Baedeker*, Anna noted the date of her first visit to Notre-Dame: November 4, 1897. She wrote her parents:

> On Thursday, I left here early and went down to Notre-Dame—just think, have been here over a month and had not been there! What a shame. I went all through the dear old place and it is beautiful and impressive—service was going on inside the enclosed choir—that made no difference except to make it more pleasant for me—I do love good church music, be it Catholic or no.
>
> In all these churches and other places, guides usually meet one and want to show you around. I shake my head and say "thank you" in French. This time I simply shook my head, so the old fellow thought I did not understand and he began a string in English. So, I said "no thank you" in English. As I went in the church an old Priest made a motion to me—I at first did not see the little sort of a switch brush he held in his hand and turned his way. Sometimes they make all visitors go round a certain way—to right or left as the case may be—but *this* was not what *he* wanted— but was going to sprinkle me with holy water. I shook my head *good fashion*. I had no idea of having my fur cape and jacket getting a shower! I guess they thought me a case, but I did not care, and after that went my way in peace.

My grandmother and Anna came to Notre-Dame in 1897 for a Christmas service. On my fortieth birthday trip, I attended a midnight mass here. This afternoon I honor family members who have supported me on this journey. When I stop to light a candle at the foot of the Virgin and child, the candle slips through my frozen Protestant fingers. I must learn the art of balancing and lighting the nubbin of wax. In this shrine to the mother of God, I bless my mother, Mary. On the way out of the cathedral, I remember the breakfast monks. For them and for the love of Paris, I light a candle at the feet of Saint Joan of Arc, Deliverer of France.

I cross the Pont au Double to the Latin Quarter, where the Trompettes de Versailles are scheduled to perform at Saint-Julien-le-Pauvre. If I can't have organ music in Notre-Dame, trumpets will suffice, but the concert now posted is the Police

Choir from Washington, DC. I'm sure the group is proficient, it's just not the music I had in mind. The tower bells of Saint-Julien-le-Pauvre ring as I turn away from the courtyard, so I flatten my spine against the vibrating stones and absorb my music for the day. Faced with the nightly hunt for an early dinner, I push open the doors of several restaurants. The waiters look up from their own plates and wave me off: "Come back in an hour, Madame." By then it will be totally dark.

I wish David were here to link arms with me and stroll along the Seine. I prop my elbows on a wall and watch a *bateau mouche* skim past Notre-Dame. The shadows of the buttresses fly backward as the boat spotlight moves forward; the cathedral becomes a pop-up postcard.

Paris has a soundtrack grooved in my memory: accordion and violin melodies from black-and-white movies and from 78-rpm recordings by Michel Legrand. Humming "Les Feuilles Mortes," I poke around in Shakespeare and Company on rue de la Bûcherie. Each book I pick up has a seal on the inside cover: zéro kilomètre Paris. This stamp refers to the marker in front of Notre-Dame, the zero point from which all distances in France are measured. Between the world wars, Sylvia Beach's original Shakespeare and Company on rue de l'Odéon was expatriate headquarters, a point from which literary distances are measured. She and Adrienne Monnier shaped the timbre of the twentieth century by nurturing Joyce, Pound, Wilder, and Hemingway. Books preserve the legends of such Paris luminaries, but each foreigner who comes to live here leaves a sliver of experience between the cobblestones. No scrubbing by sanitation men can erase our memories. The city honors immortal artists with plaques on buildings; the rest of us feel a rip in our hearts when we remember Paris.

I turn the corner onto rue de la Huchette, where Elliott Paul wrote *The Last Time I Saw Paris*. We students came here to see *The Bald Soprano* by Ionesco. Originally "the street of the roasters," the twisted walkway is a raucous remnant of medieval Paris. Insistent men in black leather jackets pull at my sleeves, hawking pizza, gyros, fondue, and shish kebabs. Street-front windows display whole pigs roasting on spits and gigantic crabs sizzling alive on fiery grates. These writhing sea creatures remind me of the Inquisition, the torture of non-recanting Protestants, and the burning of wise women skilled in the use of medicinal herbs. A wall plaque marks a later black period of French history—the Nazi execution of a resistance fighter in 1944. With a shiver of paranoia, I walk into Le Chat qui Pêche, where dinner is available. I order white fish in a cream sauce, green salad, and a crème caramel. Not stellar, but better than cold quiche from Le Marché Franprix. I take the Métro to the hotel to reenter the nineteenth century.

In June of 1898, Anna assessed her work in Paris while she prepared to travel with Edith.

June 2, 1898
Dear Edith,

About baggage—you fix yours anyway you want. I am going to make my strap and my valise hold all I need—and am not going to take *my* white clothes except two gowns. Have gotten my black Jersey *Pantaloons* and will shorten this old black skirt that I have lived in since before Xmas. Have worn nothing else except on Sunday. Then next winter it will be nice I will not have to hold it up [in the rain]. I still have on *all* my winter things and my hands are cold now. I am only going to take warm things. If I get too hot I'll simply wear *no* underclothes. I am not going to bring my black Satin or anything like I did last year. They are no good, only a care. No books, except Bible and guide books.

June 3, 1898
Went to the Beaux-Arts this morning. It was so beautiful I hated to stay inside. The sun was out. Worked all the afternoon but I do not accomplish much, no matter how I work.

June 5, 1898
My own dear Mother and Father,

You see perhaps that this [the summer address] is on my mind today. I have thought of nothing else for several days, dream of it nights etc, etc. I suppose I was born to worry for I always have something on hand—if one thing fails another jumps up and says, "Here worry over me," and I immediately embrace the opportunity.

You make me feel about as large as a small cowpea about [not being in] the Salon. If I should by hook or crook manage to get in next year, it would be wonderful! *All* the best artists in the world send there and it is awful hard to squeeze in. Really I have nothing but these charcoal drawings from the nude, so for mercy's sake don't expect to see anything when I come home. I am "practicing the scales only." I came to work and learn. Someday you may know how hard I try and why I do not get on better. All have said I improve very much, but think of where I started, right at the bottom and if I am up one peg I am glad. If I only could spend one month at home, I could work better next fall. France is all right, don't let one thought against France or the French come to your minds. *I like them.* France is as dear to me as Germany is to Edith.

June 6, 1898
Dear Edith,

I guess *you* will get warm part of the time and so will I—so I am putting in *three* shirtwaists. I have trimmed my white sailor—if you do not like it I can take off the white stuff and just have the black band. I will appear in my brand-new black Paris hat—and carry the sailor in a box. If one could only go without anything at all how charming that would be.

June 19, 1898
Dear Father,

Your dear letters came this morning while I was eating my "delicious" rolls and coffee—and I forgot all about the coffee and when I returned to my cup it was cold as anything—but that made no difference.

Now let me answer the questions first about having the [summer] money with me. I never carry much in my purse—and it is always on my mind to look out for pickpockets when I go in a crowd. The rest I wear inside. If anybody gets it they will have to *take* me first. I do not think it an "old man's idea" when you tell me about it. It is a nice spry *young* man's advice and I appreciate every word—but I do not know any better way to do—I can't put it in a Bank for the summer. I will be as careful as I know how.

June 21, 1898
Went for a lesson and Mrs. Reynolds was most encouraging, but I do not take it all in. I see what is wanting and *that* is *most important.* Washed my hair and sewed.

June 22, 1898
My, I am tired. Have been all day packing and it is most tiresome work. I am sure I do not see why my trunk and things are full. I have just about nothing and still everything is bursting.

June 24, 1898

Painted Minmine today for myself. I was glad to have something to keep
my mind quiet. I am worn out now—but must put the few things left in
my bag.

On June 25, Anna and Edith met in Cologne, Germany. They traveled through
Germany, Switzerland, and into Italy.

July 2, 1898 Heidelberg

It began to rain while we were having dinner and has not stopped. So I
will write some on *my* letter.

July 9, 1898 Rastatt

Walked about seven or eight miles, I should have not gone so far. How my
head and back did ache.

July 18, 1898 Geneva

It was so hot! Went right to Cooks and got our mail. Such a charming
letter. If I only could have one every day!! The lake was beautiful and we
sat out until the sun was quite down to see the glow on Mont Blanc. It
was so beautiful!

July 21, 1898 Chamonix

I took a mule to the top and the rest walked. We then crossed the Mer de
Glace and came down on the other side.

July 24, 1898 Territet

A quiet day at Territet. Wrote home and to my dear Friend. The sun is
beautiful and so is the lake.

July 23, 1898

Territet

Dear Mother and Father,

  We went to the Castle of Chillon. It really is a charming place and
much more interesting than I had expected. But I would not have liked to
be chained to that stone pillar with only a yard of room for six years. The
view of the lake is beautiful from every front. It is blue and green, too, and
pink according to the light on it from the sky and sun. I am hoping the

man in Lausanne will send my glasses in the early mail. He said it would take six days to make them. I do hope now my eyes will be as good as new for this is a fine Oculist. I went to the best in Europe. Dr. Dufour. I hope Father got my letter telling him to send me $100 more in care of Cooks for I will need it soon.

I think of you all a great deal and will be glad when my face is turned towards home again. I have found it impossible to make any sketches. Only staying a day or so in each place is not inducive to work. I am tired and it takes all my time seeing things and fixing my straps and things up ready for a move forward. I shall rest a week after I return to Paris before beginning work. To paint I would have to stay at least ten days in one place for I do not feel settled enough for work, you see. It is a great disappointment to me for I have my colors and papers with me but no time or energy.

Absolutely all we do is to go and see and send one letter home each week, once in two to Mlle Ballu, Edith sends a card or letter once in two weeks to Joy. That is *all* we can find time to do. If you all could be here with us how much fun we would have.

July 28, 1898 Zermatt
Another day of rain. Such luck! I want to see these beautiful things and leave before my purse is empty. Have written all the letters and post cards I *owe!!* Good, now I can write to my Darling.

July 29, 1898 Zermatt
Our mail came last night. I was so overjoyed for I did not expect *one* of mine. Today we have been all the way up to that Gornergrat! I walked and got awfully tired, but kept on. The view was superb! I could have stayed a week but of course had to leave after lunch. Snow began.

July 31, 1898 Zermatt
We leave soon so as to cross the Simplon Pass tomorrow. Today is perfect! Not a cloud in the sky. I hope the sky of life is as clear to my own Darling way off in America. God be with her and bless her always.

God be with *her*. This entry leaves no doubt about the gender of Anna's Darling. When I first looked through Anna's diary, I assumed the poems and quotations were romantic Victorian literature collected by a lonely single woman. Were they all explicit messages from Anna's Darling? Her Dear Friend had to be Henriette Ballu, but Dear D. remains a mystery.

———⊸⊛⊷———

Our Hollins Abroad summer tour lasted three months. By the end of August I was, like Anna, travel weary.

August 25, 1957
Florence, Italy
Ma chère famille,

I am giving you the honor of being the first to whom I've written on my new Olivetti typewriter, which I adore. It's green and weighs seven pounds, has French accent marks, a circumflex, and a "c" cedilla!

We made it back to Italy from Greece. Rome was fun. Very cool. At Tivoli we ran into a girl from Hollins with her husband. Of course she doesn't know me from Adam and wouldn't have recognized me anyway since I've had my hair dyed. Yes, dyed, jet black. And cut short à la Lollabrigida. Now Don't Hit The Ceiling. It looks darling. That morning Mrs. Crosby said at breakfast, "Miss Gilbert, I hope you're going to be a school teacher because you sure look like one." I knew the ponytail had to go. Some other girls were bleaching their hair. The Italians in the beauty shop couldn't believe I wanted black.

Everybody is very pleased after they recovered from the first shocked, "Can that be Susan Gilbert?" Even Mr. Crosby said it looked "Quite fetching." I'm more pleased than I've ever been over any hairdo. Had a permanent in Perugia last night for $5.

My stomach is all well now and I feel better cause the heat is not so extreme. At times though I wish I could come home for two weeks, sleep, eat, have my clothes washed, and start out anew. The thought of Spain still to go is rather frightening.

Don't be mad about my hair. It's *cute*.

Love to all,

Tu

September 17, 1957
Seville, Spain
Dear All,

You're proably worried cause I haven't written in so long. I promise to do better. I am so Sick and Tired of traveling I could scream. Oh, to be settled, clean, and straight. Spain is delightful. Not too hot but rather humid. Have seen two bullfights and I love them. Quite a sport. We go to Lisbon tomorrow and I'm terribly excited about Portugal. Our last country and I can't say I'm too sorry. Paris looks mighty nice to me. One nice thing I've gotten out of these long bus treks is that I've been able to read a lot of good books. My diary is only a month behind and it's awful cause I have no time or inclination to write. Much less wash or keep up my correspondance. Got a letter from David in Madrid and he has a plot afoot to come to N.Y.C. to greet me in January. It would be wonderful to have some help with baggage. I'm coming home with so much more than I went with.

Oh, and by the way, I'm dying my hair back natural in Lisbon. I love it black and it's a lot more becoming, but I just can't face Madame Jung's face. No really, it would have to be dyed back eventually and it's better to do it now than in the middle of Paris.

Much love to the Romans,
TuTu

Burgos, Spain
Dear All,

Just a note to let you know I'm still breathing. Nothing of great import to report except that I fell in love the other day in Portugal and I'll never see the boy again. How's that for tristesse? He's a student at the U. of Coimbra but he's Spanish and we had to talk in French. One of the few "kindred spirits" I've found on this continent and a pity to have to leave him. But that's life, ain't it? Only a few more days of this errant life but it was fun while it lasted. One of the few periods with no responsibilities or too many things to do and even tho' it was terribly tiring, a great time was had by all.

It's fall and that makes me a little homesick for the U.S. Can't wait to get back into wool. I hate these cottons with a passion.

Loads of love to all,
Tu

At the end of August 1898, Edith returned to Berlin. Anna stayed a few days in Germany before she came back to Paris. Because Madame Bazin could not hold her room over the summer, Anna moved into Madame Grégoire's pension at 9, rue Sainte-Beuve. She wrote Edith:

> Reached Paris and came right here. The cab man made a fuss when I paid him 2 francs but I really told him it was enough and walked in leaving him talking. I am on the fourth floor. Madame Grégoire has the second floor, too. That is where we eat. My room is about the size of the one at Madame Bazin's, maybe a trifle larger, and is *clean*. The girl dusts and sweeps every day, much to my satisfaction. Fare is just as good and more of it. Plenty of meat, bread and wine, so I am not compelled to eat potatoes. Madame is *very* neat—all the time pleasant and good looking. So is her son—at first—but he gets insignificant on acquaintance. There are two American men, who are *stuck up* and will not talk any English. My room is so light and nice and quiet, such a comfort. Madame Grégoire is very ladylike and nice.
>
> The cart (to take up trash I think) comes rattling up at 5 A.M. but the man does not crack his whip and abuse the horses, so I do not think of it. I sleep until 7 A.M., that ought to be enough. I try to be asleep by nine. I do want to be fat and well when I go home.

August 25, 1898
Reached Paris at 8:30 this morning. Was pretty tired and could not sleep. Rested then went straight to Cooks. Only *one* letter and that from Laura Berry. Paid Madame Bazin a visit, she had my home letters. I then wrote to Cook's here and in Geneva to see if I could hurry up my *own* letter.

August 26, 1898
Wrote home and finished my other letter, got a few things fixed in my room. The weather is charming, so cool. I am delighted. I like my room, too.

August 27, 1898
Got all ready for winter today. Then had *Tea*. After dinner I got my letters also one from Edith.

August 29, 1898

Began work at Colarossi Studio today. More men than women are there. I did not like the *tone* of one man in his treatment of our model. She's a beautiful girl, one of the prettiest I have seen posing.

August 30, 1898

Started a miniature this morning and am now ready for my afternoon work.

August 31, 1898

Worked on the head today and got some ivory to paint a sketch on in the morning. My dear letters came tonight. I was so glad!

September 1, 1898

M. Girardot was very kind. I had put the miniature out of sight as soon as he came in, so only handed him my watercolor head. But he asked for the miniature. It almost took breath away. Said that was much better.

September 2, 1898

Only work. I am going to stick at it now and try my best!

September 3, 1898

Was tired this afternoon, but gave my hat a good cleaning after studio hours.

September 4, 1898
Dear Edith,

I forgot to say we had a real pretty model this week and I made a tolerably good miniature of her. Am working from one to five at the Studio Colarossi, (where we went and they were modeling, you remember). Now the afternoon class is for draped models. Men and women work together. In the morning, I work in my room.

September 5, 1898

Went to rue du Temple for Ivory this A.M. It is so much cheaper over there. I hate the long trip, though. Then to the studio in the afternoon. A good model!

September 8, 1898

M. Girardot was there on time and said my head was better than the
body—went for the very mistake I had seen when too late almost to change.

September 9, 1898

That Geneva letter is not here yet! And I do want it so. Very warm today,
the flannels came off and will stay off now a while.

September 10, 1898

Turned cool in the night and flannels went back on this A.M. Got some
Figs, Sugar, and wine this morning. Finished my miniature today. I wish
the Prof came on Tuesdays instead of Thursday—so I would know if the
drawing is all right. My letter did come last night—and it was so sweet!

A torn piece of stationery with condensed handwriting is wedged in the journal
pages at September tenth. I have ignored this letter because the writing is like tiny
hieroglyphics or algebraic formulae written on both sides of tissue paper. With a
piece of white cardboard behind the stationery, I lean under the bedside lamp and
look through my magnifying glass. The compressed script is similar to Mlle Ballu's
printed handwriting. The opening sentence startles me:

Jonathan Dear, I have been reading Ernest and Henriette Renan's
correspondence and I was so often reminded of *ours*. I wonder if it would
be possible for English speaking people to write such letters. I have never
seen a brother and sister as affectionate in this country, but they may be as
for all of that. I thought you might like to know how devoted they were so
copied a few things.

If Mlle Ballu had an affectionate brother named Jonathan, why did Anna have
his letter? Last night I puzzled over the simulated banknote from the "Heart-Centre
Bank of Davidtown" written on May 30, 1898. The note entitled Jonathan to
"$10.00 (In Kisses) Ten Dollars." Kisses for Jonathan from Davidtown. Jonathan and
David. David and Jonathan. Of course. They were using nicknames.

I leap from the bed. A flash of intuition causes an adrenaline rush, like clouds
blowing off the shrouded Matterhorn to reveal a diamond peak. I want to shout
"Eureka!" and grab someone by the arm, but I don't think the night clerk downstairs
would understand. Mlle Ballu was not writing to her brother. Anna was Jonathan

and Mlle Ballu was David—or "Dear D." Anna's "Darling" sent the *Deutsche Liebe* book and the "dear little Photo" in May. Anna burned some letters. I assume she saved this ragged fragment because of the quotations. All I remember about the Old Testament story is that Jonathan and David's friendship was downplayed by my Sunday School teachers.

Did Henriette Ballu hear Anna's words in those written by Ernest Renan to his sister Henriette?

> "At last Dearest Henriette I have your longed for letter. Day by Day I have been on the tiptoe of expectation, watching every port."
> "Your letters are my greatest happiness. My thoughts of you are my dearest joy."
> "If the whole universe lay between us, I could not love you more, nor think of you less constantly."
> "Oh, when will we be able to tell each other all our thoughts at leisure?"
> "I thank God, dear Henriette, for giving me one human being who understands me!"
> "We will cling to each other and [keep] hope alive and let the river of life flow on! It will lead us *somewhere!*"

After the quotations, the letter continues:

There—was not their devotion beautiful? The two lived a happy life together after his correspondence ended. M. Renan is one of our most polished writers. He married Mlle Cornélie Scheffer (daughter of Ary Scheffer) but he first offered to give her up on account of his sister. This is what he told her: "I can never see you again until my sister's heart ceases to bleed at the thought of our meeting."

But his sister could not endure to have him sacrifice himself for her sake, so after the marriage they lived together and Henriette devoted herself to the "little Ary."

I have a penchant for *letters*, one reads some life in them, when they are like these, *nicht wahr?*

Sunday, July 10. Such a beautiful Sabbath, Dear, I suppose you have....

This could be the missing Geneva letter. If Anna and Henriette appropriated the Old Testament names to say they were soul mates, no wonder they did not want the snoopy Miss Weimar to intercept their letters.

Another scrap of paper has a poem written in the same cramped handwriting of the "Jonathan Dear" letter. Was Mlle Ballu giving Anna advice?

Talk happiness. The world is sad enough
Without your woes. No path is wholly rough;
Look out for the places that are smooth and clear,
And speak of those that rest the weary ear
Of earth, so hurt by one continuous strain
Of human discontent and grief and pain.

Because the poem was torn from a letter, the reverse of the page has sentence fragments:

I hope you will…affectionate with your sister, remember, it…take her by storm Dear. I have kind…it would? So I am in hopes that you…arms upon awakening. …You must…have *faith* in it Dear, try it on me…say to me…you *will* experience etc… de tout mon coeur. Kind regards to your…Same address 1712 E. 8th St. K.C.

At least I know that *de tout mon coeur* means "with all my heart." Mlle Ballu, the free-spirited Frenchwoman, encouraged Anna to be more affectionate with Edith, but I'm not sure who will be in whose "arms upon awakening." The address is one of those listed in Anna's address book under Kansas City. By tearing off parts of letters, burning others, and not putting Mlle Ballu's name in her address book, Anna edited her correspondence. Perhaps my grandmother or mother found passionate letters from Mlle Ballu and destroyed them. I know more than I did when I opened Anna's trunk, but I will never know the full story.

Another small piece of paper has a poem in Mlle Ballu's handwriting. After a moment, I get the joke.

An Arab stood by the riverside
With a donkey bearing an obelisk
He would not try to ford the tide
He had too good an ∗
        [He had too good an asterisk—ass to risk.]

After the melodramatic Renan letters and the "Talk Happiness" poem, Mlle Ballu's humor is refreshing. From these scraps of paper, I can infer that Henriette

Ballu was ardent, erudite, and had a sense of fun. I will never know how intimate she and Anna were, but I'm pleased to discover this loving presence in my great-aunt's life. The poems in Anna's journal become specific if sent by Henriette Ballu.

> *It is not because your heart is mine, mine only, mine alone.*
> *It is not because you chose me, weak and lonely for your own,*
> *Not because the earth is fairer, and the skies above you*
> *Are more radiant for the shining of your eyes that I love you!*
> *But because this human love,*
> *though true and sweet—yours and mine,*
> *Has been sent by Love more tender,*
> *more complete, more divine;*
> *That it leads our hearts to rest at last in Heaven, far above you.*
> *Do I take you as a gift that God has given and I love you.*

Adelaide Anne Proctor

Day Eight

The weather report is daunting: cloudy with a possible high of seven or eight degrees Celsius. Paris was cold and gray when we returned from our summer tour in 1957. We had logged 10,000 miles in three months. We arrived in Paris with Spanish wineskins, Italian handbags, and a permanent aversion to bus travel. One of us had dyed black hair, not quite grown out.

> Dimanche, le 29 septembre 1957
> Paris!
> Was so nice and comfortable to be "home." The smell of the apartment, the creaks in the doors, the doorbell, the shuffle of Monsieur in his bedroom slippers. All comes back with a clarity I'd forgotten. Nice to be here.

> October 1, 1957
> 15 bis, boulevard Jules Sandeau
> Dearest All,
>
> Well, made it back to icy cold Paris. I can hardly type my hands are so cold. Want immediate reply on whether you recommend Asiatic flu vaccine. There's a good bit going about. Have unpacked all winter clothes and they are too small. May be forced to buy at least a couple of skirts and maybe some shoes. Hate it tho' cause prices are so steep. The Jungs welcomed me back gaily. Yellow roses on the mantle, etc. Hope they'll turn on the heat fore long. Every night Madame heats water on the stove and we bring her our hot water bottles to fill up. My hair is now brownish

red. The Jungs approve. Here's hoping it'll be natural in January, but I'm not guaranteeing a thing.

Love to all,

TuTu

Eisenhower sent federal troops to Arkansas to enforce school integration, and the Jungs wanted to know about "Leetle Rock." In October the Soviet Union launched Sputnik into orbit, followed by Sputnik II with a dog aboard. In Paris we watched workers demonstrate for salary increases, and we exchanged money on the black market, despite warnings that the dollars went to the Communists. We returned to classes, but our time in France was dwindling.

⸻ ⬥ ⸻

Anna dreaded the cold winter and had made a bargain with God. If her father transferred money by a certain date, it was a sign that she should go home before Christmas. She continued her classes in miniature painting and life drawing at Académie Colarossi.

September 12, 1898
A good model and I do hope I will make a nice miniature of her. One more American and one English girl have come, more men too. Class, if it goes on so, will soon be full.

September 14, 1898
Girardot came today. I was glad of it for I want the drawing corrected before color goes on. He always says the head is good—but the other parts!

September 19, 1898
Had a good model this week. A man. I am going to try one in oil to please Girardot.

September 20, 1898
That English girl is so pleasant. I wish she would stay all winter. My stuck-up American still talks.

September 22, 1898
One year ago I arrived in Paris! Sick, tired, and lonely! I feel so different now—and I *know* why.

September 23, 1898

After all Girardot said my miniature was the better of the two. I might as well stick to that.

September 24, 1898

Went to the Luxembourg and saw Mr. Reynolds. I could not believe my eyes, so did not speak but started off to see his wife. Found her and will go to her on Monday and let her see what I have been doing. [Today is] Edith's Birthday. 22 years. She is having a fine time.

September 25, 1898

Went to Service and my heart was in America! Many more [Americans] have come back now.

September 25, 1898

Dear Edith,

Do not mention to the [Rome] girls that I think of going home, please. I see plainly I could not stay here during bad weather. And in houses not heated. The cough would only be worse, and result in something that could not be cured. This first little snap has used me up. I have fire, though, but no one else has.

September 26, 1898

Enjoyed my lesson with Mrs. Reynolds but it costs.

September 28, 1898

Mrs. Reynolds said I could work at home and send my things over to her if I got in trouble. I wonder if Father will send the money. Full moon tonight.

To enhance her reputation at home, Anna enrolled in Académie Julian for the month of October. She continued her study with Mrs. Reynolds.

October 1, 1898

A beautiful day but I did not go out. Worked part of the time, then fixed my hat and mended my carryall, ready to go home.

October 3, 1898

Entered at Julian's. Rooms very good, much better than I expected. Good model. Went to Mrs. Reynolds for an hour in the afternoon. Then stopped in at Colarossi's for my apron.

October 4, 1898

Tried to get a little model but she cried by the time I got her in position
so I sent her off.

October 5, 1898

The Professor came today. He only has one eye. I am afraid he is not as
good as Delécluse for he does not draw as delicately and the width of one
line might make an inch of difference according to the side taken!

October 7, 1898

Went to Mrs. Reynolds again. She was most encouraging this week. I do
hope I will succeed.

October 8, 1898

Worked all I could today, then had to rest my eyes. Washed my hair! We
got seats for the Opera.

October 9, 1898

The chapel was almost full. I thought of my own Dear D. all the time and
wished she was with me. Have written this afternoon by an open window,
now I am going to have tea!

When I read these words, first seen in my mother's attic, I realize how much
I've learned. I've found the chapel location, and I've identified Dear D. I have
written by Anna's open window, and I know, without question, how much she
loved tea. Anna and I will soon leave rue Sainte-Beuve. What else can I learn in my
last two days?

October 9, 1898
9, rue Sainte-Beuve
Dear Edith,

    I am so glad you have found the right teacher, what you say of him
[Heinrich Barth] for you was how I felt about Mrs. Reynolds. She did
not flatter and it would be useless for anyone to try that on me, for I
know too well what I cannot do. But she made me feel like trying, told
what was wrong and how to fix it, and what was right. She says I am
doing nicely and asked me to promise not to give it up. So there may be
a little hope yet.

I have been so provoked this week, the model did not say on Monday she could not take a standing pose, and began, did miserably until yesterday, just after the Professor had been and *corrected* the drawings, then had the pose changed, to sitting. She does not keep that either and nothing will be done the whole week. For one hates to go on with shadows and finish before all the mistakes in drawing have been fixed. I do not like Julian's as much as I do these other studios—and think I will come back to Colarossi when the month is up, if I do not get a letter saying to come home.

October 11, 1898
Went to Mrs. Reynolds for the last time. She goes tomorrow. She asked me to go to the Girl's Club and take her notice down. The club is so much better this fall than last.

October 12, 1898
I took the Buss ride Mme Bazin always speaks of—from the Madeleine to the Bastille. Only I got out at Place de la République for my Ivory. Paid Mme Bazin a visit later. She gave me homemade pickles!

October 17, 1898
Made a composition! But will not let anyone see.

October 18, 1898
Went to Père Lachaise today and was so pleased with all. I walked all about and enjoyed myself. I am *so* glad I happened out there. Such a charming day.

October 19, 1898
Made a sketch of my "*masterpiece*" this afternoon, the one I long to *do* for the Salon if I stay and find I get on at all.

October 19, 1898
Dear Edith,

You need not tell anybody, but I am not going to worry about going to Julian's after this month. These other studios are better, but I wanted to *say* I had worked there. That is the only reason I went. People need not know how long. I will just say I divided my time between the two winters.

That will be the truth. They need not know *how* it was divided. This Norway girl has been to Julian's two winters and says she now sees she was throwing her money out the window, for Delécluse is so much better. In America, they think Julian's is the only studio here, you know.

The crazy part is if a pupil has worked in the uptown studio and wants to come to this one, she has to pay 60 francs a month, the same as up town. While we only pay 25 francs because we have not happened to work in any other Julian's! That alone would disgust me, but some one or two actually do this. Why they do not leave is more than I can see—only because they do not know how nice it is at Delécluse, and fancy they would not care to work with men at Colarossi's. Some day I will *show* you how they act at Julian's when the Professor comes. I consider it foolish—and babyish—I believe in the Professor treating the students as equals, only not so far up the ladder—and not as schoolgirls! Catch me staying there!

October 20, 1898

Went this afternoon to Napolean's Tomb then to the Trocadéro. Looked all over the place for the two skulls—but did not find the right ones. Walked from here all the way—then rode back.

October 24, 1898

Our model is not as good as I had hoped. And they keep such a fuss about the pose that the poor man is distracted. My letters came last night. I am going home in December for Father sent the money.

October 25, 1898

My dear Edith,

Well, Edith dear—it is almost time for me to say goodbye—for the money came on Sunday night and that means that God wants me to go home to Father *now*—that is, before Xmas. If I can, I will leave on the Southwark, Saturday, Dec 10. Six more weeks here, in which I will work as hard as I can. Monday, I begin at Colarossi's again. This *month* at Julian's will only be a name if I expect to teach again. You can tell the girls I am going, no use to keep it a secret. I am sorry to leave you over here, but think it best for me to go now. Now, my plan is to get home Xmas eve if I can, but that will only be two weeks to the day from the time I leave

Antwerp, so I may pull in to Rome black and dirty on Xmas Day Sunday… I am going to frame a few of my miniatures. I almost finished mine today, had left the dress and neck as Mrs. Reynolds was anxious for me to begin a new face. In these two months, I have done seven [miniatures] besides the four charcoal drawings at Julian's.

I think if Saturday is clear, I will go to Fontainebleau maybe, for on Sunday I am going to see the Drawings at Julian's men's studio at 31 rue Dragon. It is a concours this week at *all* his studios.

You must not get homesick or blue because I go, for if you do not get a place [to teach] I hope you can stay longer. And always write home just as you do now. Not to me every other week. You can put me in a half sheet written finely with just what you want me to know and enclose in theirs. It pleases Mother for the letters to be to them.

I could not sleep Sunday night after reading the letter [from Father] because I knew I was going [home] so soon. I wish I could dismiss things from my mind once and for all when they cannot be mended, but it is impossible.

My room and berth are engaged for December 10th on the Southwark. My trunk goes a week ahead and the whole ticket from here to New York will be 257.50 [francs]. That is cheap, is it not? I *must* go now for I have already told them at home, and I do not think Father is quite well. His letters do not sound so. I had best go now, I am sure.

I am glad you all *want* me and I would love to go there [Berlin] but could not possibly afford it even if I stayed over here. I must go now for more reasons than *one*. One is—I want to be cured of this cough, it keeps me awake often two hours at a time nights—and is troublesome to say the least. You must be careful when you are not well and not practice on the organ at that time ever. It will be bad for you. Keep well and happy. I enclose the piece [of foliage] from Chopin's grave.

Your loving sister,
Anna M. Lester

October 28, 1898

Got my glasses, went to the bank, then paid the deposit on my ticket. Stopped in at Colarossi's to see if the light was good for afternoons. I want the draped model for this month.

October 30, 1898

After lunch went to Julian's Studio on rue du Dragon to see the drawings
done for the concours. Some were splendid. Such a lot of compositions. I
was pleased to see the drawings were placed as I used to for commencment
[at MBS] on easels, on the floor, too.

October 31, 1898

My letters came this A.M. Such nice ones I have felt contented all day.
This afternoon I began work at Colarossi again. Like it so much better
than at Julian's. That red tape annoyed me. A good model but I see she is
fond of the men.

⸻ ⟨⟩ ⸻

Today is my last chance for a trip out of Paris. I could visit the Basilica of Saint-
Denis, the birthplace of Gothic architecture. Anna went in June and wrote Edith:

> At St. Denis is an old cathedral where nearly all the French kings and
> queens are buried—it is a beautiful place and down in the crypt is a most
> beautiful marble statue of Marie Antoinette that is *lovely*. I wanted to hug
> and kiss her she is so sweet.

The industrial area of Saint-Denis is not enticing in today's weather, nor do I
feel compelled to hug and kiss Marie Antoinette. I'd like to go to Amiens to see the
labyrinth in the cathedral. Cathedral towns usually have markets and shops, so I'll
look for a tearoom for an afternoon treat. I do not know if the Amiens cathedral is
open today or if the labyrinth is accessible, but I am willing to gamble. I place my
photograph and a note on my bedside table, since no one in France or America
knows where I am when I leave the hotel. The freedom is exhilarating, but Gretel
wants to leave a breadcrumb trail in case "something" happens. Anna expressed a
similar fear in May:

> Went to church this A.M. Coming back, I came within an [inch] of being
> run over—as the horse dashed down the sidewalk. What would have
> become of me—I had no address with me—and Madame Bazin does not
> know Edith's [address] and Mary Young is gone!

I give Fabienne the packet of Blaikie drawings for Madame Compagnon. I
wanted to deliver it in person, but we have missed each other all week. The

Métro takes me to the Gare du Nord, the first place Anna saw in Paris. When Edith came into this *gare* from Berlin to spend Christmas at Madame Bazin's, Anna wrote instructions:

> I am afraid your train comes in at *Gare du Nord*. I feel it in my bones. But Mary says she will go with me to meet you. I am sure I do not want you to feel as *I* did the night I got here. I never will forget that arrival. I laughed over it afterward but at the time I felt like doing anything else. Horrible! Learn this in French: "Porter, will you take my baggage please" and *grab* the first one you see with a blue blouse. Be quick about it or all will be taken and you will be left. I am telling you this in case I cannot get into the place where the train stops. You pass a gate and give up your RR ticket, *then* you have to stop and have your baggage examined. Put the new books in the bottom so they will not be apt to see them. Have clothes all on top.

The Gare du Nord terminal has delicate cast iron columns supporting a roof of cloudy glass. The biting wind whips in from the open end of the building and mixes with the smell of diesel fumes. The trains line up like racehorses in a starting gate. The click-clack of the revolving departure screen brings nostalgia. In 1987 my sister Edith and I rode mountain railways to some of the places in Switzerland that our grandmother and great-aunt visited: Rigi, Zermatt, and Gornergrat. At that time we did not know their exact itinerary, but in the Zermatt museum, we searched through a July 1898 hotel registry hoping to find the names of Edith and Anna Lester. Traveling sisters share visual and culinary memories. When Edith and I mention the name "Helmut," we recall a window table in Caux, overlooking Lake Geneva. Chef Helmut served us sautéed trout with white asparagus, followed by a rainbow palette of fruit sorbets. I have enjoyed my solo trip to Paris, but no sister will share these memories with me, just as Granny Harbin was left alone with her souvenirs of the Alps.

Trains leave about every two hours for Amiens. At the ticket window I find that being over sixty qualifies me for a twenty-five percent discount. I buy a take-out *croque-monsieur*, even though the grilled cheese sandwich will wilt before train time. When my train number flips up, I walk to the platform. Did Edith and Anna walk through this same gate? I "compost" my ticket in the orange machine and find a second-class *non-fumeur* car, glad I'm not dealing with 1898 "straps" and trunks. I settle into a window seat with anticipation: I am on a European train, ticket in hand, off to an unfamiliar city. A man bounds onto the train at the last minute, loaded with boxes and gift wrap. At a table across the aisle, he spreads out paper and wraps five or six packages. We laugh as one of the greeting cards plays "Happy Birthday" every time he bumps the boxes. He leaps off at the first stop, prepared for a festive celebration.

As the train zips through the countryside, I recall how the labyrinth pattern has provided adventures in three countries. In 1994 I went to Glastonbury, England, with a group of women interested in sacred landscape. As we climbed Glastonbury Tor, our guide led us onto a pathway winding around the terraced conical hill. We circumnavigated the holy Tor as labyrinth pilgrims have done for centuries. That night, when we learned to draw the seven-circuit Cretan labyrinth, we embossed the design on our brains.

Back in America I constructed temporary labyrinths for church groups and college art classes. In 1997 my patient sister accompanied me to England to find turf mazes in Wing, Braemore, and Saffron Walden. Through the work of the Reverend Lauren Artress at Grace Cathedral in San Francisco, the medieval labyrinth design of Chartres has been reproduced on canvas and is available worldwide. Although I prefer to create the seven-circuit design outdoors, I want to walk as many interior labyrinths as possible.

A bitter wind buffets the city as I leave the Amiens station, so I take a taxi up the hill to the cathedral. The doors are bolted; the church is closed until two. For twenty frigid minutes, I take shelter in doorway alcoves, clutching my wool scarf to my throat. At last, a functionary heaves open the doors of the cathedral, and I enter with two other stalwart souls.

The labyrinth of Amiens is a black-and-white geometric pattern on the nave floor. As I feared, the design is covered with chairs. From photos in books, I know the pattern is optical art containing a Maltese cross, and through the chair legs, I can see the angled lines. The design lacks the serpentine flow of the walkway at Chartres. I devise a personality profile for labyrinth walkers. The stark Amiens design appeals to people who make crisp hospital corners on their beds and arrange their pencils in military rows. The Chartres labyrinth pleases lovers of knot gardens, overlapping rose petals, and the syncopated twists of the tango.

I want to move the chairs and walk the pattern, but the temperature is low, and the probability of Gallic wrath is high. In the central aisle of the nave, I stand on the goal of the labyrinth—a black marble octagon—to absorb its energy. The sound of my deep breathing is audible because the cathedral is very still, a contrast to the shuffling footsteps in Notre-Dame de Paris. On a warmer day, I would have basked in the sapphire blue of the stained glass.

Outside, the streets are empty. Restaurants no longer serve lunch, but a sympathetic waitress stops wiping tables to call a taxi for me. I shiver under an arcade until it arrives. When the driver charges me three times as much as I paid to get up to the cathedral, I remember how Anna told the carriage man she was not paying more than she thought appropriate. She walked off leaving him jabbering, but I am too cold to argue. I pay up, find a warm corner of the *gare* restaurant, and order hot chocolate to go with some macadamia nuts in my pocket. Not the elegant teatime experience I wanted, but my feet thaw before train time.

Seen through the train window, the landscape flashes past in theatrical stage sets. Light descends in baroque stripes behind a proscenium arch of gold and pink clouds. Farms, villages, and church towers flow across the horizon against a Tiepolo backdrop. As the train glides into the station, the dome of Sacré-Coeur looms on its hill in Montmartre, silhouetted against the lowering sun. The Gare du Nord was the last place Anna saw in Paris; Frances Blaikie and Amy Steedman accompanied her to this station to say farewell. The three friends never again shared a cup of tea.

A flight of stairs leads from the arrival platform to the RER line; the fast train takes me to the Luxembourg Gardens gates. Shafts of sunlight funnel up rue Soufflot to spotlight the dome of the Panthéon. I understand why photographers worship the diagonal Paris light.

At the Café Orbital across the street, messages from family and friends await me. After sending a final e-mail, I start to leave the computer terminal. On a whim, I sit back down and access Yahoo! on the Internet. I enter "Jonathan and David" in the search line. Can I find pertinent Bible passages about the Old Testament figures? Before I can blink, lists of Web sites pop up with citations from the Book of Samuel: Jonathan and David knit together; Nothing so comforted David like Jonathan's presence; Sweeter than the love of woman; Jonathan loved David: Homosexuality in Biblical Times. Here is cyber-confirmation of the nicknames of Anna Lester and Henriette Ballu. I turn around to see if anyone has been looking over my shoulder, then I shut down the computer and walk out of Café Orbital.

The sun's last rays slip through the locked gates of the jardin du Luxembourg, and the Eiffel Tower sparkles in the distance against an India ink sky. Gingko leaves skitter through the iron fence onto the sidewalk. I scoop up a few for my gingko-loving friends. Students with backpacks stride along the pavement, headed for café warmth. Men and women hurry home from work, armed with briefcases and baguettes. Feeling the loneliness of the city as it closes down for a winter night, I pull my beret over my ears and lean into the wind.

At the Café Vavin, it is the hour of coffee and cigarettes, but a young woman is making crêpes at a stand on the sidewalk. She prepares a cheese and egg crêpe for me, and we agree that she has the warmest job on this cold night. From Le Marché Franprix I choose fruit and cookies and nod to the heavy-breathing man in the doorway. Back in the warmth of the hotel, I get a glass of wine from the bar and balance it into the elevator. Having no desire to go back out for a real dinner, I take a hot bath, rub cream on my feet, and watch crazy French TV game shows like *What's My Line?* Other choices include *Urgences* (*E.R.*) in French, a Kevin Costner movie about the Battle of Hastings, and the ubiquitous *Baywatch* in German. I catch part of a riverboat gambling movie, which has been dubbed from English into German with French subtitles. The heroine sings, "Polly wolly doodle all the day"—untranslatable into either German or French.

My skill in French has improved daily. My responses come from the reservoir of words and phrases stored forty years ago in the French cupboard of my brain. I think, Oh yes, *pamplemousse*, and roll the sound around in my mouth as if it were the actual grapefruit. Some words taste good on the tongue. Franglais and sign language help when talking to a waiter about the menu. He and I reach an understanding about *which* part of the *boeuf* or *veau* is featured in the *plat du jour*.

Tomorrow, on my final day in Paris, I want to re-walk Anna's *quartier*. I would also like to locate 9, impasse du Maine, Mrs. Reynolds's address. Other places hover on the outskirts of my mind, but my brain is turning to gruel. In the morning, I must review my finances, look for gifts, and think about packing. I have one day to meet Madame Compagnon and learn the history of the Hôtel Sainte-Beuve.

I don't want to leave Paris without eating some *coquilles Saint-Jacques*. In sidewalk fish markets, I have seen scallops splayed on their shells like pilgrim oblations at Compostella. In 1957 Nina and I dared quicksilver tides to collect sandy scallop shells at the base of Mont Saint-Michel. David and I ate *coquilles Saint-Jacques* in a small restaurant on île de Ré. Nothing tastes sweeter than these *coquilles* straight from the sea. Any scallop would surpass the Café Vavin cold cheese and egg crêpe—my elegant dinner for the evening. In her sardonic way, Anna would have said it was "Fine!"

November 3, 1898

The Professor came and I understood most of what he told me. No one to explain. He seems most kind and interested in the work.

November 6, 1898

Day of all Days—Fontainebleau! Most glorious—color—light—air—and everything. I enjoyed it fully. Sunset was beautiful.

November 10, 1898

9, rue Sainte-Beuve

My dear Edith,

Your letter has just come from my own little Girl and I am struck with your last wish: "Dream of your own true love." How can my own little fortune teller tell me of whom to dream? Think right hard and let me know, please. I am sorry your Sunday was not a success, for mine was a *glorious* one! I got up at 6 A.M. and went with these two sisters and a German girl to Fontainebleau. The day was simply perfect! Magnificent sun and oh my, the colors of that forest. I never saw such a place. The colors were simply beyond words. And we reached the top of a hill just as the sun went down in gorgeous colors. Saw Rosa Bonheur's house in the distance, came near Millet's, so I ought to have a little inspiration for work this week, don't you think? We did not get back here until quarter of nine, then I was tired but satisfied with my day. My cough is *much* better. It must be this charming weather, one long, long Indian summer day ever since I returned on August 25. Wouldn't it be glorious if this does last until December 8? On the ship I will not need an extra shawl for I will have two and the rug, then my jacket and fur for my neck and I expect to put on an extra union suit over this shirt, so I will be stuffed to death.

You may be sure I am going to eat a lot when I go home. I have an appetite now and so have to eat. It may be the oil and wine I am taking that is doing the cough good. I am on my third pint, think of that. I wish I could send you some of the good home things, but I will not tell you about them, that will make you hungry. No, I am not *depriving myself* of anything under the sun. Does that satisfy you? Think of having all one wants!

I guess I will have to return to five-finger exercises [on the piano] so as to take some of the *stillness* out of the house. I could not take your place with Mother but I do expect to be as *sweet* as I know how to be *all the time* and not fly off the handle once. How will that do, dear?

Thursday P.M. I had to go to dinner then, as usual, went straight to bed. I was so awfully extravagant this morning that *that*, or something else, has tired me out. I went downtown [rue du Temple] for the frames for my miniatures. Got beauties, more than I had miniatures for, because I intend doing some at home, and the frames are so much better and cheaper here. Now I am wondering how on earth I am to get into New York with them and not pay duty.

I have no Will [Mrs. Reynolds's husband] to put them in his overcoat pockets and I am afraid if I try to put *18* in my pocket they will break and I do not want to pay any duty. *All* I have bought over here would not come to $75 and they say we can carry $100 worth and no duty but I do not know if frames are included.

You are to come home next summer, the last of June or in July if you prefer and spend the summer any way you want—even if you stay no longer it will cost less than staying [in Berlin] if you come on winter rates and stay home until winter rates begin again. This is if you do not get a position. You know I have told you often, I did not want you to feel you had any debt [to me]. If we can keep up the Insurance for 20 years then I will have enough for old age and I hope to be able to support myself that much longer.

I do not relish leaving my little girl on this side of the water, but I feel it my *duty* to go home now. Good night and what should I say? Dream of *your* handsome young love that is to bring you joy and happiness all your life? That God may give you peace and joy and love, is my hearty desire. Let me put my arms around you and tell you *all* my heart contains for my own sweet little sister, *then* kiss you.

November 13, 1898

Went to the Bois to hear the music after lunch. An awful crowd. Got a letter from Laura Berry. She wants to go home on the same boat with me.

November 14, 1898

Letters! They are disappointed I did not come [home] in November, but I said Xmas at first. A beautiful model in our room and a pretty little girl in the watercolor room. Would like to have both if possible.

November 15, 1898
Dear Edith,

We have a lovely model this week, only seventeen. Says she does not pose nude. The one we had week before last tried to commit suicide since. I hope the bad drawings had nothing to do with her feelings. She is now in the hospital. The men do provoke me so—being familiar with the models—if they would let them alone it would be better.

I do not expect to try for a position [to teach]. If they should offer me a big salary at Shorter that *might* tempt me, but they will not, I am sure. Then too, they need a new studio. What I want is to stay at home and take a few *orders* instead of Pupils. I was thinking of sending a few miniatures to Savannah for exhibition and in that way get some [orders] or some tapestry work. I was not thinking of *making* the money for you to stay [in Berlin]. I think I have enough laid by now for a year more—if [Earnest] Hutcheson thinks it is to your advantage. There is no use for me to go home and hold my hands, for I would be miserable. I want to work all of the time—in some way—I *must* be busy to be contented at all—and if the work brings in a little money—I certainly will not refuse to take it and say thanky too.

———◈———

In November 1957 I began to ponder what my life would be like when I returned to Georgia. One afternoon a friend and I had tea at the Ritz Hotel with some of my mother's acquaintances from Atlanta. They described their two-week continental tour and said, "Well, now we've *done* Europe!" After my months in classrooms, Métros, theaters, and museums, I saw the distance between the person I had become and the world I had left behind.

Samedi, le 2 novembre 1957
I hadn't seen Atlanta society in that light before. I don't belong in that type of group. What am I going to do? What's my life going to be after this year? Am I going to settle back into Rome life and stagnate or is that

what I *should* do. ("Heureux qui comme Ulysse…") Took Granny for example. Happiness in old age because of roots built for a lifetime. A defined position in society. A job well done. A life well lived. Beloved of all. Three years in Berlin taken into account. Influence on *me* of her European *séjour*. Can I really be happy without my roots? The big question. I know I can't wander all my life. Don't cut ties, you'll need them *un de ces jours*…

November 7, 1957
15 bis, boulevard Jules Sandeau
Dear Famille,

Life moves on as usual. School has commenced and things are really popping. Martha Dix came to visit, loves Paris and is full of the enthusiasm that we all arrived with. My enthusiasm is a little dimmed, not to mention my staying power. Went to see the National Ballet of Checkoslovackia (I never could spell it). Sunday to church, to Louvre, and to a Tchaikowsky concert. In additon to 8 hours lecture in the mornings I have 9 hours of practical work in French and phonetics and an art course at the British Institute and several courses at the École du Louvre. The worst part is the hours spent in transit every day. Saw Antonio and his Spanish Ballet, reminded me of Spain. But last night was the best. Went with Mrs. Terry and Nina to see The Diary of Anne Frank. It was the most moving play I've ever seen. Going to see Faust with Martha Dix. What about Sputnik the Second?

I met a nice boy from California who's here in the Air Force and who has a turquoise Austin Healy sports car(!) I figure if I spend all my time doing all the things I want to and fill every minute I won't feel so bad about coming home. The time is SO SHORT it scares me. I can't wait to get home but I sure do hate to leave. Am scared to death I'll never get back. Am studying Asiatic Art. Think I'll go to India next. It's cold here— wet and damp and chilly and disheartening and winter. The hair's not growing as fast as it should and I'm so sick of my clothes I could scream. But will be brave. Send my love to Granny.

Love to all,

Tu

November 18, 1957

Dear Family,

    We may sail on the Mauretania on the 18th [of January] instead of on the Elizabeth on the 22nd. No one seems to know. Typical. Cooking classes great. Can't wait to get home and practice. Saw La Traviata last night. Going to the Ballet on Wed. Hearing Brailowsky play Chopin next week and Rubenstein the next. Culture coming out of the ears. There are rumors that we'll have a strike tomorrow. No gas or electricity. Or professors. The best excuse for not going to class is not living close enuf to walk. Esp if the prof ain't gonna show. Am actually getting excited about coming home. I've about had enough, even though I love it.

Love to all,
TuTu

———⋖⊚⊶——

    Midnight. Time for bed, but my mind is on Anna's last days in Paris. Did she see Mlle Ballu when she returned to America? I need a confidante with whom I can discuss their friendship. Since it is only six o'clock in America, I call my sister and tell her how I missed her on the train this morning. Speaking English is a relief; I babble about the two sides of Anna Lester.

    "I think Sister Anna was a workaholic, but there are these love poems in the journal. Do you think Mlle Ballu sent them all? Sister Anna sent Mlle Ballu a book for Christmas called *The Prince of the House of David*, but it got delayed, and she was really upset about it in April. In January, Anna got a dear little poem from Staunton, and a dear little photo in May…"

    "Slow down. What was the name of that book again?"

    "The Prince of the House of David."

    "Hold on a sec." Edith drops the phone, and I count the crackling transatlantic seconds until she returns.

    "I've *got* it!"

    "Got what?"

    "The Prince of the House of David!"

    "You're kidding."

    "Granny Harbin gave her copy of the book to me in 1960. The inscription says that it was a gift from her mother and father for Christmas 1886. It seems to be the life of Jesus told by a female Jew. It was on the shelf in my guest room. I'll bring it to you for Christmas."

"Can't wait. But there's more…"

I tell Edith my deductions about Jonathan and David. We wonder if Anna picked the House of David book because of Henriette's nickname. We don't want to taint what may have been an innocent, platonic friendship. Maybe Victorian women exchanged poetry in a subterranean river of affection. We're glad Anna had one affectionate relationship in addition to the one with Moses. After I sever the connection to my sister, the room is still as marble. One of Anna's poems rocks me to sleep.

In Absence

Watch her kindly, stars.
From the sweet protecting skies
Follow her with tender eyes,
Look so lovingly that she
Cannot choose but think of me.
Watch her kindly, stars!

Soothe her sweetly, night.
On her eyes, o'er wearied, press
The tired lids with light caress.
Let that shadowy hand of thine
Ever in her dreams seem mine.
Soothe her sweetly, night!

Wake her gently, morn!
Kiss her softly, winds.
Softly that she may not miss
Any sweet, accustomed bliss.
On her lips, her eyes, her face,
Till I come to take your place,
Kiss and kiss her, winds!

Phoebe Cary

Day Nine

Tuesday, November 17, 1998

Roses on the rue de Chevreuse

After breakfast I wait in my room in case Madame Compagnon arrives at the hotel. As I arrange my clothes and purchases, I imagine Anna packing her trunk, perhaps in this same room. One hundred years ago today, Frances Blaikie and Amy Steedman moved into the room next door. Their enthusiasm and vitality brightened Anna's final weeks in Paris. Thanks to Miss Blaikie's drawings, I can picture their activities.

November 18, 1898

These Scotch girls seem very pleasant, come in often. When I was ready for my bath they put an invitation to tea tomorrow under my door— funny. I *could* not open the door.

November 19, 1898

Went to tea and had a very pleasant time.

November 20, 1898

Went to church with the two Scotch girls. Then we went to the Luxembourg. Wore my new Hat!

November 23, 1898

Went after Studio with those girls to get some Rhum.

November 23, 1898

9, rue Sainte-Beuve

Dear Edith,

Let me tell you about these girls next door. They are nice and just as friendly as can be. They planned to go to see Sarah Bernhardt with the new Norwegians. So the two [Norwegian] sisters were to buy the tickets for [last] Saturday night. Well at dinner on Friday, they said they had good seats for Saturday, 7 francs.

I did not see them next day until one came to the Studio nearly 3 P.M. They had been out with an old lady friend who was passing through Paris. So we came back together and had a nice time at tea. I left them to dress for the theater, as we were to have dinner at 6:30. Everybody in the house was going out but me—up here—and Mr. McKnight on the 2nd floor. They started off in fine spirits, wished I could go, but I could not afford 7 francs to see her [Bernhardt] again.

I went to bed at 8 P.M. Before 9 they came back, asked if I was in bed, said they wanted to pound somebody—for their tickets were dated 18th [November] for *Friday* night so were no good! I was awfully sorry for them but they did [act] so funny I had to laugh. Well when the [Norwegian] sister came in at 12:30 and heard the mistake, they had a great time in their room. She was so distressed she could not sleep at all. I finally got to sleep after one—had been in bed a long time but slept little.

The next morning Madame Grégoire told Miss Steedman to write Sarah a note and explain how the tickets were bought for her and she did not see them until she got to the theater—which was the truth for she simply put them in her pocket a few minutes before leaving the house. Well after a touching note was written—to bring tears from a stone— enough, she said, [so] we three went to [chapel] service. After lunch got stamps and mailed the note then went to the Luxembourg.

Yesterday at lunch the answer came. Sarah was "tray contont" to give them the "entrée personal" and enclosed invitations for 3 seats. In the *Parquet!* mind you. Wasn't that fine? We simply shouted and clapped. Now they will have to go full dress and ride in a cab both ways for it is awfully cold. It is a good thing Sarah did not include me in that invitation for tonight, for I could not go low neck to my grandmother's wedding—it is so cold—I would land in the grave pretty soon afterwards.

Lovingly,

Anna M. Lester

November 24, 1898 Thanksgiving Day
Dear Edith,

The funniest American man has come here, Mr. McKnight's friend. He looks like a Chinaman and drags his words. I simply cannot keep my face straight if I look his way. So they [the "Scotch girls"] call him Miss Lester's friend, "Joke." And they nearly die laughing at him themselves. I really am afraid he or Madame or Mr. McKnight will catch on.

The girls had a lovely time last night—went low neck and said they were the only ones there in evening dress. Everybody had on *hats* even. So as soon as they took their seats opera glasses were launched [on them] from all directions. I told them never mind, they were taken for some distinguished friends of Sarah's. They got hot of course in two seconds—so did not feel *cold* anymore. They came in here on their way to their room at lunch and gave me *violets* for Thanksgiving.

Madame Grégoire had Turkey stuffed with chestnuts and Pumpkin pie for dinner. Then asked us to stay and play games after dinner. The girls did but the two men took themselves off! I had invited the two Scotch girls to eggnog and we were on pins to leave—it was no fun at all until Mlle Beadker sang—the German girl. She has a fine voice, I tell you, has been singing in the concerts in Germany.

We finally got in here at quarter after ten. I got a soup plate spoon and fork from Madame, and they had a bowl—so we made five eggs—for the three and it was fine. Used Jamaica Rhum. Miss Steedman said the eggnog was like "eating white satin." I remarked I had never tasted that, so she said she ate it by the yard.

November 26, 1898
Dear Edith,

Miss Steedman is the one I like the best, and think what a chance I am missing. She goes to Italy the middle of February to Florence to meet her mother, then to Rome. She passes through Milan, back to Venice in April, etc. Just exactly what *I* wanted to do—and she dreads the trip alone, though she has been down three winters. If I was going to be here it would be *the* chance, for she seems to like me somehow. They are the only girls I have really felt like being friendly with. The others are so stiff and cold.

I have bought Miss Beall a *silk* dress! You know I promised her a black silk if she would be good to Mother and Father until I could get back. I got Mother a lovely chiffon neck thing and a dear little handbag. Bought some flowers for future hats, a piece of chamois, a wicker carpet beater, a veil, black gloves, and a half-dozen bone salt spoons. Then I was *dead* broke and came away. Yesterday I got Ivory for a year, one frame for 10 francs and 3 cheap ones. And photos and cards. Now if I buy anything more I'll feel like going and hanging myself for I really do not know now how these are going to get home. Got a note from Laura Berry. She wants to go [in room] with me in Antwerp, also in New York.

Keep well and happy and have all the fun you can along with work. These are your best days for enjoyment. I am so much obliged to you for your good wishes for my birthday and the letter case. But you must not do that. I told you our summer was our birthdays. Get something you want for yourself in Berlin for my Xmas for you. If you get what suits, you will enjoy it more. Happy dreams my dear little sister and all the good luck one can have. Much love and kisses from your loving sister.

November 26, 1898
The last day at the Studio and it really made me feel sad. I do hate so to give up my work now.

November 27, 1898
Went to church in the morning. In the afternoon I took tea in the next room and then stayed until nearly dinnertime. Miss Steedman has some pretty sketches in Watercolor of places in Italy. Oh, I did want to go to Italy so much!

November 28, 1898
My dear Edith,

I am not *leaving you.* I am no earthly use to you here in Paris, and I could not stay in Berlin, so you will enjoy a letter from Rome, Georgia, each week as much as you would one from Roma, Italy. And even if I stayed in Italy this winter I could not wait until July, for the money I set aside for *my* expenses is giving out, so it seems necessary to go home. I cannot promise *not* to teach, for I guess that will be what I will do next fall. I *must* support myself you know to be contented, as long as I am able to do so. Now the amount I had for *your* expenses will not be touched except for you. I hate to go home first, but see no way out of it. Goodbye with ever so much love and kisses.

P.S. *After tea!* I do not know that I meant exactly that *my* part of the money was "giving out." I should have said I have decided to use mine in another way, now that I feel they need me at home. I suppose God is sending me home to save a disappointment in the spring. For if I stayed, my heart was set on getting in the Salon. Now I want *you* to accomplish what has been impossible for me—*success!*

Ten days before she left Europe, Anna accepted the end of her art study in Paris: she would not exhibit in the Salon. Illness and a needy father won over artistic determination. Twenty-two-year-old Edith now shouldered Anna's truncated dreams in addition to her own. How much of their combined ambitions filtered down to me?

November 29, 1898
Went back to the Bon Marché and got all I could. In the afternoon I made tea ready for the girls when they came in at four.

November 30, 1898
Began to pack a little. Then after lunch went to see Miss Lakjer. Took her to the Louvre then to tea at the Liverpool tea room.

—— ⊰⊱ ——

Fabienne says that Madame Compagnon may not arrive until afternoon, so I will go see where Anna saved money on supplies for her miniatures. Her address book gives street numbers for a frame supplier named David's and for an ivory factory on rue du Temple. I start out on my last Métro journey. From place de la République, I walk down rue du Temple, where the window displays of beads, jewelry, and cheap scarves remind me of the garment district of New York. The courtyard at number 187 probably looks as it did when Anna came here to the ivory factory, but I see no sign of David's frame shop at number 191.

Elderly men and women sit on benches in the square du Temple, so I cross the street to join them. Though sunny, the park has a tang of dead vegetation and aging skin. The facade of a nearby building contains a *cadran solaire*. The sun's shadow moves across the face of the dial, nibbling the minutes of my last Paris morning.

In a nearby Monoprix store, the merchandise is less expensive than at the Bon Marché. I buy linen dish towels for the women in my family and truffles for chocoholic friends. With the heavy package straining my shoulder muscles, I return to my *quartier.*

In the median of Boulevard Raspail, sunshine illuminates the bronze statue of Balzac. Auguste Rodin created his *Monument à Balzac* amid controversy and delay, finally exhibiting it in the Salon of 1898. Anna's catalog has a photo of the Balzac statue. Did she know the furor Rodin's statue caused in Paris art circles? The critics compared it to a sack of flour, a pile of melting snow, a seal, or a colossal fetus. More charitable was the comment that Rodin portrayed Balzac in his dressing gown. Some said the statue was innovative and prophetic. I see Balzac as a giant redwood stump leaning into the wind.

After I photograph *Monument à Balzac,* I speak to a man in an apron outside a corner restaurant. He is shucking oysters at a table piled with *fruits de mer* on ice. I point to the menu on the doorway.

"Coquilles Saint-Jacques?"

"Entrez, Madame! Entrez!"

I read the name: La Rotonde, one of the legendary restaurants in Montparnasse. Along with Le Dôme and Le Select, La Rotonde was café home to writers and artists. I feel like a bag lady as I haul my plastic Monoprix sack into the elegant space. The mirrored ceiling and walls reflect my charcoal jacket, black knit cap, and thick-soled shoes. Again, Madame Are-vay attempts to glide with grace onto a red velvet banquette.

No one seems in a hurry in a French restaurant. Businessmen flash gold rings as they sip coffee and tap cigarettes on ashtrays. Out on boulevard du Montparnasse, taxis and busses screech and honk in 1998 Paris, but I imagine an expatriate writer at a sidewalk table, dawdling for hours over one *café-crème.*

For my last lunch in Paris, I am within proper dining hours and ready to savor the fruits of the sea. I choose *chèvre salade* followed by *Saint-Jacques à la Provençale.* The scallops are pearl ambrosia from the ocean, so fresh they ooze seawater. For dessert I have a *soufflé glacé avec sauce mandarin impérial*—a frozen orange mousse sauced with enough liqueur to dizzy my head. When I blink out into the sunlight, the oysterman inquires about my search for *coquilles.* I arch my eyebrows, nod my head, and saunter down boulevard Raspail to rest.

le 28 novembre 1957 Thanksgiving Day

Went to church at the American Cathedral. Dean Riddle preached: We're too complacent. Give thanks but don't stagnate. Then to lunch at the American Embassy, turkey, etc. Then to Cours Practique with Madame Tessier. On the way home I stopped for thé at the Ranelagh. Bought me some violets.

Saturday, December 14, 1957

Went to catch bus and saw crowds gathering on corners, awaiting the arrival of IKE from Orly [for NATO conference]. And seeing how I can't resist crowds, I joined in. Have never been so cold in my life. A bitter gray windy day. *Finally*, he arrived, *standing up* in an open-top car, waving to the crowds. Shouts of "Bravo Ike!" and "Vive Ike!" and I yelled, too. Was quite touched and impressed. With a spirit like that in front of us, there's hope. Seems some 10,000 Parisians were along his route to welcome him. Recalled for many the entrance of the armies of liberation.

December 17, 1957

15 bis, boulevard Jules Sandeau

Dear All,

Brief this will be cause I'm sleepy. Leave Saturday night with a ski group for Saint-Anton, Austria. Am very excited about a white Christmas. Have been slightly flu-y. Sore throat, cold, but seem better now. I stayed in 3 days.

Town all excited about the NATO conference. Ike came to church at the Cathedral Sunday for special NATO service. I was nine rows behind him. John Foster Dulles read the psalm. Monsieur Jung is furious at us for publishing the failure of our "pamplemousse" of a Sputnik. Would love to be home for Xmas. Doesn't seem like it over here. The lack of commercialism is surprising. I love it over here but I've about had enough for this dose. If I could come home for a coupla months, get straightened out and come *back*, that'd be a different story. Only one more month to go. Time flies, to be original. Must stop. Wish you could see my hair. It looks great! Ditto figure. Have lost the surplus.

Love to all,

TuTu

"Madame Are-vay! Madame Compagnon est arrivée!" Fabienne telephones from the reception desk.

"Je descends, tout de suite."

After eight days in Paris, I meet the owner of the Hôtel Sainte-Beuve. Madame Bobette Compagnon is an energetic businesswoman with high cheekbones and a blond pageboy. A gold chain and a silk scarf accent her tailored black pantsuit. She is ecstatic about the sketches by Frances Blaikie and the 1898 accounts of life at 9, rue Sainte-Beuve. After Anna's time, the address had an unsavory reputation. Madame Compagnon delighted the neighbors when she converted the building into an upscale hotel with David Hicks interiors. One client of the former "hotel" was not pleased with her changes. A dapper elderly gentleman appeared at the hotel door one day, claiming that Madame Compagnon's renovations had destroyed his amorous memories. He said the nickname of the previous establishment was "the hotel of one-hundred-thousand tremors." The ghosts of Anna Lester and the "Scotch girls" witnessed some shocking sights if they revisited 9, rue Sainte-Beuve during that phase.

I learn that rue Sainte-Beuve bears the name of Charles-Augustin Sainte-Beuve, journalist, poet, and grand master of literary criticism. He lived around the corner on rue Notre-Dame-des-Champs but claimed this was "his" street. A portrait of the corpulent writer hangs in the hotel *cabine de téléphone*. Madame Compagnon tells me about Sainte-Beuve and Victor Hugo, who also lived on rue Notre-Dame-des-Champs for a time. The men were good friends—until Sainte-Beuve had an affair with Madame Adèle Hugo.

After my conversation with Madame Compagnon, I go to my room. How will I spend my final hours in Paris? I turn the pages of Anna's address book, noting the pensions and academies I've found: Bazin, Berthier, Grégoire, Colarossi, Delécluse, Julian. Have I missed anything significant? As if lit by a strobe light, one address pulses on the page: The Girl's Club at 4, rue de Chevreuse. Anna told her parents about the club when she first moved to Montparnasse:

> I went to the St. Luke's Chapel on Sunday morning and enjoyed the
> service so much. It is just back of The Girl's Club. Do you know they have
> tea (English Breakfast) every afternoon at the club *free*. Some English Lady
> gives it, but I haven't got the cheek to go. I went once and it was *good!* But
> I felt strange [like a] stray cat.

"St. Luke's Chapel." "Just back of The Girl's Club." I'm tired but alert enough to feel the cogs in my brain engage. On Friday I learned that Saint Luke's Chapel was behind the wall at 5, rue de la Grande Chaumière. If the church was in *back* of the Girl's Club, the club address must be on the next street over. Yes, the map shows that rue de Chevreuse connects with rue Notre-Dame-des-Champs, one block past rue de la Grande Chaumière. Anna mentions the club in her letters, but I never thought of looking for the address. I absolve myself. I could not have squeezed more into the past few days, but I have time for one last search. In a few minutes, I'm striding along rue Notre-Dame-des-Champs.

On rue de Chevreuse, I expect to find a locked door or a demolished building, but at number 4, a brass doorplate says Reid Hall. When I push open the wooden door, I find a group of young people in an entry hall; the building must still be a student center. Glass doors open from the foyer into a courtyard where pink roses catch the last rays of sun. Students in duffel coats sit in slat-bottomed park chairs around green garden tables. Jasmine vines grow up the sides of the buildings; the potted plants and fir trees could be on a country estate.

As the sunbeams leave the roses, I follow a path to the rear of the property. Does it lead to rue de la Grande Chaumière? Even on tiptoe, I can't muffle the crunch of my shoes on gravel. I may be trespassing, but asking permission could involve bureaucratic negotiations, and the light is fading. The iron gate at the end of the path is locked, but I can see over it to the Maison Gaudin building, the stained glass factory at 6, rue de la Grande Chaumière. I am standing *behind* the wall at number 5. Four days ago, I stood on the other side of this wall, before I found out it was the address of Saint Luke's Chapel. The small church where Anna, Frances, and Amy worshipped was here, in the back garden of the Girl's Club. The only remnant of a building is a wooden storage shed.

With my hands on the gate, I plant my feet on the earth of Saint Luke's Chapel and visualize lines converging at this spot. One line goes straight behind me to Reid Hall, evidently the Girl's Club in 1898. My left shoulder points across rue de la Grande Chaumière to Académie Colarossi; Académie Delécluse was down the hill and to my right. Two lines shoot left up to the boulevard Montparnasse pensions of Berthier and Bazin. Several blocks ahead of me is rue Sainte-Beuve, and further still is the Académie Julian address on rue du Cherche-Midi. My right shoulder points toward the Musée du Luxembourg and on to the Louvre. If I drew these lines on a map of the *quartier*, they would cross in a rough star or an asterisk. By standing where the lines intersect, I have found the spiritual center of Anna Lester's Paris—the goal of my nine-day labyrinth journey.

The air is without sound. I am in one of the pockets of dead calm found occasionally in Paris streets when buildings buffer traffic and noise. Into the holy twilight, I whisper the names of Anna Lester, Amy Steedman, and Frances Blaikie. Rue de la Grande-Chaumière becomes a street scene from a nineteenth-century play. Under my direction, the ladies walk through the gate with their prayer books to worship at Saint Luke's Chapel. Across the street they carry their portfolios and aprons to Académie Colarossi to sketch the nude models. They sip free tea in the garden before walking home to rue Sainte-Beuve.

Many clues led me to Paris and to these women: Mlle Ballu's 1898 envelope, Anna's journal and letters, Miss Blaikie's cartoon drawings. Perhaps the ladies of rue Sainte-Beuve have moved me around on a Ouija board. Cheered when I found pieces of their puzzle. Tugged me through the garden to this wall and gate. Do they sit on cloud balcony seats, clapping and yelling "Brava!" as they did for Sarah Bernhardt? Does Sister Anna want to go home with me or hang out back here a bit longer? She has no constraints of time or flight schedules. I pray that in Heaven she is a healthy, satisfied woman, whipping up eggnog for her friends.

I bid the ladies *Au revoir, Auf Wiedersehen*. What do they have up their leg-of-mutton sleeves for our next sighting? I retrace my steps through the tranquil garden. On my right are classroom buildings; on the left a tree grows through the roof of a dark green building. Back in the stone-floored foyer, students chat in several languages behind me as I study a bulletin board to find out more about Reid Hall. This could be the same posting place where Anna removed Mrs. Reynold's class notice in October 1898. There are schedules listed for American colleges, including the Hollins Abroad program. I now remember that Reid Hall became Hollins Abroad headquarters long after I left Paris.

"May I help you?" The voice startles me.

"Yes, *oui*, perhaps, *peut-être*." I turn and see a short woman wearing a paisley shawl. She is Madame Tchistoganow, the manager of Reid Hall. The name explains her Russian accent.

"*Ma grand-tante était ici en 1898…*" I begin. My Sister Anna tale gets me invited into her office, where we speak in French and English. I learn the history of Reid Hall.

The building was an eighteenth-century hunting lodge built by the Duke de Chevreuse. Later it became the Institution Keller, the first Protestant school in Paris, whose most famous pupil was André Gide. In 1893 Mrs. Whitelaw Reid, the wife of an American diplomat, started a club for female American art and music students studying in Paris. During World War I, the buildings served as an army hospital for wounded soldiers; after the war, the American University Women's Paris Centre was here until Mrs. Reid gave the property to Columbia University. Several American universities use these facilities for their study abroad programs.

Madame Tchistoganow gives me a postcard of a 1900 painting. Two women sip tea in the garden of the club; they could be Anna and her friends, refreshing themselves after art lessons. I wish I could join them for a cup of English Breakfast and thank them for my nine days in Paris. Even if Anna felt like a "stray cat" at the Girl's Club when she first arrived, she said the club was much better her second year. How delightful to find this haven for students, the building and courtyard still in use, one hundred years after Anna was here. When I opened the door to Reid Hall, I dropped a compressed paper flower into a glass of water. A rose garden blossomed with information. I came very close to missing this experience.

Madame Tchistoganow remembers Hollins Abroad personnel from my era— Mr. Stuart Degginger, Mlle Paulette de Ram, and Mlle Marguerite Prinet. I recite for Madame Tchistoganow a poem we memorized at the British Institute in 1957. The professor exaggerated the syllables and told us to purse our lazy southern lips: "*Avec une jolie petite bouche, mesdemoiselles!*"

La vie est brève	Life is short
Un peu d'amour	A little love
Un peu de rêve	A little dream
Et puis, Bonjour!	And then, good day!
La vie est vaine	Life is vain
Un peu d'espoir	A little hope
Un peu de haine	A little hate
Et puis, Bonsoir!	And then, good night!

I have a copy of a similar verse from Anna's diary. The poem is a synopsis of her life:

A little work, a little play
To keep us going, and so, good day!
A little warmth, a little light
Of love's bestowing, and so good night!
A little fun, to match the sorrow
Of each day's growing, and so good morrow!
A little trust that when we die
We reap our sowing! And so, good bye!

du Maurier

We think the author is George du Maurier, who wrote *Trilby* in 1894. Anna may have read his story of a Paris model who falls under the spell of the hypnotist Swengali. Madame Tchistoganow recommends another book and writes the title on a card: *Montparnasse Vivant* by Crespelle. I thank her for her generosity and go out into the dark to search for the Crespelle book at bookstores on boulevard du Montparnasse. I turn down rue de la Grande Chaumière; I remember there was a bookstore at number 10. Anciens Livres shares the address of Académie Colarossi. The store's logo is one of the Nazca drawings from Peru: a monkey whose tail curls in a spiral. How did I miss this labyrinth symbol when I walked by here several days ago?

The bookstore's proprietor is François Roulmann, a dark-haired young man in a crewneck sweater. In addition to old books and music, his passion is the history of Montparnasse. He has a copy of *Montparnasse Vivant,* but the out-of-print book is beyond my price range. When I tell him of my Anna quest and my interest in the 1898 art studios on this street, he pulls out his postcard collection. The first card is a picture of number 2, rue Léopold-Robert. I point at Madame Bazin's balcony house: "*L'adresse de ma grand-tante!*" At the turn of the century, the ground floor housed a *pâtisserie* and a *boulangerie*, where Anna might have shopped. Next, he shows me a street scene of rue de la Grande Chaumière. Another card pictures a studio of artists at the Académie Colarossi with a nude model holding a pose. Here are contemporary photos of Anna's life.

When I ask the address of Académie Colarossi, Monsieur Roulmann says it was here, at number 10, rue de la Grande Chaumière, *dans la cour*. In the courtyard. Behind the door I found locked on Friday.

I share my recent knowledge that Hemingway's son was baptized at Saint Luke's Chapel, located across the street at number 5.

"*Ah, oui? Vraiment?*" He looks through his files and finds an 1893 photo album, which belonged to residents across the street from number 5. We turn the pages. One photograph, taken from an upstairs window, looks into the space behind the Girl's Club back garden wall. At that time two open gateways pierced the wall; horses and carriages stand in a courtyard before a one-story structure running parallel to the wall. The windows are square panes of stained glass, and a wooden cross tops the pediment over the entrance.

"*La chapelle!*" we say in unison. Monsieur Roulmann had not noticed the chapel in the photograph. I added to his knowledge, and he added to mine. I now know what Anna's church looked like. This *gentil* man lets me take the postcards and photos to a copy machine. I leave a deposit, dash to Copifac, and squeeze in the door a minute before the store closes. After taking the originals back to Anciens Livres, I turn down rue de la Grande Chaumière for the last time. At the wooden door of number 10, I push the bell and the latch clicks open. The entryway is black as charcoal, but I see the outline of a building in the courtyard. Was this Académie Colarossi? At least I know where to resume my search on my next trip to Paris.

In the waning minutes of my final afternoon, I found important information. This justifies my staying more than a week in Paris, but it is also a metaphor for life. We only start to understand things when time is running out. On her deathbed, Gertrude Stein asked, "What is the answer?" Receiving no reply, she said, "Well, then, what is the question?" Formulating the precise question is the first step toward illumination, whether one is at Delphi or on rue de la Grande-Chaumière.

On my way back to the hotel, I pass Portobello, an antique store at 53, rue Notre–Dame-des-Champs. I have seen this attractive shop several times but have not entered. Eager to extract one last experience from the day, I go in and admire monogrammed linens, kitchen pottery, and bone-handled cutlery tied with ribbons. An unusual silver teapot sits on a crowded table. Egg-shaped, with a black handle, the pot is the right size for a single serving of coffee or tea. Anna added a postscript to her letter to Edith on November 17, 1898:

> Did I tell you I went to the Bon Marché on Saturday A.M. and got some gloves—then bought the blue Tea Pot and two cups. Now how on earth *are* they to get home?

On November 17, 1998, I buy the silver pot as a souvenir of my nine days in Paris; our family traditions repeat. Back in the lobby of the Hôtel Sainte-Beuve, I sip a last cup of *thé citron* at Anna's Paris address. At a nearby table, Madame Compagnon works on her accounts. When two of her friends come in, she introduces me, and they find my quest intriguing. The enthusiastic Madame Compagnon waves Frances Blaikie's drawings in the air and talks of having them framed. The French gentleman gives me the title of a resource book about early Paris streets plus the name of his niece, who works at the Michael Carlos Museum in Atlanta. The worlds of France and Georgia converge; the nineteenth century telescopes into the present. I think Great-Aunt Anna is pleased I made this pilgrimage and delved into her world. I am satisfied.

December 4, 1898

9, rue Sainte-Beuve

My dear Mother and Father,

I got up early this morning and went to the first service then came back, had my coffee and bread. At the church hour the two girls went with me. It seems so funny to have anyone take any interest in what I do. Yesterday they came in an hour ahead of me, so when they heard me unlock the hall door, opened theirs and insisted on my coming in there to have tea. They know my teapot is [packed] on its way to America. They are very kind I must say, and had they been here all the time it would have been so different. We are going to the Opera on my last night here, to hear Faust, for they wanted me to go some place at night with them. They have been most kind to me ever since they came, and for a week now have made me tea every afternoon when they had theirs. No one else has seemed to strike my fancy since I came here.

After lunch I went to the Luxembourg—a most beautiful day and some of the flowers are still blooming in the Garden, some trees green. Children all sizes and ages playing out. Edith sends "Oceans of love" to you both. Do you think I can bring that much?

Keep well and happy and be ready to meet me. Much love for your dear selves.

I am your loving child,

Anna M. Lester

December 3-6, 1898

My own dear Edith,

I have gotten my trunk all ready and am now waiting for the man, and you may imagine how restless I am—for you know I do not *like* to *wait*—for anything. I wonder why he does not come. I got an answer from both places in Antwerp, but rather think I will go to Hotel des Flandres—8 francs for everything. The other place is fine but they do not have an omnibus and the fare may not be so good. Have not seen Laura [Berry] or her sister—I suppose they expected me to show them about, but I really could not do it—I have been on the rush all the time as it is, then would wake up at three and four in the mornings—I do hate so to do that—I got my new hat in the trunk, also everything else. So it is awfully heavy—I got a strong cord to tie it up—they do not seem to keep rope here but this is strong—so when the man comes I will have him tie it for me. I am afraid I will be on my head by night if he does not come, for then the trunk may not get there in time for the boat.

After lunch: The man came for my trunk while I was at lunch, tied it up for me and took it off, after giving me a receipt. I think at three o'clock I will go to the Bon Marché and see all the departments, kitchens, etc. The washwoman did not bring my shirt on Saturday, now says I forgot to put it in! I shall have to wear this fellow a long time if the other does not turn up—for I do not want to buy new ones now—too bad for her to do so at the last minute, is it not? I do not realize one bit yet that I am really going. I will, I guess, one week from this hour—when I am out on the big water.

On Monday, I am going to see Madame Bazin. Then I will have Tuesday and Wednesday for the Louvre and Luxembourg to pay a farewell visit.

These girls went with me on Thursday to see Marie Bashkirtseff's studio. She has been dead about ten years and everything is just as she left it and very interesting. Then we went to one of Julian's studios. The girls then treated me to tea, at the Liverpool Tea Room. If I went often it would spoil me for anything else. It is the only good home tea I have tasted and the cake is not bad. They liked the place so much I would like to take them there one afternoon, especially as they insist on going to the Gare to see me off on Thursday. You would be sure to like them—they are full of fun and life, still work hard. If I only had some pretty watercolors like Miss Steedman has, and could sketch funny things as Miss Blaikie does. They seemed to like the miniatures, though. I must go now and mail this note to Laura. Goodbye, dear.

6:45 P.M.: I mailed the note and then paid a visit to the Bon Marché. At the reading room at 3:30 a man comes and takes anyone who wants to go all over the place, to the kitchens, dining rooms and all. It was quite interesting, then gave each a little book on the history of the store. Then I bought two pairs of gloves and looked the place over for some little things for Mary and Joy, but I saw nothing I could get. I am sure they will expect me to bring some little things. I want all the other things I have for myself. Greedy—am I not?

This morning Madame asked me if I wanted these two men, "My Joke," and Mr. McKnight, to tie my trunk. I thanked her and declined, but told those girls of it at lunch—so Miss Blaikie has drawn me and my trunk, helping the "Joke" tie it up. He's putting his whole weight on the string and with feet on the end of trunk, stands off horizontally in the air. I wonder how on earth she does it anyway. Born in her, I guess.

"The Joke" ties up Anna's trunk

I must say good night now and wish you happy dreams. Do not think of me as being at home, imagine me still in Paris working, will you?

Monday, 11:30: I have done most of my mending and am now waiting for lunch, but I do not want any. I am afraid I am going to be sea sick—for I feel a little so now. I think it is because I got over tired last week and went out in the bad weather. It made me lose my appetite, at least it was that or stopping at the studio, for from that day I have not been hungry once. I am going to the Bon Marché later this afternoon to get my vest, and will look again for some little thing for Joy. She likes fancy things, does she not?

Mlle Kroepelein showed us her miniature painting on Saturday night. She has only done one these last six weeks, but it is lovely and puts mine very in the shade. She has copied mostly and would not let us see *any* she did from life. Works in a different way entirely from me, with slick Ivory and does it over and over, while I go for the effect at first. Mrs. Reynolds likes my way the best and to work from life, I should think so. No one would come to pose six weeks every afternoon.

I went to the Luxembourg, came in just before 12 and the man with the little [letter] case from you was just behind me on the stairs. I am so much obliged as it is just what I have needed and wanted a long time. Miss Blaikie will put my initials on the little band across the shield for me. She has her instruments for doing it on leather.

What shall I take for the Cablegramme?

Bon—would mean all went well, not sick, *everything good!*

Fair—not quite so good in all respects but *satisfied*

Sorry—means seasick, but still alive and right side up

How will that do?

Think of my going to the Opera the *last* night! It is well I do not leave until 12:40 the next day. This afternoon at 4 we go to the Liverpool Tea Room. You ought to taste that tea, it is fine. I just put my letter in my new case and it will go across with me, for company. I do wish I had my own little sister to go herself but I feel you are getting more good and real pleasure by staying here. Imagine me with you all of the time and let me squeeze you and kiss you to my hearts content, will you? Even if it does "tickle." I may mail this on my way out this afternoon, then in Antwerp I'll send either a letter or a postal to let you know I am that far on safely.

I haven't an idea what I have written in this letter for I began Saturday while waiting for that man. Don't you hope they will not make me pay any duty? That would provoke me. I got two little grey wool jackets at the Bon Marché to wear with the German ones we got. So, I hope I will be warm enough. Have taken every precaution and left out warm things. So do not worry. I guess anyway I will have to stay in the berth most of the time, too cold to be on deck.

Take good care of your dear self, and think of the nice times we will have next time we come and go to Italy in the winter, then spend June in Venice, July and August in Chamonix, Interlaken and Zermatt. God bless you in your work and watch over you and keep you from harm always and bring you safely home to us.

Goodbye my own little girl, and always remember that your sister loves you very, very much. Now give me a long kiss to last until I get home.

Your own sister,

Anna M. Lester

P.S.

The fire decided to burn by dinnertime, so afterwards it was warm. Those girls asked to see my miniatures at dinner and after I was in my room came in with a sketch of my arrival in New York, with Alpenstock in my hand, punching an old man in the head. A porter with my two bags and five men struggling with my trunk and cannot manage it, it is so heavy. The Miss Blaikie gave it to me, also one of me at the Bon Marché buying black pantaloons.

I showed them the miniatures and they seemed to like them. Then after dancing the Highland Fling for me, in their slippers and trousers, they left me to sweet repose. They send their love to you and want to know if you do not see a great improvement in me since they came. It rains and is dark as Egypt this morning. I wonder if I can see to pack my trunk. I'll keep the sketches for you to see when you come home.

Miss Lester's arrival in N.Y.—   Nov. 1898.

Miss Lester's arrival in New York

"Noirs Pantalons pour dames"

Black Pantaloons for Ladies

December 6, 1898

Finished my letters in the morning then at 3:30 we, the two Scotch girls and I, went up town and to the Liverpool Tea room. They seemed to enjoy it very much and I know I did.

Out for the Afternoon, December 6, 1898

December 7, 1898 [Anna's last day in Paris]

Went and got my ticket and then to the Louvre for the last time. My letters came in the morning and one made me most wretched. After lunch I mailed my letters then tried to fix my things. Had tea then dressed for the Opera. After we came back we made Eggnog.

After saying goodbye to Miss Blaikie and Miss Steedman at the Gare du Nord on December 8, Anna Lester and Laura Berry went to Antwerp to board the SS *Southwark* of the Red Star Line. They sailed on December 10, 1898. On that day in Paris, diplomats signed the peace treaty ending the Spanish-American War. One of the signers for the United States was Mr. Whitlaw Reid, husband of the founder of the Girl's Club. Anna had booked room 35, berth 1, on the upper deck of the SS *Southwark*. She promised to let Edith know if this was a good stateroom to request for her return trip.

December 9, 1898 [Anna's 36th birthday]

Antwerp

Rain, rain, rain! Took a cab and went to the Red Star place and paid for our trunks then out to the museum and spent the morning. After lunch to the Cathedral, got photos, then for a walk. Got my money changed into American.

December 9, 1898

Antwerp

My own dear little Sister,

Antwerp is weeping for you today, rain in sheets and buckets. Keep bright and cheerful. I have delivered your love to Antwerp in general and Rubens in particular. I hope you will have better weather and not take any more colds this winter. Be very careful of yourself. I feel awfully *old* today—almost forty! Think of it.

God bless my dear little sister and give her all the good things this world can supply, "an own true love" included. Only be sure he loves *you* more than you love him—at any rate, let him think so.

Now kiss me your sweetest kiss and let me do the same and squeeze you as much as I can. Goodbye with my best love and wishes for a happy Xmas and a joyous New Year.

Your loving sister,

Anna M. Lester

December 10, 1898 Antwerp

Got up early and went to the boat at 8 A.M. My letters were so *very* nice! I just read and read them over and over.

December 11, 1898 Aboard *Southwark*

Nice weather but nothing to do—and I *was* so blue. Not ill but not very comfortable.

December 12, 1898

All days are alike. I sleep late and only get up in time for lunch—so the day will be shorter.

December 13, 1898

Cold. Snow! I did not dare to stay long on deck.

December 14, 1898

Awfully cold, so I walked for dear life over an hour, then came in.

December 15, 1898

Making good time so we hope to reach New York on time.

December 16, 1898

Better weather, not so cold. I walk all I can.

December 17, 1898

Have written a little, not much for I do not feel like staying inside.

December 18, 1898

Finished my letters now except one. Have been out a good deal today.

December 19, 1898

A charming day. Beautiful sunset! Saw Nantucket light after dinner.

December 20, 1898 New York City

Reached New York before time. Mr. Masters met us and was so kind. Got up to the M. L.[Margaret Louisa] Home at 12:10. After lunch we went shopping and it seemed good to be on land again. Mailed my letters.

December 21, 1898 New York City

Finished shopping, then had a few spare minutes before the train time. Left at 4:20 P.M. A bad day, much fog, and streets seemed so dirty.

December 22, 1898 Atlanta, Georgia

Late in Atlanta so had to stay all night there. Did not relish that at all. Hotel dirty and servants not polite but the fare is good. Sent Father a telegram.

December 23, 1898 Rome, Georgia

Got home at 10:30! Father met me at the train. Cousin Mattie and Lutie were here with Mother and stayed to dinner. Moses, Danny and Dickens knew me, and all got kissed.

Waste no tears upon the blotted records of lost years,
but turn the leaf and smile—
Ah! Smile to see the fair white pages that are left for thee.

Ella Wheeler Wilcox

Coda

Things that Abide
I know that love never is wasted
Nor truth, nor the breath of a prayer;
And the thought that goes forth as a blessing
Must live, as a joy in the air.

Lucy Larcom

For my last breakfast in Paris, I have a cup of hot chocolate in my room. The croissants don't arrive this early, so I have toast and jam. A taxi speeds me through the gray city to Charles de Gaulle airport, where I spend my last francs on French magazines, specialty teas, and chocolate.

As I settle into my seat, I wrap the memories of my trip around me like a down comforter. I did it. *Toute seule*, I did it. The next ground my feet touch will be my native Georgia. When Anna left Paris, she intended to get well and return to Europe to paint. I make a list for my next trip: number 10, rue de la Grande Chaumière, the Musée d'Orsay, the Cluny Museum, Fontainebleau, the Paris Observatory. I want to know if Mademoiselle Prinet was kin to R. X. Prinet? Where did Mrs. Reynolds live and where was the Liverpool Tea Room?

Questions about Mlle Ballu won't be answered in Paris; I may have to go to Kansas. If I visit Scotland, would Miss Blaikie and Miss Steedman guide me around? Eliza Mary Lester might say I've started a "life work," but this trip seems as inevitable as falling in love with David Harvey and as much a part of my path as studying with Frances Niederer at Hollins and with Virginia Dudley at Shorter.

What have I created this week? If I were a pastry chef I might visualize a jelly roll or a Buche de Noël. My ingredients were biography, memoir, and history, rolled up in the phyllo crust of Paris. When I slice the pastry, each day becomes a spiral pinwheel of my life layered with Anna's. The fourth dimension is spiritual: Sister Anna's life is plaited with mine, as tightly intertwined as her braids in my grandmother's attic. I have siphoned Anna into the twentieth century; her story has given my life new direction. I consider it an equal exchange.

The flight attendants distribute headphones, but I have my own interior sound system. On one memory channel I hear Anna's words to my grandmother: "For if I stayed, my heart was set on getting in the Salon. Now I want *you* to accomplish what has been impossible for me—*success!*"

When Anna crossed the ocean, she left behind her dream of Paris honors. Perhaps it's time for me to abandon my fantasy of a Mount Olympus retrospective. Artist friends and I laugh as we set aside work from each phase of our careers for the mythical "retrospective at the Guggenheim-Whitney-MOMA-Hirschorn" where we will be, at last, recognized for our life's production. Anna Lester did not receive the Salon credentials she coveted, and I will not have a museum retrospective, but every artist contribues a filament to the fabric of art. With great pleasure, I followed Anna's slim thread through the streets of Paris. Is this what immortality is, the piggybacking of one generation onto another?

Instead of abandoning my artwork, I could curate my own retrospective. Who knows the work better than I? In my house and studio I have enough sculpture to fill a gallery. I can tie up my three-dimensional career with ribbon, or in the case of *my* work, with strong rope. I'll close my studio, give away the crates, tanks, boxes, and gears, and then go back to Paris.

The beverage cart rolls down the aisle. No wine for me, thanks, I'm high on the churnings of my mind. I close my eyes and let images flow from my past. In junkyards I collected phallic objects for antiwar statements. Other pieces about the male ego required obelisks, and my "Junk Woman" character was pleased to "measure" them. After a poem series about the wives of famous men, I dressed as the wife of Melvin Dewey, the obsessive classifier of information. The performance, "Mrs. Dewey Decimates the System," was both library history and the humorous tirade of an angry housewife. In my autobiographical slide show, *Rôle Call*, I transition from coy "Southern Belle" to the sword-wielding "Junk Woman." "Monk Woman" represents my inner journey into spiritual feminism; "The Lunatic Moth" is the crazy butterfly, last seen on the observation deck of the Empire State Building.

Some audience members have cringed at my explicit themes—just as the people of Rome were probably too modest to look at Anna's nude drawings. It might have been easier to create my sculpture and costumed characters in San Francisco or Soho, but I've relished breaking convention in my hometown. No tapestry. No flowers. Just saying what I wanted to say in whatever form I chose.

I've just completed a trans-century project, and I'm off on a retrospective tangent, but before I can reimmerse myself in Anna's life, I need to close a phase of my own. I want to see my art in one room—perhaps in the Moon Gallery, where I had my first solo show. I like the symmetry.

Before my first show in Washington I pasted this quotation from Elizabeth Hardwick in my journal: "It wasn't such an easy step for women. Any creation of art is a totally gratuitous act. Nobody cares if you do it or not. It's up to you." Anna and I made art for the pleasure of creation and for the survival of our souls. She could have led a placid spinster existence in Rome, caring for her aging parents and knitting afghans. I could have baked beans and grown roses. I am daughter, wife, mother, and grandmother, but I am also sculptor, performer, and writer. Anna chose New York and Paris. This week I also chose Paris, where I've tasted Anna's frustrations and delights. I set out on an ancestral search to share with my family, but the byproduct is a hoard of exquisite, private memories: juicy scallops from the sea, gold leaves in Père Lachaise, the fantôme in room number 9, and the crunch of gravel on the path to the back gate of Reid Hall.

For a French literature class in 1957, I memorized a poem by Joachim du Bellay. I think of it every time I return from a trip, but today it seems especially appropriate for me and for Anna. I've made my own translation.

Les Regrets

Heureux qui, comme Ulysse, a fait un beau voyage
Ou comme celui-là qui conquit la Toison,
Et puis est retourné plein d'usage et raison,
Vivre entre ses parents le reste de son âge!

Happy is she who, like Ulysses,
made a great voyage
Or, like the one who conquered the Golden Fleece,
Then returned full of customs and reason
To live among her ancestors the rest of her life.

In January 1958, when the *Mauretania* docked in New York harbor, David
Harvey was standing on the pier. He had skipped classes at Georgia Tech to meet my
ship. After a year apart, our reunion was joyous. When this plane lands in Atlanta,
David will again be waiting, and so will the ancestors.

———————

On my first morning home, I wake up clutching a dream of Paris. After David
goes to work, I unpack my souvenirs. Wearing my Bon Marché hat, I walk around
the house gathering Anna's possessions. I took photocopies of her papers to Paris;
today I touch the actual flyers from Académie Colarossi and Académie Julian. One
receipt has Madame Bazin's signature beside the paid rent. A miniature portrait of a
baby is signed A. L. Lester, Paris 1898. Did Anna buy the frame on the rue du
Temple? Did she use this piece of charcoal to draw at Delécluse?

I place the silver teapot I bought in Paris next to Anna's blue teapot on Aunt
Joy's tea table. I prop Miss Blaikie's invitation to tea on a small easel. It's morning in
Georgia but teatime in Paris. After the water comes to a rolling boil, I pour cups of
English Breakfast for me and Sister Anna. Following the custom on the *troisième
étage*, Miss Blaikie and Miss Steedman are requested to bring their own cups.

———————

When Anna returned home, she unpacked her Paris treasures and set up
her studio.

December 24, 1898 Rome, Georgia
Went to the store and did a little shopping for Father. Met a number of
people down town who spoke and said they were glad I have come home.
Mailed a letter in the P.M.

December 25, 1898
Father and I went to the new Episcopal Church. Lutie and Mr. Allen took
dinner here. We had a good dinner.

December 26, 1898
Began to put away my things and Lila came, then Mary, so I gave up the
job until next day.

December 27, 1898

Am fixing my studio. And unpacking all my things. A lot of dust!

December 28, 1898

Some work. And still the people come to see me.

December 30, 1898

Have almost finished my cleaning for a while.

December 31, 1898

Went to see Lutie and Cousin Mattie. Mailed my letter and finished the Studio. Now on Monday I can frame my miniatures. Goodbye old year—

End of Year 1898

The best thing I can do for my friend is to be his friend. I have no wealth to bestow on him. If he knows I am happy in loving him he will be satisfied. Is not friendship divine in this?

On Christmas Day 1898, Anna and my great-grandfather attended the first service in the new Saint Peter's Episcopal Church in Rome. I see them walking up the stone steps to the church that I attend. Anna wears her Paris hat trimmed with white dove feathers and violets. She carries a small black Book of Common Prayer.

For Saint Peter's centennial on Christmas Day 1998, I place a poinsettia on the altar in memory of Anna McNulty Lester. I, too, wear my Paris hat to church. When I take Anna's prayer book to her memorial window in the south transept, a beam from the winter solstice sun illuminates the blue stained glass. She is glad I am home, and so am I.

Anna's journal ended on December 31, 1898. After that date I have no letters other than this one, which describes her life in Rome. Did she dream of Paris as she was making her required social calls?

Sunday, January 29, 1899

309 East Third Street

Rome, Georgia

My dear Edith,

I finished your letter on Tuesday night last time. After I went upstairs I read your letter over then burned it. Early Wednesday morning I went to Dr. Wills, had him smooth off the filling and told him I did not suppose I could ever use the tooth.

I decided it was such a beautiful day I would pay my East Rome visits. Walked over. Got to Mrs. Gammon's at 10 o'clock. She had not been here [to call], but I thought I better not pass by. While there, the two Miss Kingsberrys of Atlanta came in. Then I left and went next door to see Mrs. Stillwell and Laura Gammon. They both seemed glad to see me. Then I went over to return Alice Park's visit. It was a quarter of twelve by the time I got to Mrs. Reynolds. I stayed there until half past then made a break for the streetcar line and caught the car at the depot 20 minutes of one. Rode to the Masonic temple and came up by Mrs. Kincaid's. Came home and had dinner then Mother and I started again, Lutie with us, to see Mrs. Vandiver. She was out, so mother went to Cousin Mattie's and Lutie and I went to see Miss Battie Shropsire—she was out—then while I waited for Lutie to see if Mrs. Hanks was at home, Cousin Mattie passed me in the buggy with Mrs. Sanford. Mrs. Hanks was out so Lutie and I walked to the Baptist Church together. She went to Mrs. Gardner's. I came home. I went upstairs for a nap but could not sleep, then I would cough and was so tired, but I wanted to pay *all* my calls and not go any more until fall!

Thursday, I got mother off to spend the day with Lutie, then after dinner Miss Beall was to go to Mrs. Seab Wright's and I to Mrs. Clemmons. Dr. Harbin says she must not eat anything, no fruit of any kind, so I only took a few little things for Lucille and Anna Louise. I came back and worked on the miniature, then Lutie came in the afternoon and at 4 o'clock Father came home nervous and with a cold, so he had to be amused. I found out he took cold by getting up and walking around in the middle of the night "looking for burglars." Such nonsense. I tried to make him promise never to do so again! But he will not promise!

Oh, wonder of wonders, and here I always forget to tell you. What *do* you suppose I have succeeded in doing? You could not guess if you did until your hair was grey. But for some three weeks now, we have had breakfast at *6:30* instead of *6!!* It is 7 o'clock often when father leaves the house now instead of a minute or so after 6. I stay *in bed* until 6. Isn't that fine not to be in such a rush?

Lola came by and said Cousin Mattie was sick in bed, so I went there a while. The ride used her up of course, then that night as she was trying to get sugar out of the bottom of the barrel, she tried to fall in but was too fat, so got sick and had to send for Dr. Johnson.

On Saturday A.M. I got an invitation to Miss Terhune's for Wednesday Feb 1st to a reception for the Misses Kingsberry. I wrote a note and declined, much to the dissatisfaction of both Father and Mother, but if I am not going into society, I am *not*. That is all. So I expect to refuse *all* [invitations] that come and not say a word to them hereafter.

Father is *all* in the notion of your coming home as soon as possible this summer. I keep telling him to let you stay while you can, etc. but his mind is on our having a class! Between you and me, I simply consented to teach to *quiet* him. He seemed bent on it for some reason. I do not quite know what unless to show the town people I *can* get a class. I would not have anyone know this for a pretty. I had *no idea* of beginning [to teach] now, and didn't want to, but I saw no way out of it. I have begun, would like at least 5 pupils—that would be $50 and help a good deal.

I believe everybody sent love to you—all I saw, I mean. I am decidedly *not* in Society in future! My miniature is nearly finished, will get it off this week I hope, then I want *real* orders. I hope you are quite well. Tell me everything on a separate slip.

> Much love and kisses for my dear little Sister.
> Anna M. Lester

Although Edith Lester's teachers in Berlin urged her to stay another year, she returned to America in the summer of 1899 and accepted a position on the music faculty at Agnes Scott Institute in Decatur, Georgia.

In January 1900, Anna received a holiday card from Frances Blaikie and Amy Steedman:

To our Miss Lester from Rowdy and Amy.

Later in the year, Frances Blaikie and Amy Steedman wrote to Anna.

Blackwaterfoot, Shiskin, Arran. Scotland

7 September 1900

Our dear Miss Lester,

    I expect you will think we are both dead or at least have quite forgotten about you, but you are wrong. We are very much alive and have been thinking a good deal about you and trying to get time to write. I don't believe we have ever said thank you either for your last letter of Jan 7th or for those nice Easter cards. I do wonder how you are, you didn't sound up to much last time you wrote. I wish you could be here. Arran is an island off the west coast of Scotland where there are nothing but wee whitewashed cottages and little toy farms. It is lovely to be here with nothing to do but bathe and read and tramp among the heather and have an all round good old lazy time. We spend a good deal of our time looking for white heather. We ought to be pretty lucky after this as each one of us has found some. I shall enclose a bit to bring luck to you—with our Best Love.

Do you know we are going back to Paris for 3 months this winter? We took a flat in the Boulevard Edgar Quinet, then discovered that it contained neither towels, sheets, blankets, pillows nor anything else. Of course it would have been too ruinous to have taken all those things with us, so there was nothing else but to give it up again and ask Madame Grégoire if she could have us. She can, so we'll be back in our same old room and wishing all the time that our dear Miss Lester was in the next room.

Both Miss Kroepelien and Miss Betke are engaged and *of course* you know—but I am afraid to tell you just *in case* you may not have heard— Your Joke is—married. At least so Miss Betke says, but of course she may be wrong. Let us hope so for your sake. All the old people are away from Madame's, I think, let us hope there may be as nice ones next winter, but that isn't likely. Amy has been doing something in the exhibiting line this year. She had one sketch in the Glasgow Ex [Exhibition], one in Stirling, and one in Edinburgh. Two of these she sold, which isn't bad for a beginning is it. Everyone seems to be getting married or doing something silly, soon there will be no one left. I think I shall come and live in Rome, Georgia, U.S.A.

This is ME now as Rowdy has let me have an innings [*sic*]. I think she has told you all there is to tell, only I want to tell you how I WISH you were going to be in Paris this winter. Not because of Egg-nog or all the good things you used to give us, but just because of *you*. I wonder how you are getting on. I do hope you are stronger and able to get to work again. Have you been making any plum cakes lately? Rowdy and I are very flourishing and looking forward tremendously to Paris. We will write and tell you all about everything there. One of the places where we will miss you most is in the little church. Do you remember how we used to kick you and say Vice Versa when the President was prayed for before the Queen? Please do write to us, we shall pine for letters in Paris—same old address you know.

> VERY much love to
> OUR DEAR Miss Lester from
> Amy and Frances

Six weeks after the "Scotch girls" wrote this letter, Anna Lester died from tuberculosis. The only details of her death come from her obituary, although my aunt told me she'd heard that Sister Anna died on the sleeping porch.

October 18, 1900, The Rome Tribune

The Death of Miss Lester

The brightness of a glorious October day was dimmed yesterday for the family and friends of Miss Anna M. Lester whose pure soul passed into the great beyond.

Her devoted mother had only left her a few moments to get her breakfast when upon returning she found her sleeping her last sleep. It was about 6 o'clock when she passed away so calmly and quietly at the home of her parents, Mr. and Mrs. B. S. Lester on East Third Street. Though her death came as a shock to her parents and friends, they had realized that the end was not far off. She had been in declining health for several years but during the past three months rallied from the dreaded disease of consumption, and her friends were hopeful that she might recover. Since Thursday of last week she had grown weaker and weaker, until she gradually faded away like a flower.

Miss Lester was a loving and devoted daughter and sister. Naturally very quiet and reserved in her disposition only those who knew her well appreciated to the fullest extent her many beautiful traits of character. She was a consecrated Christian woman of whom the Master said: "Blessed are the pure in heart, for they shall see God."

After a funeral at 309 East Third Street, Anna McNulty Lester was buried near Sister Minnie in Myrtle Hill Cemetery. Edith Lester returned to her teaching duties and wrote home:

Agnes Scott Institute

Decatur, Georgia

Dear Mama and Papa,

I thought just before I left home and didn't have time to tell you that I think the best thing to put on the tombstone will be "Auf Wiedersehen," for it was Sister's favorite of all words used at parting. I remember when she saw it on the German tombstones she said she thought it such an appropriate and sweet sentiment. It means, "until we meet again." You might just have the name and dates and this one word underneath. If you object to the foreign language don't use it at all, but I think "Auf Wiedersehen" is so simple and sweet and means so much, and she was so fond of it.

———

In October 1900, Amy Steedman and Frances Blaikie returned to 9, rue Sainte-Beuve. After learning of Anna's death, they wrote to Edith Lester from Madame Grégoire's pension:

November 6, 1900

9, rue Sainte-Beuve

My dear Miss Lester,

The "Rome Tribune" was only forwarded to us today from Scotland, and I have no words to tell you what the news it contained meant to us both. I can't even yet believe it is true, for I never realized that our dear Miss Lester was dangerously ill. Her letters were always so cheery and bright about herself. Since we came to Paris two weeks ago we have talked so constantly of her and missed her so badly. You know she had the room next to us, and when we arrived in Paris two years ago, very strange, and very much alone, she was just a good angel to us, and I shall never forget her kindness. I think you will understand when I tell you that the news today went right down in my heart for she made me love her as I do few people I have known all my life. I know she spoilt us badly but it was the sort of spoiling that makes the world a nicer place to live in and makes one a better sort of person. I am glad to think I knew her even for that short time and I know her influence will always help us in our Paris life, especially. I am very, very sorry for you and send my reallest sympathy. Madame Grégoire asked me to say how sorry she was and to send her sympathy. I know you will forgive me for troubling you with this letter, and for Miss Lester's sake will let me send my love.

Amy Steedman

I wish I could show you some of the sympathy I feel for you, but I can only send my love and say that we have lost one of our best friends.

Frances M. B. Blaikie

A letter from my grandmother indicates that Anna saw Henriette Ballu at least once before she died.

October 25, 1900
Agnes Scott Institute
Decatur, Georgia
My own dear Mama,

    Mlle came to see me on Tuesday afternoon and she does not think Sister destroyed her will, for she told Mlle that she had made it, when they were in Atlanta. Mlle said Sister wanted her to have all of the miniatures she made of her. I can get them at Christmas. There is one place I did not look thoroughly, and that was in that little box on the lower part of the desk where Sister kept some of her miniature materials. You remember I told you that I had not found the little package of miniatures I brought to Atlanta for Sister. Mlle said she took them back home, and maybe you will find them and the will in that little box.

I find an undated letter from Mlle Ballu. The signature verifies my assumptions about her handwriting.

My dear Mr. and Mrs. Lester,

    The little allegory which I enclose reminds me so much of Anna's life that I send it to you. She wanted her father to have this slip about "worry" which you will also notice with this.

Sincerely yours,

Henriette Ballu

I don't know what the little allegory was, but I found a "worry" quotation typewritten in the purple ink that I think Mlle Ballu used.

Only the serene soul is strong. Every moment of worry weakens the soul for its daily combat. One's environment may be very disagreeable, but there is a reason for that environment. A great part of the strength of life consists in the degree with which we get into harmony with our appointed environment. Let us say: God put me among these scenes, these people, these opportunities, these duties. He is neither absent-minded nor incompetent. This is exactly the place He means me to be in, the place I am capable of filling: there is no mistake, My life is in its proper setting.

I can appropriate these words. I believe I am in my "appointed environment," doing what I am meant to do. Confirmation comes from a small book I find on my shelf. When we divided my mother's possessions, I chose this white leather volume because it is embossed with violets. I've never read it.

The booklet, *What is Worth While?*, contains the text of a speech by Anna Robertson Brown, PhD, to the Philadelphia Branch of the Association of Collegiate Alumnae in 1893. Dr. Brown discusses the dilemma faced by college-educated women: how to balance the love and care of others with our intellectual passions. As I read the book, I recognize the language. The "worry" quotation came from this book. The coicidence delights me. Anna and the ladies are still feeding me clues and putting books in my hands. The book was also the source for the typewritten words I found before I went to Paris: "Let us hang our life on the line, as painters say, and look at it honestly."

When I first read these words, I pictured a clothesline art display. Now I know that "on the line" means hung at eye level, the most prestigious position for a painting in the Salon.

Life's Calendar
We know this life is but a longer year, and it will blossom bright in other springs.

Gerald Massey

ACKNOWLEDGMENTS

Many people contributed to this project. I thank the women of WHIM: Bambi Berry, Mildred Greear, Nancy Griffin, and Rena Patton. In New York: J. David Farmer and Stephen Edidin at the Dahesh Museum, and Stephanie Cassidy at the Art Students' League. Catherine Fehrer, Gabriel Weisberg, Marie Lathers, and Louly Konz responded to inquiries. At Hollins: Nina Terry Thorp, Frances Niederer, Jake and Trudy Wheeler, and the late Lewis Thompson. In Staunton: William Pollard, archivist at Mary Baldwin College. At Berry College: Gus deBerdt, Virginia Troy, Tommy and Mary Ann Mew, Sandra Meeks, Amy Summerlin, Vincent Grégoire and le groupe du Mardi Soir. I thank Maryse James, Jan Petersen, Marny Busbin, Sherrie Bacon, Sutton Bacon, Bill Fortenberry, Jon Hershey, Randa Mixon, Allen Bell at RACA, Alice Enloe, Dr. C. J. Wyatt, Cheryl Ranwez, the Rome Music Lovers' Club, W. C. Owen, Ralph Helzer, Ashley Summers, Liz Fisher, Mary Sib Banks. Rebecca Skelton restored the trunk. Paul O'Mara took the author's photo. Nancy L. Smith made the map. I thank Susan Cofer and Kappy Ackerman for their support and Chuck Perry for his advice. In France: Bobette Compagnon preserved number 9, rue Sainte-Beuve; without her foresight, this book would not exist. I thank Jean-Pierre Egurreguy and his staff, Cécile and Mathieu, for their continued welcome at the Hôtel Sainte-Beuve. Also: Jamey Keaten, Fabienne Copelli, Lilia Tchistoganow, Annick Scouten, Paulette de Ram Vigneron. François Roulmann shared his archives; Marguerite Prinet gave me a book about her kinsman, R. X. Prinet. In 2000 Phyllis Theroux lured me to Scotland, where Dr. Tom Barron and Dr. Jim Strachan hosted me in Amy Steedman's house in Edinburgh. Alison and Charles Melville opened the door to Frances Blaikie's home and directed me to her grave.

I'm grateful to Margie Harbin and my Harbin cousins, especially the estate of Mary Shelor Harbin. Special people who did not live to see the book: Mary and Warren Gilbert, Elizabeth W. Harbin, Nancy C. Berry, Anna Marie Kent, Athlene Forsyth, Jeanne and Al Braselton. I am indebted to my editor, Mindy Wilson, for her vision and skill. Hans Rogers, Tracy Cole, and Debbie Stubbs at Caldwell Printing turned the words into a book. Great thanks to Peter and Suzy Gilbert, co-survivors of the attic; to Larry Ethridge for his enthusiasm; and to my sister, Edith Ethridge, who has shared the journey. My children, Mary and Walt Beaver, Katherine and Tim Kenum, and Jaynee and David Harvey III, have been part of my art adventures. David Harvey has provided love and support for 46 years and has made all things possible.

Susan Gilbert Harvey is a visual and performance artist whose work has been exhibited nationally. She graduated from Hollins College and studied advanced design with Virginia Dudley at Shorter College. Susan and David Harvey live in historic downtown Rome, Georgia. With this edition of *Tea with Sister Anna: a Paris journal,* Susan Gilbert Harvey celebrates the 50th anniversary of the Hollins Abroad-Paris program of Hollins University.